FALLGIRLS

Classical and Contemporary Social Theory

Series Editor: Stjepan G. Mestrovic, Texas A&M University, USA

Classical and Contemporary Social Theory publishes rigorous scholarly work that re-discovers the relevance of social theory for contemporary times, demonstrating the enduring importance of theory for modern social issues. The series covers social theory in a broad sense, inviting contributions on both 'classical' and modern theory, thus encompassing sociology, without being confined to a single discipline. As such, work from across the social sciences is welcome, provided that volumes address the social context of particular issues, subjects, or figures and offer new understandings of social reality and the contribution of a theorist or school to our understanding of it. The series considers significant new appraisals of established thinkers or schools, comparative works or contributions that discuss a particular social issue or phenomenon in relation to the work of specific theorists or theoretical approaches. Contributions are welcome that assess broad strands of thought within certain schools or across the work of a number of thinkers, but always with an eye toward contributing to contemporary understandings of social issues and contexts.

Fallgirls
Gender and the Framing of Torture at Abu Ghraib

RYAN ASHLEY CALDWELL
Soka University of America, USA

ASHGATE

Published by
Ashgate Publishing Limited
Wey Court East
Union Road
Farnham
Surrey, GU9 7PT
England

Ashgate Publishing Company
Suite 420
101 Cherry Street
Burlington
VT 05401-4405
USA

www.ashgate.com

British Library Cataloguing in Publication Data
Caldwell, Ryan Ashley.
 Fallgirls : gender and the framing of torture at Abu
 Ghraib.
 1. Abu Ghraib Prison. 2. Prisoners of war--Abuse of--
 Iraq. 3. Iraq War, 2003- --Prisoners and prisons,
 American. 4. Iraq War, 2003- --Participation, Female.
 5. United States--Armed Forces--Women. 6. Trials
 (Military offenses)--United States. 7. Courts martial and
 courts inquiry--United States. 8. England, Lynndie--
 Trials, litigation, etc. 9. Harman, Sabrina--Trials,
 litigation, etc. 10. Women soldiers in mass media.
 11. Torture in mass media.
 I. Title
 956.7'04431-dc23

Library of Congress Cataloging-in-Publication Data
Caldwell, Ryan Ashley.
 Fallgirls : gender and the framing of torture at Abu Ghraib / by Ryan Ashley Caldwell.
  p. cm.
 Includes bibliographical references and index.
 ISBN 978-1-4094-2969-2 (hbk) -- ISBN 978-1-4094-2970-8 (ebk)
1. Abu Ghraib Prison. 2. Prisoners of war--Abuse of--Iraq. 3. Iraq War, 2003--Psychological
 aspects. 4. Torture--Iraq. 5. Women and war--United States. 6. Control (Psychology)
 7. Women in war. 8. Feminist theory. I. Title.

 DS79.76.C346 2011
 956.7044'37--dc23

2011040756

ISBN 9781409429692 (hbk)
ISBN 9781409429708 (ebk)

MIX
Paper from
responsible sources
FSC® C018575
www.fsc.org

Printed and bound in Great Britain by the
MPG Books Group, UK.

Fall.girl (*noun . slang)*
1. A fallgirl is a person of feminine gender who is used as a scapegoat or easy victim to take the blame for someone else's actions. **2.** An individual said to "take the fall" in terms of responsibility for another's exploits.

For my mother.

*And, in loving memory of
Joseph Morton Ransdell
and Stuart Jay Hysom.*

I truly miss you both.

Contents

List of Figures

List of Abbreviations

ACLU	American Civil Liberties Union
BIAP/BIOP	Baghdad International Airport
CIA	Central Intelligence Agency
CID	Criminal Investigative Division
CJTF-7	Combined Joint Task Force-7
CPA	Coalition Provisional Authority
DADT	"Don't Ask, Don't Tell"
DFAC	Dining Facility
EPW	Enemy Prisoner of War
FM	*Field Manual*
Gitmo	Guantanamo Bay, Cuba
HMMWV	Humvee motor vehicle
ICO	Iraqi Correctional Officers
ICRC	International Committee of the Red Cross
ICRP	Theater Interrogation and Counter-Resistance Policies
IR	Internment Resettlement
JAG	Judge Advocate General
MEDVAC	Medical Evacuation
MI	Military Intelligence
MKTS	Military Knowledge and Testing Standard
MP	Military Police
MPI	Military Police Investigator
MRE	Meal Ready-to-Eat
NCO	Non-Commissioned Officer
OGA	Other Governmental Agencies
OIC	Officer in Charge
PSD	Personal Security Detail
PT	Physical Training
PTSD	Post-Traumatic Stress Disorder
ROT	Record of Trial
SHA32	Sabrina Harman Article 32 Hearing, Camp Victory Base, Iraq
SHCM	Sabrina Harman Courts-Martial, Fort Hood, TX
UCMJ	Uniform Code of Military Justice

List of Significant Personnel

"Rotten Apples" from the Military Police

- Corporal Charles Graner, 372nd MP, Military Police Officer, NCO of night shift for 1A (10 years in prison, released after six and a half years on August 6, 2011).
- Private Ivan L. Frederick, 372nd MP, Military Police Officer, NCO IC for night shift at the hard site (eight years prison, released October 2007).
- Specialist Jeremy Sivits, 372nd MP, Military Police Officer (one year prison)
- Specialist Sabrina Harman, 372nd MP, Military Police Officer (three months prison).
- Private First Class Lynndie England (three years prison).
- Sergeant Javal Davis, 372nd MP, Military Police Officer (six months prison).
- Specialist Meghan Ambuhl, 372nd MP, Military Police Officer (discharged).

"Rotten Apples" from the Military Intelligence

- Specialist Armin Cruz, 325th Military Intelligence Battalion (sentenced to one year).
- Specialist Roman Krol, 325th Military Intelligence Battalion (sentenced to 10 months).

Whistleblowers

- Sergeant Ken Davis, 372nd Military Police Company.
- Specialist Joseph Darby, 372nd Military Police.

Commanders at Abu Ghraib and in Iraq

- Captain Donald J. Reese, Company Commander at Abu Ghraib, 372nd MP.
- Major David DiNenna, Supply Officer and in charge of prisoner operations at Abu Ghraib.
- Lieutenant General Ricardo Sanchez, the General who was Commander of all military units in Iraq.
- Major General Barbara Fast, in charge of Military Intelligence in Iraq.

- Major General Geoffrey Miller, the General who was Commander of Guantanamo and who came to Abu Ghraib in order to "Gitmoize" the prison in the fall of 2003.
- Colonel Thomas Pappas, Brigadier Commander, one of the disputed Commanders at Abu Ghraib.
- Lieutenant Colonel Stephen Jordan, one of the disputed Commanders at Abu Ghraib.
- Lieutenant Colonel Jerry Phillabaum, one of the disputed Commanders at Abu Ghraib.
- Captain Carolyn Wood, one of the Intelligence Officers at Abu Ghraib, who came from Afghanistan.
- Colonel (former Brigadier General) Janis Karpinski, in charge of all of the prisons in Iraq.

Other Military Police and Military Intelligence at Abu Ghraib

- Staff Sergeant Ivan L. Frederick, 372nd Military Police, Senior NCO night shift at Abu Ghraib (testified against others for the prosecution).
- Specialist Matthew K Wisdom, 372nd Military Police Officer.
- Sergeant Robert F. Jones, 372nd Military Police (Wisdom's Immediate superior).
- Specialist Israel Rivera, 325th Military Intelligence Battalion (testimony in exchange for immunity).
- Master Sergeant Bryan Lipinski, 372nd Military Police Officer.
- Sergeant Hydrue Joyner, 372nd Military Police Officer, in charge of the day shift at Abu Ghraib.

Series Editor's Preface

Most people think they know all that there is to know about the Abu Ghraib torture scandal: the "bad apples" (referring to a handful of allegedly corrupt soldiers) allegedly had fair trials; they went to jail for allegedly committing acts of torture; and as far as the public, law, and academia are concerned—the case is closed. But as my friend and colleague in philosophy, Professor John McDermott is fond of saying: "The world does not speak in Aristotelian clarity." Clarity is dangerous, because it closes the doors of perception. Genuine perception of an event or an issue must include the elements which lie on the fringes of consciousness and on the peripheries of what is seemingly known. Dr. Ryan Ashley Caldwell researched, analyzed, and wrote this book on Abu Ghraib in the spirit McDermott describes, as he was, and remains one of her mentors. McDermott's approach is a remnant of a distinguished tradition in philosophy and sociology that dates back to the late 1880s, the era of William James, Emile Durkheim, and other classical theorists who laid the groundwork for discovering and re-discovering the social world. My own mentor, David Riesman, similarly advised his students that the social world as well as social theory must be re-discovered continuously.

This is because the bulk of our "discoveries" about the social world and social issues in this, our hyper-modern age, are based upon first impressions, which are disseminated by the information media and the Internet more quickly and thoroughly than previous generations could have imagined. Discussions are thereby closed before they have a chance to be opened. The moment that the White House labeled the accused soldiers in the Abu Ghraib drama as "rotten apples"— the designation that made its way around the world in a matter of seconds—their fates were sealed, and the full horizon of possible explanations for the scandal was closed with the exclusive focus on them, and not their superiors or their social environment. One must re-discover the original truths, which the media's "discovery" of the scandal obfuscated for generations to come. Thus, Dr. Caldwell analyzes court documents and the ROT for the accused soldiers. This seemingly obvious step in the research process—to examine the actual, sworn testimonies of the accused and of witnesses—is not obvious at all. It is shocking that in our digitalized, information-laden age, there is no central repository in existence for the ROT. By law, the ROT are public documents, but are not truly accessible to the public. The purportedly public ROT are extremely difficult to obtain. Dr. Caldwell was a member of the defense teams of two of the soldiers charged in the Abu Ghraib scandal, Sabrina Harman and Lynndie England. In this role, she had access to them and to other witnesses, as well as their attorneys, their trials, and to precious information such as the ROT which eluded the media and society's opinion-makers.

I shall not review here the genuine discoveries Dr. Caldwell makes and shares in this book. What is striking is her curiosity, scrupulous attention to detail, and sensitivity to what various actors actually said about the abuse, command climate, and social climate at Abu Ghraib—as well as *how* they said what they said. The facts she lays out challenge existing preconceptions which have been frozen into dogma: The court-martialed female soldiers did not strike anyone, and did not torture anyone. They were convicted mainly for taking and posing in photographs, under the direction of male superiors. In sum, the convicted female soldiers were the "fallgirls" or scapegoats for abuse that was orchestrated at the White House and by lawyers, high-ranking officers, and intelligence personnel in the stratosphere of the chain of command above them. These real architects of the evils at Abu Ghraib will most likely never be charged with any crimes.

Worse yet, the center versus the periphery of the Abu Ghraib saga have been inverted. The government and the media would have one believe that the fallgirls, and other low-ranking soldiers at Abu Ghraib, were at the center of the abuse, while the high-level architects remained passive, helpless, and unknowing on the fringes of the story. The truth is that the seemingly peripheral and high-ranking characters in this story are the real protagonists and bear the real responsibility not only for the abuse, but for creating the dysfunctional social climate at Abu Ghraib which led to and maintained the abuse.

In addition to documenting the full, contextual account of what happened at Abu Ghraib—including the fringes, margins, and periphery of the received story—Dr. Caldwell re-discovers the social theories necessary to comprehend what happened at Abu Ghraib. One should keep in mind that social scientists do not hold a monopoly on theories for explaining events. Lawyers, journalists, politicians and other professional groups all draw upon or develop theories to explain this and other events. Indeed, the prosecution and defense attorneys had their own, opposing theories at the Abu Ghraib trials regarding key concepts such as choice, responsibility, procedure, and so on. Lawyers routinely concoct ad hoc sociologies and psychologies of their own, which would never be accepted without discussion in academia. Dr. Caldwell's unique contribution in this volume falls under the broad umbrella of theories known as feminism and gender studies— and more specifically, how these theories impacted legal and other theories. She looks to the neglected margins and periphery of social theory for concepts which could capture the complexity of the Abu Ghraib drama in a meaningful way. Thus, she begins with the nearly forgotten distinction made by Talcott Parsons between instrumental, goals-means functions (ascribed to males) and expressive functions (ascribed to females). Most contemporary feminists seem to assume that this is a sexist distinction which no longer applies to contemporary society. But Dr. Caldwell argues convincingly that this distinction still operates in the U.S. military, and thereby opens up new vistas for understanding. A brief summary of her discoveries would be that the fallgirls were exploited by the male commanders precisely because they were female, and would thereby heighten the shame experienced by male Iraqi inmates at Abu Ghraib. She calls this the instrumental use of expressive torture.

In her analysis as a whole, she invents many new concepts to capture the twisted use of homoerotic, sexual, and gender-based, expressive themes in instrumental, rational, goal-means techniques. The significance of her new theoretical perspective is that the sexual perversion at Abu Ghraib can no longer be dismissed as the aberrant behavior of a few individuals. Rather, this climate of perversion was the product of carefully-crafted interrogation "techniques" which aimed at the misuse of gender, expressive functions, and sexuality for the purposes of torture. Additionally, Dr. Caldwell walks the reader through other peripheries of social thought, including that of Michel Foucault, Judith Butler, Jean Baudrillard, among others, in an attempt to understand the spectacle of Abu Ghraib.

Dr. Caldwell's book is the first in Ashgate's Classical and Contemporary Social Theory Series. It is an exemplar of the kind of sociological theorizing which put sociology on the intellectual map in the first place. It is the sociology of discovery, not of lifeless propositions intended for hypothesis testing and "falsification." Dr. Caldwell seeks the truth about Abu Ghraib, and in the process, demonstrates that this truth is complex, ambiguous, and deserving of our attention and discussion. The reader should be prepared for discoveries in this book which will be surprising and disturbing, as all discoveries are.

Stjepan G. Mestrovic, Texas A&M University

Preface

Our responsibility is much greater than we might have supposed, because it involves all mankind.

Jean-Paul Sartre, *Existentialism and Human Emotions* (1957)

I wrote this book based on my experiences as a researcher in sociology for the trials of Lynndie England and Sabrina Harman, and as a co-expert witness and researcher for the defense. As I participated in these trials with Dr. Stjepan Mestrovic, many different themes became apparent to me. Issues of power, gender, control, punishment, deceit, to name a few, were manifest in both the trials and the stories that were shared with me about Abu Ghraib. I knew then that there was more to Abu Ghraib then was being reported in the media and that it was my job to further convey these stories in ways that I knew how. I knew almost immediately that my reading of this abuse would apply a critical power perspective that used gender as a primary point of departure. This I could do.

So, why? Well I am interested in both justice and the sociology of knowledge, and how truth is created within culture, the courtroom, through dialog, and within institutions, such as the military. I found it fascinating that a huge institution such as the U.S. military could blame the events of Abu Ghraib on seven low-ranking soldiers, and claim no responsibility, no knowledge of these happenings going on whatsoever. Something did not seem right. (And then came the Levin-McCain Report in 2008.)

I am trained as a social and cultural theorist, and also as a feminist philosopher, and so, the focus of this book is a social and cultural theoretical analysis of the empirical data regarding the prison abuse that occurred at Abu Ghraib prison in Iraq by American forces. The empirical data provided is drawn primarily from my first-hand qualitative research that involved participant-observation of Lynndie England's and Sabrina Harman's courts-martials, interaction with soldiers and officers, and analysis of documents pertaining to the trials as well as the photographs of abuse themselves, among other things.[1,2] Few, if any, have looked at the mass of empirical data surrounding Abu Ghraib through the lens of social theory and

---

1 Although I mostly consider gender and power in this book as significant explanations for the abuse at Abu Ghraib, in other publications I apply additional theoretical viewpoints, and consider for instance the anomic social climate as well as the varied experiences of Reisman's lacking moral compass. This line of thinking is best laid out in Stjepan Mestrovic's book *The Trials of Abu Ghraib* (2007) and other joint publications with him.

2 I was the only female, feminist, academic who was not only in the courtroom at the England and Harman trials, but who ate meals with the defendants, sat through conferences

gender. *Fallgirls* provides the following: an examination of the photographs of abuse that were leaked to the press in the fall of 2003; a first-hand analysis of both Lynndie England's and Sabrina Harman's courts-martial (two of the "rotten apples"); a discussion of the body associated with punishment and torture, and also as marked in ways of identification; an evaluation and critique of existing feminist analyses of Abu Ghraib; and finally a one-on-one interview with Sabrina Harman.

My approach to understanding gender is that gender as a sociological concept is multifaceted, based on power relations, and has to do with performances of individual, cultural and symbolic meaning constructions, where identity is constituted through these performances. *Gendering* is something that is "done" (either something we do, or something that is done to us), it is a process and an action, and a metaphysical transformation so to speak. Gendering is always in reference to a "code" such as a context, a culture, or a symbol rich with meaning, and these "codes" have to do with power. Bodies can be gendered, so can roles, expectations, spaces and environments, commands, organizations and institutions, fashions, theoretical viewpoints, and advertisements, to name a few. In this way, gender is a *process metaphysics*,[3] a system of becoming, a performance process, an adjective of sorts, a means for identity construction, as well as a tool or thematic for analysis. Gender functions as code with power infused within its understandings—where even the analysis of power itself can be examined and understood as "gendered."[4] What I think is most important within discussions of gender is not only theoretically important conversations about gender (its "code") rich with detail and example, but also critical engagement and thought about how gender is policed, produced by and for us, consumed, and other ways power makes complex the relations of gender.

Although this book deals with sensitive and emotionally disturbing issues— torture, abuse, sadism, abandonment, and other distressing topics—I make sense of Abu Ghraib through the lens of a social scientist, a sociologist, a feminist and a philosopher. This approach does, however, have its unique aspects. First, I view the "rotten apples" as persons, and not as they have been characterized in the media— as "poisoned apples." Like most people, I do not condone the abuse, and actually deplore it; nonetheless, I am trying to understand the circumstances surrounding the

---

with attorneys, talked to relatives, talked to other soldiers, read sworn statements that were never made public, reviewed court martial transcripts, etc.

3   This notion of 'process metaphysics' is inspired by William James' philosophical metaphysics, where he describes reality as literally states of becoming—hence, a process. I argue that gender works similarly.

4   Social construction is a theoretical concept used to understand and explain social reality, and I take it as a theoretical presupposition that individuals experience a shared sense of reality that is itself socially constructed in terms of power differentials. By this, I mean that what individuals and society perceive and understand as "reality" is a product of the social interactions of individuals and groups with others, as well as with the previously established "reality" that has been beforehand socially objectified. Through these interactions, people continually create a shared reality experience, thereby ultimately establishing a shared social epistemology.

abuse. Second, I favor the approach of looking at a social climate, environment and context above and beyond simply a lone individual for responsibility. Third, I look at laws as social constructions that might not always be applied in practice (such as the Geneva Conventions *should have applied* in Iraq, but there was confusion). Fourth, I discuss gender and social theory throughout, and as a means of understanding Abu Ghraib. Given that the U.S. military is not a bastion of feminism, this analysis is important for several reasons: showing how power functions within Abu Ghraib and also for interpreting and illuminating the gendered and homoerotic torture that took place there as well.

I am grateful to the soldiers for sharing with me their experiences of what happened at Abu Ghraib. I am most thankful to Sabrina Harman for allowing me to interview her and also for sharing photographs for this book with me. Harman is a down-to-earth individual with a sacred bond to animals (which I share!). Additionally, the professionalism of the legal teams was quite impressive and I am especially grateful for all of the information and unclassified documents that they provided during the trials. Thank you specifically to Frank Spinner, Captain Patsy Takemura, Captain Catherine Krull, and Captain Jonathan Crisp. In my limited experience with all of you it was an absolute honor and pleasure.

I would like to personally thank the following individuals for discussions and help pertaining to this book: Keith Kerr, Kristi Wilson, Tomas Crowder-Taraborrelli, John McDermott, Alex McIntosh, Don Albrecht, Cletus Dalglish-Schommer, James Spady, Orin Kirshner, Aneil Rallin, Enrico Mariotti, James Chouinard, Rachel Romero, and my fantastic student research assistant Mohammad Ali Ahsan for his tireless work. I could not have finished this project without your assistance, Ali. I appreciate greatly the previous mentorship I have received from Alice Sowaal, Mark Webb, Joseph Ransdell, Ed Averill, Karann Durland, Rod Stewart, and Mark Hebert. I am also grateful to my family and friends, and especially Lucy Ransdell, for all of their support throughout this project. Additionally, many thanks to Diana Phillip and Will Harrell of the ACLU, Texas who taught me very early on in my academic career (during an internship and then later, as a member of the Texas State Board of Directors) about justice and accountability within the prison and jail system of Texas. It is so strange to look backward in time and have it all make perfect sense! Also, many thanks to Neil Jordan and Philip Stirups for all of their assistance with this project.

The most important inspiration and absolute support for this project comes from my friend, mentor and dissertation chair, Stjepan G. Mestrovic. He has always taught me to believe in myself, to ask questions of situations, to never take the obvious explanation as truth, to seek for deeper analysis, and to push myself further. Mestrovic also taught me to love social theory and to readily engage theorists in conversation within my very own head—and I do! I am forever indebted to him for revealing to me how to use social theory in a constructive way in order to help others. I *appreciate your help*, Mestrovic. I fashion myself after you as a professor each day.

Prologue: So What Really Happened at Abu Ghraib?

After viewing the photos of abuse at Abu Ghraib at the hands of American soldiers, over 16,000 of which have never been seen by the public, I remember thinking things would never be the same from this point forward. What had happened? How could this behavior be explained? What would be the aftereffects of this abuse and these photographs, knowing that from this moment on the world would refer to this instant in time as the flash when America lost its claim to "doing good" in Iraq.[1] I remember trying to imagine myself actually at Abu Ghraib prison in the fall of 2003, turning my head to see past the physical abuse and into the faces of the onlookers in their cells, envisaging their fear, dread and anxiety. I also tried to imagine what it must have been like for the soldiers there, how the social environment was experienced at Abu Ghraib by all, and what day to day life must have been like given the horrible surroundings of the prison I have come to understand. I am still trying to make sense of the abuse at Abu Ghraib, and to tell a story of Abu Ghraib that has not readily been told. It is this endeavor to fully understand the whys and hows that drives my sociological research in war crimes, in order to understand how power operates within military institutions, and the associated contextualized experiences of all members involved within the social environment. *So what really happened at Abu Ghraib?*

Media depictions, popular perception, and academic explanations for the infamous torture at Abu Ghraib at the hands of American soldiers have utilized conceptions of chaos as a means to describe and explain the abuse. For this reason, many read and understand the abuse and torture of prisoners at Abu Ghraib as being about the actions of a handful of rogue soldiers, namely the "rotten apples" operating in an environment of chaos. The government's own theory of the abuse is that there were originally seven rogue soldiers with moral failures, who just went out on their own and engaged in misconduct. In fact, former defense secretary Donald Rumsfeld's 800-page book *Known and Unknown* (2011) argues that the abuse at Abu Ghraib was isolated and uses the "rogue soldier" approach for understanding the abuse itself, claiming that soldiers went outside of the bounds of approved policy. However, Rumsfeld's book has drawn scrutiny from the ACLU who claims that Rumsfeld is "rewriting history" in his approach, and that abuses

---

1   There were 281 photographs used at exhibits, from five different cameras, that were pertinent to the courts-martials associated with the "rotten apples" (Special Agent Brent Pack, Computer Crime Investigative Unit, U.S. Army, Harman CM, May 13, 2005).

were not only widespread in Iraq, but also that "government documents show the methods used at Abu Ghraib were the same ones that Mr. Rumsfeld approved".[2]

Looking at the U.S. government's own reports (for example see the Levin-McCain report)[3] shows that the U.S. government deals with conspiracy, deception and intrigue, and suggests that we should not blindly accept the characterizations of these so-called "rotten apple" soldiers without question (Danner 2004, Strasser 2004). These reports state that the abuse *was not at the hands of a few rogue soldiers, and was instead ordered and orchestrated from much higher in the chain of command*—all of the way up to the White House itself.

An expert witness in sociology, Dr. Stjepan Mestrovic, points out at several of the "rotten apple" trials that there were leadership, training, discipline, chain of command, resource, environmental and socio-cultural issues that need to be considered in order to get a full picture of the context of Abu Ghraib, and how some abuse was *inevitable* given these conditions. In this way, I and others argue that the "rogue soldier" explanation for abuse is demonstratively false—magical thinking in fact—even though it was used by the government's prosecutors at each and every "rotten apple" trial, and is still put forward today by some as a means for justification.[4] Says the defense counsel at the Harman trial, "you don't have seven soldiers who were basically out there on their own like a bunch of cowboys just having their way with Iraqi detainees" (SHCM). Consequently, I think that we should be more critical of what happened at Abu Ghraib. Instead of pinning the abuse on lower-level soldiers, arguing that they acted alone and with no direction, I offer an alternative reading of this abuse in terms of gender and power to describe what caused these events so as to provide an additional narrative about what happened at Abu Ghraib.

Abu Ghraib Prison

Abu Ghraib prison is known as Saddam Hussein's infamous torture chamber and was the site of weekly executions under his regime where political dissidents were tortured. Located about 20 miles west of Baghdad, Amnesty International has

---

2   See "Rumsfeld Memoir Draws Criticism from ACLU Over Abu Ghraib Depiction," FoxNews.com, February 3, 2011. http://www.foxnews.com/politics/2011/02/03/rumsfeld-memoir-draws-criticism-aclu-abu-ghraib-depiction/

3   http://levin.senate.gov/newsroom/release.cfm?id=305735

4   In fact, the ACLU and Human Rights First filed in 2005 in federal courts in the Northern District of Illinois (*Ali et al., vs. Rumsfeld*) that Rumsfeld personally approved unlawful interrogation techniques and failed to stop torture at Abu Ghraib, therefore abdicating his legal duties and violating the U.S. Constitution, federal statutes and international law. See "ACLU and Human Rights Sue Defense Secretary Rumsfeld Over U.S. Torture Policies" at http://www.aclu.org/national-security/aclu-and-human-rights-first-sue-defense-secretary-rumsfeld-over-us-torture-policie

Figure P.1   Abu Ghraib Prison

Source: Photograph provided courtesy of the author.

repeatedly documented human rights violations at this huge prison (about the size of an average airport), which was described as having vile living conditions. In October of 2002, Hussein declared a general amnesty for all prisoners in Abu Ghraib and they were subsequently released. When American occupation forces invaded Iraq in 2003 and overthrew the Iraqi regime, like most other places around Bagdad during that time period, the prison too was ransacked, looted, and abandoned. Soon afterward however, the American military took over the prison itself and continued running it, albeit not a common tactic, in the middle of an active war zone as a holding and detention facility, renaming it the Baghdad Central Confinement/Collections Facility. In June of 2003, Brigadier General Janis Karpinski was ordered to restore Hussein's prison, and in her words:

> We did our best to marginalize the old hellhole. While we rehabilitated Abu Ghraib in stages, starting with cellblocks 1A and 1B, we kept most of our Iraqi inmates in compounds of tents … We started to draw down our biggest facility at Abu Ghraib, Camp Ganci (named, like all of our camps, for a policeman or fireman affiliated with the 800th who had died on 9/11) … The commanders had created a monster at Abu Ghraib, but they felt no real need to bolster our resources for dealing with these thousands of incarcerated Iraqi citizens, most of them innocent bystanders swept up by the attempts to stop a growing insurgency. (Karpinski 2005: 183-191)

The hard site of Abu Ghraib, or the actual hard standing building with a foundation is built with brick and concrete. The hard site housed tier 1A and 1B and the rest of the regular prison wings; however, it was tier 1A where the MI and CID holds were located, as these were the prisoners who were supposed to be high value detainees. Interestingly, we now know that none of these prisoners had any actionable intelligence whatsoever, and that these prisoners were mostly local criminals that were picked up in street sweeps during raids.

Captain Donald J. Reese, the 372nd Military Police Commander since December 2002, stated in court that one wing of the hard site had Military Intelligence, and the other had Military Police who were responsible for taking care of the prisoners and transporting them within the compound. It was tier 1A where the "rotten apples," most of whom were from the 372nd Military Police Company, were assigned to work the night shift—a curious assignment for the 372nd, as their training was as a combat support unit for supply route and convey security escorts, and not at all as prison guards. Says Reese, "The Iraqi detainees were there for different reasons. Some inmates were there as MI holds, CID holds, and Iraqi on Iraqi criminals. There was a mix of detainees" (June 24, 2002, SHCM). However, this "mix" also included women and children detained at Abu Ghraib in tier 1B, a crime that is explicit in the Geneva Conventions. In addition, there were tent and fence prisons surrounded with Constantine wire around the prison compound that extended the prison itself. Camp Ganci housed common, general population prisoners, such as Iraqi on Iraqi crimes, who are not believed to have military intelligence value. The other tent prison within Abu Ghraib was Camp Vigilant and this area housed high value/priority detainees ("insurgents"). However, Abu Ghraib was not just a prison—it was an Army base called FOB (Forward Operating Base) Abu Ghraib, and contained non-prison related troops and services.

Although it was the spring of 2004 when the photos of abuse at the hands of American military soldiers were leaked to the media, the abuse itself (and thus the infamous photographs) took place in the fall of 2003. By the spring of 2004, several military investigations into the abuse were under way. In May of 2004, United States President George W. Bush announced plans to demolish Abu Ghraib prison. However, Attorney Paul Bergrin (viewed as the lead defense attorney in the pool of attorneys representing the "rotten apples") objected to this closure, claiming that the prison was a crime scene and could not be demolished. Judge Colonel James Pohl, the judge for all of the "rotten apple" companion cases, agreed and stopped the demolition of Abu Ghraib, contrary to the wishes of President George W. Bush and his request to destroy Abu Ghraib prison. Also in the summer of 2003, Major General Geoffrey Miller came to Abu Ghraib from Guantanamo Bay, Cuba for the expressed purpose to make the prison more like Guantanamo Bay Detention Camp, or to "Gitmoize" Abu Ghraib (Mestrovic 2007). Between May of 2004 and September 2005, seven soldiers (the so-called "rotten apples") were charged and convicted with various violations of the *Uniform Code of Military Justice* (UCMJ) such as dereliction of duty, maltreatment of prisoners, and conspiracy, among other

Figure P.2   Abu Ghraib prison cell

Source: Photograph provided courtesy of the author.

violations. While some officers were reprimanded or demoted, such as now Colonel Karpinski, for the abuse at Abu Ghraib, not a single commissioned officer was ever charged or prosecuted with a crime, and in fact several were promoted. Indeed, Abu Ghraib is one of the world's most notorious prisons, where memories of terror and torture at the hands of not only Saddam Hussein, but also American occupation forces and other interrogators reveals the history of suffering within its walls. The obvious two questions that surface are: How did American occupation forces perpetuate suffering at this notorious prison? And why?

Gender Categories as Code

Over the last 20-30 years, gender has become an important focus for analysis in the social sciences. Feminists, gender and social theorists, those concerned with women's issues, and others, have analyzed society and culture using gender as a focus for understanding many different phenomena. In order to show how different social theorists come to interrogate gender in different ways concerning Abu Ghraib, I present my notion of gender in order to provide a theoretical mechanism of comparison and entry into discussions about gender and power within social theory. Throughout this discussion, what is clear is that sociologically, gender has been, and continues to be socially constructed in different ways throughout our social-theoretical cannon, and I am quick to point out that the reality of these social constructions has always been about power. I draw out the gender suppositions of social theorists such as Talcott Parsons, Michel Foucault, Jean Baudrillard, Judith Butler, and Philip Zimbardo—some of the most well-known names in social theory, yet many of who are not really considered gender theorists at all (except of course Judith Butler). However, I argue that all of these theorists conceptualize power and gender in different ways given their theories of the social and cultural world and my project aims to outline the gender variations within these theories, and also the consequences that these understandings have for explaining the abuse at Abu Ghraib. In addition, coupling these social theorists' ideas with the gendered nature of the military, it is possible to obtain a new perspective and thus explanation for what happened at Abu Ghraib and the associated courts-martials. Gender thus remains an important means for analysis within this project, woven through social theory and accounts of power, as gender is the vehicle I use to explain the abuse at Abu Ghraib and the events of the courts-martials themselves.

I view gender as something that we are socialized to within a culture, where social and cultural norms prescribe the boundaries for categorical understandings of "masculinity" and "femininity." These gender norms, or the socially constructed rules of "masculinity" and "femininity," are basically the set of conventions that a culture uses to make sense of gender for the individuals of that specific culture. I call these conventions "gender code" as they supply the cultural translations or shared set of meanings that a culture uses to make sense of gender performances. (Literally, these normative gender codes "de-code" the meanings associated with gender so as to inform and prescribe for the larger dominant culture.)

These gender rules or codes are not natural, in that they did not derive from biology or divine law. Instead, they are a shared, symbolic, and agreed upon set of practices that have been reified over time by a group of people who share a culture—that is, they are socially constructed.[5] In this way, we imagine categories as a certain general measure for conceptualizing gender, and we pass this kind of knowledge on through our social interactions and socialization practices, as our gender code is thus conceived of as a process that we learn from our culture. This process informs our behavior (how we act), our viewpoint (how we see the world and others), and our perspective (our outlook or how we think). This gender code gets inside of our minds and starts to function such that it might begin to feel like something natural, normal, or even like it has always somehow continuously been there informing our every move, decision and way of seeing. Some say that our gender perspective is similar to wearing a pair of glasses with a specific prescription, in that this pair of glasses causes us to see the world in a certain way. After a while, with these culturally informed gender glasses on, gender itself becomes unquestioned and assumed correct, such that the normative assumptions

---

5   Social constructionists work to document and analyze the *processes* through which social reality is constructed, and how that constructed reality begins to work back upon society itself.

and socializations that we use, inscribe, share with others, etc., is actually the "truth" of gender. In some ways, gendering can be conceived of as a ritual practice associated with categorizing, cultural meaning creation, and identity.

However, understanding gender is not just as easy as understanding a rule book of norms associated with culture; in fact, it gets even more confusing, because all of these gender divisions and gender rules—or the politics of gender—are socially constructed and vary based upon specific cultures, complex discourses, time periods, or contexts, and are imbued with power such as hierarchies and stratifications. First, this means that what one culture views as the norm for understanding gender might be different, or even completely opposite, from another cultural understanding of gender. Hence, it is quite possible then to have varied, different, and opposing systematic cultural approaches to gender. What one culture views as feminine or masculine might be socially constructed differently in dissimilar cultures. This mostly applies to gender roles, where what is considered to be "masculine" labor in one culture is identified as "feminine" in another, or vice versa. Second, even varied time periods within same cultures may have different conceptions of gender, which can be seen with changing concerns over women's rights in different waves of feminism, as well as changing gendered fashions, to name a few. Third, gender can be understood in certain contexts as either strictly associated with some standard or law, such that gender is defined in a rigid way, such as within stereotypes, fantasy, or archetypes; or, gender can be critically challenged as conforming to a certain law (such as heterosexuality) or in reference to some dominant standard for value (such as patriarchy), where it is claimed that this law or standard constrains the ability to render certain projects of gender viable or valuable (Butler 1993b; Rubin [1975(2002)]). Finally, one thing that is certain about gender is that it does indeed become entangled with power differentials and structures, such that how we locate ourselves within the geography of feminist theory and in terms of gender is political.[6] Indeed, we should not assume that all women of the same culture experience that culture in exactly the same way, even though they are all women existing within the same cultural context. Drawing from the idea that the "personal is political," I think that viewing gender as one component of an intersected identity is important, where race and ethnicity, class, sexual orientation, nationality, religion, among other identities are considered when determining the level of subordination a person will experience in any culture. These identities function as additional schema intersecting with gender to provide a crucial understanding of cultural stratification.[7] What is actually different for each individual in any gender performance is the subjective experience within their context that creates a differing gendered epistemology, as an individual's

---

6   I am indebted to Victoria Rosner for this notion of feminist theory and gender theory as geography.

7   Another way to understand this is in terms of "gender capital," where reward and social status or value follows what is viewed as the legitimate empirical cash value for gender identity performance within that specific context alone.

gender identity is affected by their other and varied identities, which thus impacts one's ability to construct their gender project in the first place.[8] In this way, gender conceptualizations change, gender itself is multifaceted and fluid, *yet also* has a staged and referenced standard. One could go so far as to say that the code for gender is thus so malleable to the point of theoretical inconsistency (being that it culminates in the actual lack of a code at all), as it seems to represent nothing stable. Gender is both performatively and radically constructed, but is also socially understood according to rules, norms, discourse, and power, as these provide the basis for social value within the larger population. These social constructions of normative gender codes are basically the language of gender that allows for gender translations to be made at the cultural level so that conversations about gender can exist; however, these norms are and should be critically questioned.

Although I find that the theoretical perspective of social construction is a valuable starting point for understanding gender, as it allows for the varied conceptualizations of gender to be brought forth, I also add that a critical power analysis that outlines how power functions to determine or limit conceptualizations of gender is also imperative to theorize in that it shows that, within different perspectives, cultural or otherwise, the possibilities for thinking (or not thinking) about gender exist.[9] So, for example, when we consider the many places that gender codes exist, such as the marketplace (where we shop for things like toys, clothing, and fragrances), we realize that from a very early age ideas about gender are passed onto our children through these cultural spaces. Specifically, gender socialization occurs based on how we treat our children differently, how we interact with them, how we encourage them to interact with others, the kinds of toys we purchase for our children to play with, the activities we encourage them to engage in, and so forth. As Cynthia Enloe (2000) rightly points out regarding the gendering of toys, the G.I. Joe action figure is called a soldier, while the G.I. Jane female version is not called a soldier, but instead is described as a *doll* "in authentic military gear" or even a "female action figure" (Enloe 2000: 10). This is a tremendous socially constructed message regarding gender, and one that is based in social value (doll versus soldier) that deserves an analysis focused on power.

So, I looked into the toys that even I played with as a youth with my brother, and I found that Hasbro toys is commemorating the G.I. Joe series with a 25th anniversary edition of figurines, and two of these are the leading female characters of

---

8 Although it is the case that we all have the freedom to conceive of our gender performances in the existentially free and authentic way Sartre would have approved of, it is not the case that we can all freely realize these conceptions given the constraints of our own material world and contextual surroundings. Sometimes it is the case that we are limited by our very circumstances themselves (Davenport 1980).

9 This is especially important for conceiving of gender queer categories, discussions revolving around intersexed identities, transgender identities, drag identities of all kinds, and other gender specific identities perhaps connected with categories of sex and gender, and others.

the original G.I. Joe series—Scarlett and Lady Jaye. I remember both sexy females from my childhood—both are members of counter intelligence, but Scarlett was the first female member of the G.I. Joe team. Scarlett has a prestigious university degree, practices law, is a ninja, and fights with a crossbow; but, the focus is on her looks, as she is notably quoted as saying "Beauty may only be skin deep, but lethal is to the bone."[10] Lady Jaye, like Scarlett, is a busty covert operations specialist, who also has a degree from a prominent university, and whose special skill is *impersonation* of all kinds. (Given the description used by Hasbro of female soldier toys, one might ask if Lady Jaye's skill is to impersonate a masculine toy soldier.) We can learn a lot from these toys and perhaps the messages that children learn about their gendered toys translate into larger cultural beliefs about gender such as the following: females are not soldiers but are instead dressing-up in costume so as to impersonate soldiers; the authenticity about female soldiers such as G.I. Jane is her outfit and not her identity, skill, intelligence, or qualifications; females in military gear are in "military" drag, performing a constituted identity illusion; sexualized females use their looks as weapons (even if they are intelligent); and lastly because G.I. Jane is labeled as a doll and not a soldier, it is unlikely that she will be taken seriously either within the military or on the playground (as we *all know* that boys do not play with dolls in the narrowly socially constructed world of U.S. gender code). I think this is what Enloe (2000) means when she argues that American's relationship with the U.S. military is of "women soldiers," where this means soldiers in lipstick and high heels—as feminine but militarized (Barbie in her military uniform outfit, simply waiting for the next outfit), and not as fighters with guns. This is where our narrow versions of gender socializations lead—to G.I. Jane being subjugated on the merry-go-round and beyond.

It is now possible to see that with the added analysis of power, in addition to theoretical social construction, the intricate workings of oppression, domination, subordination, and control associated with gender become comprehensible. Another example that is even more lucid is that even cultural gender norms sometimes function as oppressing mechanisms within *"genderscaping"*[11] (or the individual's construction of gender), for within culture, gender is policed by reference to cultural norms, and these norms function to both make sense of the world, and also to give value to those individuals who perform gender in such a way to constitute their identities according to the ways prescribed by the reified and enforced norms of a given culture. (In a sense, this is a form of "gender capital" in the sense of Bourdieu's [1980] 'social capital'.) The individuals who "do" gender correctly and according to the norms or code of the culture to which they belong

---

10   http://www.yojoe.com/action/93/scarlett2.shtml

11   I came up with this notion of "genderscaping" after considering Veblen and his work *Theory of the Leisure Class* ([1899]1994) and his idea that social value comes to the individual via the well-manicured lawn. In the same way, the well-formed gender garners social recognition and thus value by being "landscaped" in the correct and socially approved way as well.

are given admittance into the larger and "dominant group," while those who do not "do" gender according to the norms are seen as "other" or are out-group individuals with regard to dominant culture's understanding of gender, and thus value, reward, etc. How is cultural gender status decided and assigned? So you may ask, *who* gets to determine how gender is socially constructed within society, and why would this matter? Who is the architect and provides the blueprints for socially approved and socially valued "genderscaping"? This question has to do with power structures and power differentials, which is a major focus of analysis in *Fallgirls*.

A system of social control thus springs out of these cultural norms for gender, where those with the ability to garner social power (the social elites or members of the dominant group) are more able to define and delineate the boundaries and definitions for these cultural gender norms, or what becomes defined as the culturally valuable gender code (i.e., genderscape). This code comes to define gender "reality," and although this "reality" is itself shared among the members of a culture, it is a limiting one because it narrowly defines gender in terms of a select defined set of gender options, or bias, instead of leaving gender possibilities open to creative conceptualizations.[12] Again, those who "fit" into or embrace the narrow standards and prescriptions for gender are given social value and social reward in the form of recognition and significance, recompense, and worth within a given culture. We receive cues from our social surroundings, peers, and other members of our shared culture if we are doing gender correctly in the form of positive and negative sanctions. This can be in the form of a positive wink of the eye, a negative name-calling, or something even more drastic such as a negative physical attack or even hate crime. In this way, there are positive and negative consequences for performing gender, and with respect to cultural gender norms, or the "code" for gender.[13]

But what about individuals who "do" gender differently than the norms of their culture? Or, what if the reverse is true in that gender is "done" to us, in that we are forced into normative cultural categories or gendered boxes for understanding by others? After all, sometimes it is these norms alone that limit gender conceptualizations—such as the case with transgender individuals, drag queens and kings, intersexed, gender queer, or those who understand their gender outside of a heterosexual matrix or who have their gender forced upon them.[14]

---

12   Some theorists such as Jean-Paul Sartre's keyhole example in *Nausea* ([1938]1964) and Audre Lorde's (1984) example in "The Master's Tools Will Never Dismantle the Master's House" point out that it is the oppressed that truly understand this system of norms best which thereby dictate their own gender domination.

13   You can see for yourself, have a male friend wear a skirt in public to see the reactions of others for not performing "masculine fashion" correctly or as a female, hold the door for a large group of men (especially men over 30) and insist that they all go through before you. See if any men put up a fight for performing "feminine courtesy" experiments.

14   One really important thing to remember is that the term 'heterosexual' also has a genealogical history, and Foucault project in the *History of Sexuality* (1978) reminds us of that.

Those who push back at gender normative categories view these categories as troublesome, limiting, lacking, etc., and want to see them either redefined or done away with totally. Assuming these individuals have gender performances that are outside of the cultural norms for gender, we can say that their gender productions have the possibility to transform normative and limiting standards of gender in that they reconceptualize the limits and boundaries for gender understandings. However, prior to these reconceptualizations, it is usually the case that these individuals are not given value within the existing cultural schema of gender value and representation (Caldwell 2009).[15]

This brings up the tension that keeps reappearing—*is there a fixed normative standard for gender, or is gender multifaceted and fluid?* It might seem upon first inspection that it should be one or the other, but what is happening here is that power is influencing our analysis on both the micro and macro level, both at the larger cultural picture and the smaller level of individual analysis. *Perhaps the answer is that gender is both—it is both policed and fluid.* Hence, power here too is the variable that aids in explaining this anomaly *vis-à-vis* gender identity. Does this mean that gender is meaningless? Absolutely not! Indeed, the very fact that gender is something that is contested, policed, and based in power differentials shows its very importance!

Gender therefore is about constitutively performing a certain part of identity that for some gives admittance and value into dominant culture's system of worth; nonetheless, gender becomes something that we all "do" each day in order to establish identity (Caldwell 2009). Each of us "genders" ourselves everyday through our actions of subscribing, performing, associating, and reifying the established gender norms of our culture, or questioning these norms by establishing an alternative model. This happens when we put certain clothing on our bodies, when we perform certain roles, when we symbolically fashion our bodies in a way to denote a gendered identity, when we enter into power relationships with one another, among many other social interactions that can be described as gendered or in gendered terms. Gender is thus something we "do," a process metaphysics—we put it on, all of us, each day, just like a costume or symbol that we identify with, in order to belong, to make sense of ourselves and others, or to question the very system of gender itself. I suppose we can say that the notion of gender norms and rules are somewhat misleading as themselves being strict and fixed, or as having guiding principles. Perhaps the only norm that gender does have is that when thinking gender (queer or otherwise), power relations are involved. These are the aspects of gender that I hope to bring out in *Fallgirls,* so as to make evident how power works both subtly and not so subtly in discussions about gender, and in order to show the multiple meanings associated with gender and Abu Ghraib.[16]

---

15   Judith Butler calls these "abjects," as these individuals are literally not theorized within the normative gender paradigm (1993b).

16   I see this project located at the intersection of sociology, social and cultural theory, women's studies, and critical theory. Consequently, I incorporate cultural studies, feminist

Social Value and Representation

Simone de Beauvoir, in her iconic book *The Second Sex* ([1949]1952), writes that woman is defined in terms of the category of man, and as the "other." What this means is that "man" and "woman" are binary categories, and that "man" is set up as first, primary, natural and normal, and "woman" is secondary to all of those qualities and generally seen as lacking all that is "man" or "masculine." Beauvoir's entire discussion centers around the topic of how to constitute "subjecthood" given this secondary status, that of "woman" being defined in terms of "man," which really provides a key insight into an understanding of oppressive modes of identity in terms of reference. If one group is defined in terms of another group, where the elite group has the power to define and shape the social reality for the oppressed group, social inequalities arise regarding value, autonomy, cultural representation and worth, to name a few. So for instance, Laura Sjoberg claims that "women soldiers were not *soldiers* but *women soldiers*; their gender marked their identity on the battlefield" (Sjoberg 2007). I actually disagree with Sjoberg's assessment about gender, and argue that women as soldiers have their gender defined *for* them, as they *are marked* in terms of a lack, and thus do not have the power to instantiate their gender identity as such. In this way, gender is *done* to these female soldiers instead of these soldiers having the ability to gender themselves, thereby marking their identity autonomously and free of coercive power. (This is along the same lines as Edward Said's notion of Orientalism (Said 1978), where he argues that the Orient is represented, constructed by, and in relation to the West, where the Orient is all that is inferior, alien and "other".)[17]

Given the problem of this kind of biased social construction of reality, feminists aim to understand and uncover the ways in which members of society come to know and simultaneously create "social reality," so as to identify and expand on the ways in which women come to be represented within society. Feminists argue against a phallocentric (or male dominated) ordering of society, which privileges the socially powerful male subjectivity, and argue instead for the equality of the sexes, where woman is not defined in terms of, or in reference to man. Likewise, feminists make a case for the realization and representations of women's diverse

---

and sociological theory (modern and postmodern), and feminist philosophy so as to provide a theoretical analysis of the abuse at Abu Ghraib and the subsequent courts-martial focused on gender.

17   Interestingly, R.W. Connell (1995) discusses this process of instantiating identity with his distinction between hegemonic and subordinated masculinities, where hegemonic masculinities *feminize* other masculinities in an attempt to maintain power and control through the act of dominance. Sjoberg (2007) points to this example later in her article to elucidate the relationship between the USA and Iraq; however, I suggest we not only think of prisoner relations in this sense (as feminized, through torture and also power), but also how women are gendered within the military, as gender-instantiated by men—literally feminized in terms of their relational power to masculinity. This was my experience of the U.S. military.

experiences given the idea of intersected identities (race and ethnicity, class, gender, nationality, sexual orientation, etc.), and show how these intersected identities actually shape the ways in which women experience different kinds of subjugation. Feminists locate the origin of male dominance in patriarchal cultures within the social, economic, and political spheres of society, and are interested in the ideological processes that legitimize and perpetuate female subordination. As a result, it seems that the term 'feminist' implies a specific politicized understanding of "woman," namely as members of a subjugated social group, albeit within different contexts. Although some theorists argue that women do indeed see the world differently *because* they are women (nature), others simply claim that women experience the world differently in terms of power (culture), although even this is varied. It is this latter approach that I take.

Accordingly, feminist social theorists question the gendered hierarchy of cultures that privilege males, as this endeavor questions the social theory cannon's universal voice that represents masculine biases. In Chapter 1, "It was not Lucifer Achieved: Zimbardo, Women, and Abu Ghraib," I argue that one way American society is sexed and gendered is within science, where cultural biases are imported from dominant culture by scientists, and are impressed into theory and ways of knowing (Harding 1991). This can be seen in research design, as demonstrated through the study of men in social scientific research to the exclusion of "woman as subject" in similar experiments. This section shows that by using a gender-sensitive analysis, which accounts for sex, gender, and sexuality, one can come to a thicker understanding of social phenomena, including deeper understandings of both The Stanford Prison Study and the abuse at Abu Ghraib prison.

The Stanford Prison Study was aimed at researching if certain environments evoked certain behaviors—in this case, did a prison somehow generate violent behavior? Interestingly, Philip Zimbardo argues that the narratives from which to understand the abuse at Abu Ghraib can be found through an analysis of group conformity and obedience to authority, and in terms of his 1971 Stanford Prison Study. One might argue that still a further understanding of this abuse can be found in Stanley Milgram's social-psychological study on obedience. However, neither of these experiments in obedience and authority uses a critical gender-sensitive analysis as a means for interpreting the abuse at Abu Ghraib.

Using gender as a tool for analysis, it is possible to provide a richer understanding of the gendered masculine, and heterosexist nature of the American military. Although I fully support the separation within queer theory of heterosexuality from gender for understanding gender constructions, I found that because the military functions as a heterosexual entity, masculinity is forcibly aligned with heterosexuality for its understanding. Because of forced heterosexuality "by law" given "Don't Ask, Don't Tell", gender and sexuality are connected in the military as part of the normative code for gender identity.[18] The "*code of cultural masculinity,*"

---

18   Even though law is certain to change regarding Don't Ask, Don't Tell (DADT), discriminatory practices are still embedded within the military and larger culture towards

where both masculinity and heterosexuality function together as powerful cultural ideology, was demonstrated at both locations, the "Stanford Prison" and also at Abu Ghraib. At both locations, sexualized and homoerotic torture techniques and forced feminization existed as torture techniques, which exploited notions of both masculinity and fears concerning homosexuality.[19] Zimbardo's paradigm cannot explain these (sex, gender, sexuality) phenomena sufficiently, where gender and sexuality are themselves used against prisoners and *as torture techniques*.

This chapter shows that by using a gender-sensitive analysis, which accounts for power and heterosexuality, additional elucidations about both Zimbardo's study and also Abu Ghraib are evidenced. I critique Zimbardo's Stanford Prison Study using the realities of Abu Ghraib, and show how data from England's and Harman's trial evidence the importance for considering gender within the context of war crime studies—from the Stanford Prison Experiment to Abu Ghraib.

Narrative and "Genderscaping"

As a feminist I argue for an account of gender that is radically constructed and constitutively performative (Butler [1990] 1999, Butler 1993b), one that allows for all interpretations of gender conceptions, gender-queer productions (Caldwell 2009), drag, trans, radical inclusion, postmodern spectacle, reward, value, space for consideration, among other plans for genderscaping. However, not all gender systems allow for radical possibility and inclusion.[20] For example, one existing and limiting structure of gender relations occurs within the military, where the oppressive and suffocating gender code can be used to make further sense of the abuse at Abu Ghraib and the subsequent courts-martial's of Lynndie England and Sabrina Harman.

Gender categories provide descriptions of gender characteristics, where both masculine and feminine symbolic narratives and "codes" have been culturally employed to describe social phenomena. For example, in modern patriarchal societies some narratives describe gender in terms of binaries, associating

---

LGBTQ individuals, and just as racism and sexism still exists *even though* laws prohibit discrimination, I believe that homophobia and associated discriminatory practices will still follow when DADT is repealed, and that heterosexuality will continue to inform gender understandings within heterosexist spaces.

19   Even within larger culture there is the idea that what it means to be male is to be "masculine," and that this is also to be "heterosexual." This is the stereotype that queer theory aims to get rid of in order to open up one's ability to conceive of and thus perform one's gender identity.

20   I am grateful for this notion of possibility in my theorizing to John J. McDermott and his tireless lectures regarding existentialism and also William James. His words still imprint my thought.

masculinity with all that is essential, rational, reasonable, strong, orderly, active, controlled, and logical. Conversely, femininity is associated with all that is emotional, chaotic, weak, inconsistent, inessential, passive, uncontrolled, and irrational. Notice that this binary system is an arrangement of opposites, where masculine descriptions and traits are positively valued, and feminine qualities have less value. This value system has been socially constructed in terms of a gendered opposition and serves as a frame of reference when conceptualizing cultural understandings and meanings associated with gender.

One of the problems of defining gender in terms of strict binary codes is that the narratives associated with these codes is problematic both for gender constructions and also for social value and power distributions within a society. To dictate a standard for everyone, from which gender should be parsed, determines a fixed blueprint for construction that leaves little room for gender flexibility. This is evidence of the limiting nature of binary gender categories in that only certain characteristics are available for gender construction, where masculinity and femininity are thought about in strict and contradictory ways. Additionally, the consequences of this kind of arrangement are that those who are gendered "masculine" are given more social value, prestige, status, privilege, power, and opportunity within patriarchal societies over those who are "feminine." This is oppressive gender theorizing from the initial establishment of these gender categories themselves.

Nonetheless, these binaries in fact inform the very ways that we do and have (uncritically, I might add) to think about subjects, individuals (their properties and qualities), and subjectivities. Narratives using gendered language have even been expanded for use to describe places and spaces, paradigms, sex categories, roles and bodies, among other things. That is the power of narrative—it functions as an ongoing and foundational storyline or backdrop from which we come to know and understand how the socially constructed reality of the world emerges. The consequence of these narratives is that they are the basis of stereotypes about gender within American culture.

One of the gender narratives that I am concerned with specifically is that of the stereotypical association between sex and gender. Interestingly, one of the reasons that these gender binaries are based on stereotypes is that gender categories are usually associated with sex categories. When I refer to sex categories I mean those categories that describe and are thus usually coded to denote sexed males and females. This means that masculinity has a culturally informed narrative such that for its categorical conceptualization it is associated with guys, maleness, or the male subjectivity, while femininity is associated with girls, women, or the female subjectivity. What is more, the attributes that are associated by conceptually connecting the binary categories come to also represent sexed individuals through their gendered connection, and thus stereotypes about gender are applied to understandings of sex. In American culture, this association between sex and gender is so conceptually automatic that it may even sound strange to question its separation.

This is the socially constructed sex and gender connection that I am referring to that we, as socialized individuals, pass on to our children and reify ourselves through our interactions and unquestioned gendered assumptions. It is this *narrative of gender* that becomes the story that we come to believe as the truth of the social world. It is almost as if gender is on autopilot, such that no questioning of these associations takes place. We pass these connections along through our interactions as if they were truths about gender, that man should be masculine and that woman should be feminine, and that for some reason these are the only prescriptions and options we have in our culture for gender. This baseline of gender is the starting point from which conceptualizations about gender arise, and this baseline serves as literally the starting point or gender narrative creation myth for American society. I am not saying that these are correct starting points, but that these exist in conception only (remember, it is necessary to be critical).

What is interesting is that the U.S. military operates using a similar version of this creation myth of gender on a daily basis, which does little more than perpetuate outdated stereotypes of both gender and sex (and their forged association). Looking at the data surrounding Abu Ghraib, I show how the use of theoretical gendered binaries actually helps to make sense of some of the abuse at the prison and the associated courts-martial, which I argue was the result of gendered deviance.

Power coupled with gender has been used to control bodies, and I show how torture, abuse, and other deviances in the name of gender were carried out upon the body at Abu Ghraib. Historically, women's bodies have been controlled by patriarchal power in areas such as marriage, sexuality, and in legislation over abortion, among other places. However, power and control over the body can also affect sexed male bodies, where feminization of these male bodies serves to humiliate and mock cultural constructions of masculinity itself. In this way, power is used to torture both the body and mind.

In Chapter 2, "Abu Ghraib and the "Rationalization" of Rationality: Uses of the Masculine and Feminine Symbolic Narrative," rationality and chaos as descriptors are explored to show that both have implications for understanding deviance in terms of gender. Many do not understand the full deviance that occurred at Abu Ghraib because this unique reading of the abuse is nonexistent in academic and lay publication. Through this analysis, I argue that a gendered mutation of rationality has rationalized the furtherance of torture at Abu Ghraib.

In this chapter, I apply a binary theoretical analysis of the abuse at Abu Ghraib and the following courts-martials. Although this is a limiting paradigm for understanding gender, the theoretical use of binaries and these binary stereotypes are a minimum starting point for gender analysis and critique. What is more, the U.S. military functions using these binary stereotypes in a non-critical manner. I associate modernity with masculinity, and divide modernity into two parts using my alternate reading of Chris Rojek's "masculine" Modernity 1 and "feminine" Modernity 2.

Within this chapter, I also describe Abu Ghraib's built and created environment, and how this setting lacked modernist masculine rationality. Also, I address Foucault's theory of modern forms of punishment, and argue that at Abu Ghraib, power was used to punish *both* the body *and* soul. This is in contrast to Foucault's theorizing about modern forms of discipline, and is associated with a critical discussion regarding gender, power and punishment for the following reasons: Iraqi women and children were held at Abu Ghraib; forced feminization of prisoners was used as torture; gender humiliation as a weapon was used against prisoners; nicknames were given to detainees in an attempt to control through masculinist power; soldiers, both male and female, suffer from PTSD given their experiences at Abu Ghraib; among other examples provided. These examples count as a form of gendered torture and deviance, and should be read through a critical gendered analysis.

Parsonian Gender Roles: A Thing of the Past?[21]

One aspect of society that is frequently analyzed using gender is the division of social power between men and women. These realized power differentials manifest themselves in the ways that society is organized, as they directly inform a schema of social order and value. In patriarchal societies, what I call gender ideology, or the set of cultural beliefs, values, and attitudes that favor the interests of the powerful masculine gender, come to function as dogma in that they foundationally constitute, justify, and legitimate positions of power.[22] Additionally, in patriarchal societies, males are given social power, opportunities, value, and rewards unequal to women, where women receive less of these benefits given their subordinate statuses.

Consider the doctrine of separate spheres as an example, where actual space is divided according to gender and also according to modernist binaries. Public space, or the space used for rational, political thinking is associated with males and masculinity, and historically has the associated benefits such as the right to vote, the right to own land, paid labor, and the right to education—all rights and opportunities that women did not initially have equal to their male counterparts in the United States. Private space or the domestic sphere, also known as the female or feminine sphere within this dichotomy, is associated with child rearing, the maintenance of the home, and all things having to do with the family and domesticity. In this way, certain types of labor, social value, and prescribed gender roles manifest from these social divisions of space. Quite literally, because of how social space is divided, a

---

21   Previous research on Parsons and Abu Ghraib was printed in Sage's journal *Cultural Sociology* in 2008 and was nominated for SAGE's Prize for Innovation and Excellence 2008, "The Role of Gender in 'Expressive' Abuse at Abu Ghraib." I want to thank Sage for allowing me to expand on this initial research with these new ideas and additional data.

22   This is a general understanding of power, as not all females or males come to understand gendered-power in similar ways given the intersection of other kinds of identity along with gender identity.

prescribed genderscaping is forced upon individuals within society in such a way that specific roles for masculinity and femininity are stipulated within culture as seemingly associated with each sex and the division of both space *and* the family. For some social theorists, this form of social control through the use of gender and sex specifically informs how they describe and understand social roles.

Nonetheless, sometimes it is the case that theories need to be expanded upon in order to explain certain social and cultural phenomena. In Chapter 3, "*The Abuse Was Reported*: Parsonian Gender Roles and Abu Ghraib Transfigurations," I show how Talcott Parsons' theory of instrumental and expressive gender roles illustrates what took place at Abu Ghraib in gendered terms. For Parsons, his notion of gender roles is fundamentally based on the idea that men are rationally instrumental and focused on means/goals, while women are emotionally expressive and focused on group cohesion. Overall, these complimentary roles "function" in terms of the total social system's stability, whether you are imagining a family structure or a military prison. However, at Abu Ghraib, the gender role experiences deviated from Parsons' theorizing, and with regard to the reporting of abuse, where both expressive and instrumental roles functioned in gendered ways that Parsons did not imagine given his theories. A new and creative reading of Parsons allows for original theoretical terms to be applied to Abu Ghraib in order to understand how soldiers, and even some of the "rotten apples" reported abuse. Terms are developed to demonstrate this additional gendered interpretation, such as the *instrumental perceived reporting of abuse* (where abuse is reported in the perceived belief the chain of command will respond, yet with a failed goal/means outcome), the *expressive non-reporting of abuse* (where abuse is *not* reported because of fear associated with the consequences of reporting and other expressive reasons), and the *instrumental actual reporting of abuse* (where abuse is reported with an actual means/goal or end outcome). In this way, we should not be so ready to accept stereotypical gendered accounts of society without question.

My aim in this chapter is to show that responsibility for abuse is a collective thing—not only at the individual level, but also at the higher levels of command responsibility. It is this kind of critical analysis of abuse responsibility that was needed at Abu Ghraib and during the trials themselves. Also, I am not sure that anyone knows outside of the trials that *abuse was reported*—and even by the soldiers who would later face charges of courts-martial.

Postmodern Gender "Realness"

Like *The Velveteen Rabbit* (1976), I am concerned with how the notion of "real" is constructed, and how power relates to this conception of "realness." As I have been arguing so far, gender is defined as being "real" in terms of some "code" for meaning. In Chapter 4, "The Significance of Identity Simulacra and Gender Hyperreality: The American Military and the Case of Abu Ghraib," I am interested in how what is considered theoretically "real" instructs the formation of conceptual and organizational paradigms, and especially categories for thinking about sex and gender. Considering the military as an example, some of these categories include: how sexed bodies are made sense of, how gendered bodies are made sense of, how militarized gender relations serve to enforce how soldiers understand their gender, how the military context limits the conceptions for gender "doings," and so forth. Reflecting upon the women connected with Abu Ghraib Prison and the associated trials, what then was theoretically *real* and what were postmodern *simulacra* about their gender performances as well as their roles? Using postmodern theory as a perspective for understanding notions of "realness," it is possible to make clear how exactly gender identity and identity in general can be understood as something that is produced in relation to a socially constructed code of "realness."

Feminists and postmodernists alike have questioned this "design" (this "real") in terms of its problematic theoretical construction, and specifically with reference to gender and race inequalities, assumptions of heterosexuality, and the primary positing of whiteness. At the center of this project is the elucidation of the ways in which our world is parsed, separated and categorized, such that an understanding of the organizational schema (the "real"), forced upon that which is being conceived of (thereby making its conception "real"), is itself dissected and critiqued (and for the postmodernist, deconstructed). It is for these reasons that I put into conversation Jean Baudrillard and Judith Butler, who both have theories of gender, and I consider both theories when describing gender understandings at Abu Ghraib as simulacrum in their construction, but real in their consequences.

For Baudrillard, gender identity is about cultural signs, where identity culminates in the grabbing and identifying with the many available free-floating simulacra. He does not view gender as something "real," and instead sees gender as hyperreal—that which has no referential origin or reality apart from a self-legitimating system (self-referentially valid). When individuals conform and contort their identities to the hyperreal categories of gender, or when identities are understood in terms of some gender "code," these identities can be understood as succumbing to *rule by simulacra of reality*. Consequently, although Baudrillard claims that "realness" is dominated by a simulacrum of reality, he provides the means necessary for discussing the hyperreality of gender category simulations.

For Butler, gender is understood similarly to that of Baudrillard, however Butler allows for an analysis of power, where the policing of self-presentation is in terms of social norms. She argues that surveillance itself constrains our behavior and appearance formations, and that gender is a performative identity (which constitutes subjecthood) that can be conceptualized in terms of value with regards to its legitimating practices. Gender for Butler is thus an act of "doing" that is understood with regard to a socially constructed standard, which I argue is at base level a simulacra of reality. This means that, for Butler, "realness" regarding gender identity is something that comes from culture in terms of a normative system of value for identity realness (i.e., the heterosexual matrix for value).[23] Hence, gender is simulacra for Butler, as for Baudrillard, in that it is neither a representation of reality, nor a description of reality, as "reality" can only be found in the cultural representation itself and within the consequences of these representations.

At Abu Ghraib, the postmodern deconstructed and imploded meanings of gender function in that they elucidate not only the consequences of gender for individuals, but also help explain the chaos of the prison using a gendered perspective. I develop the terms *simulacra gender code*, *power simulacra*, and *rule by simulacra of reality* to describe the gender processes and consequences of the following examples: the metrosexual soldier, the phenomena of drag at Abu Ghraib, the idea that "drag-techniques" were used to torture, and that gender simulacra and seduction played a role in the courtroom, among other examples.

Feminist Analyses of Abu Ghraib

Much of the analysis of the photographs of abuse at Abu Ghraib has relied on a lack on data for the interpretations of the photographs themselves, and especially media interpretations. While it is true that I was indeed privileged in gaining access to a courtroom that many were restricted from, and therefore had an insider status with regard to the data of the trials, I am still somewhat confused about the lack of knowledge and the amount of assumptions that have been made regarding the women of Abu Ghraib. I am specifically concerned with the kind of feminist analysis that would so blindly rely on media and other sources while not considering either their objectivity or possible biases, and also analyses of the abuse at Abu Ghraib that does not either consider context or power as significant variables for analysis, as we are trained to do. I think it is time for conversations about these women—these Fallgirls, as I have named them. Thus, in Chapter 5, "The Fallgirls of Abu Ghraib: Feminist Analyses and the Importance of Context" I attempt to critique findings in terms of my experiences at both the trials and also given my interactions with soldiers at the various courts-martial I attended. Additionally, I repeatedly point out the importance of context for analysis of these events, and try to make sense of some of the events associated with Abu Ghraib in terms of context and gender so as to provider a richer analysis and understanding of these events.

I do want to mention that as a feminist, I was somewhat shocked when I read some of the interpretations that feminists made of the photographs that pictured women at Abu Ghraib. Sometimes these soldiers were unfairly described in ways that did not match up with courtroom testimony, and so I attempt to fill in some of these gaps. However, other times there are clear mistakes in simple shallow feminist analysis that I would not expect from leading feminist scholars—some

---

23   Although, to be sure, Butler is in no way advocating for this oppressive heterosexual matrix. Quite the opposite. See *Undoing Gender* (Butler 2004).

who I have read and looked up to for years, as do other academics and activists, as *did* some of these women I write about in this book. This is about power, and specifically the power of image, and as feminists, we are taught to know about the importance regarding frames of reference and how these are necessary for interpretation of the "facts" of women's lives. Actions take place in contexts and some feminists have interpreted these actions and these women of Abu Ghraib outside of context, and without all of the correct contextual facts. This is not responsible theorizing. To make matters worse, some of these feminists still go around touting these incorrect facts at college graduation speeches and other lectures. Feminists, listen up ... It is time to *stop framing* the *Fallgirls* of Abu Ghraib.

My Little Protector Once Assaulter

As a means to understand the impact of what happened at Abu Ghraib (both at the prison and also the effect it had on one soldier), in Chapter 8, "Conversations with Sabrina Harman," I provide sections of a series of conversations I had with Harman over summer, 2011. Within this conversation several themes become apparent: how homophobia exists within the military; the homoerotic and sexual nature of the military; how fear and PTSD exist for one soldier after the events at Abu Ghraib; sexism in the military; trauma in war; friendships with Iraqi prisoners and children; and the emotions associated with the events of Abu Ghraib, among other topics.

Conclusion

Fallgirls is a book about conspiracy, deceit and intrigue on the part of the American government. The government's version is that there were "seven rotten apples" who were responsible for the abuse at Abu Ghraib, and that these rogue soldiers were the masterminds behind the invention of prisoner interrogation, torture and brutality. However, the government's own report's show that these soldiers were trained by their higher-ups in interrogation and torture techniques. If anything, the Levin-McCain report exposes the U.S. government and its successful attempt to "project" conspiracy charges onto the "rotten apples" in the form of guilty sentences at their many different courts-martials. In this way, it was the U.S. government that engaged in conspiracy, deceit and intrigue, whereas the women of Abu Ghraib have been framed as the *Fallgirls*, the "rotten apples" and scapegoats by the government, media, and certain feminists.

Defense Counsel's Opening Statements

Sabrina Harman Courts-Martial, Civilian Defense Attorney Frank Spinner, May 12, 2005, Fort Hood, Texas

CDC: This case is about a lot more than some still photos of what happened in Abu Ghraib. This case is about how the Army took a young woman, who decided to enlist in the reserves, in July of 2002, just after she completed basic training, how she started serving her country, her obligation faithfully. Only shortly thereafter, only six months later activated to report to Iraq. It's about what she experienced when she was assigned over there. And it's about the failure of leadership in the Army to give her the training and the resources to perform the task that she was assigned.

...

What I would like to do is take a little bit of time to step back and look at the context in which these events occurred.

...

You see, here's the problem, how hard is it to look at some pictures and say wow that looks bad, that looks wrong?

...

So who are some of the players that were called up to active duty and sent over to Iraq? Well there's a Captain Reese, the Company Commander, he'll be called to testify as a witness for the defense; some names that you may hear but they may not appear as witnesses I'm going to mention as well: Captain Brinson, Captain Brinson was the officer in charge of the night shift. There's some other individuals who were assigned to the prison but they were not part of the 372nd, but they played a role with Colonel Pappas who was the Head of Military Intelligence Operations and Lieutenant Colonel Jordan. I don't anticipate that either of them would be here to testify, but their names may come up in the course of the evidence that you hear. Higher up the chain of command you're going to hear the name Lieutenant Colonel Philabaum and the role he played, and then General Karpinski. Now, with respect to the actual nightshift you've gotten some of those names, I'm not sure if you got them all, but let's just go over who worked on the nightshift. The people that were deployed earlier, a Staff Sergeant Frederick and Staff Sergeant Allen those were the senior NCOs working the shift. Then there's Corporal Graner and as—between Frederick and Graner you are going to certainly see them depicted in some of these pictures that are—had been addressed. Sergeant Davis— Javal Davis, also working the nightshift. Then there was Specialist Ambuhl along with Specialist Harman. By date of rank and I may be wrong on this but at least as the evidence plays out I think it will show you that Specialist Harman was the lowest ranking guard that worked on the nightshift.

In any event, this unit is activated and they undergo several months of training preparing them to go to Iraq. Finally, I think it's around March of 2003 they were actually deployed to Iraq. Now, understand that these are not corrections officers. This unit—this combat unit was military police. What you're going to learn is that they were stationed in Al Hillah and the idea was to train local Iraqis, police officers, and establishing law and order and maintaining it in that community. And so there was a period of time before this unit ever went to Abu Ghraib where they were fulfilling the duties to which they were trained, and assigned. They do not arrive—this unit does not arrive at Abu Ghraib until October of 2003. They are given a task, in particular, Specialist Harman along with the others I named are given the task of guarding what is perhaps the most dangerous part of the prison. Now what are you going to learn about this Tier 1A and Tier 1B? You're going to find out that *this is not like a normal prison* when the maximum custody, minimum custody—or medium custody and minimum custody in some prison in the United States or even Fort Leavenworth the USDD. This was a prison. A former prison maintained and run by Saddam Hussein that basically was taken over by the Army. And in this prison it was overcrowded. That's in part why they had camps and tents set up outside the hard site. You're going to learn that there were more prisoners coming into this facility than they had guards and resources to secure them and maintain them.

I anticipate that Captain Reese is going to tell you that the ratio of guards to detainees was well below a regular prison. Captain Reese is going to tell you that this people were not trained to be corrections officers or guards. But as you bring the focus down and narrow it on that part of the prison, Tier 1A and Tier 1B, you're also going to be aware that *this was a very unusual environment,* because unlike the civilian facility where you might have maximum security, everybody is a serious criminal and all that sort of thing, you're going to find out in Tier 1A that they had people who were suspected terrorists. You're going to find out that they had some very dangerous people locked down. People being held for military intelligence interrogations. People being held for interrogations by other government agencies. You're going to find out that CID—Army CID had some of their own prisoners who were being held there for various types of offenses. And surprisingly, you will find out that the next group of cells, Tier 1B, were women and juveniles being held in the same part of the prison and that at some point because of the overflow in Tier 1A, some of these really bad people were being moved along—next to the women and children and that one of the primary tasks that Specialist Harman was assigned, was guarding the women and the juveniles. The evidence will show you that in many respects, Specialist Harman, was on the peripheral of the primary duties—of the duties that were being assigned to this particular shift.

I anticipate that between then Corporal Graner and then Staff Sergeant Frederick, they're going to come in, they're going to tell you that they were the primary interface with military intelligence. And they're going to talk about the duty to soften up detainees who were there being interrogated by military intelligence. But what does this tell you? It tells you that, again, this was not like some civilian, military prison—or civilian prison or military prison, where people who have been convicted of crimes and are just occupying space, serving their sentencing. This was an institution where there were ongoing intelligence activities for which Specialist Harman was not trained.

You're going to learn that when their unit arrived at Abu Ghraib and the hand off from the company that was there before them that there were a number of things going on. Now, the government has shown you some pictures and they've talked about how on 7 November they stripped these detainees and the initial emotional impact is that, wow, that's terrible. Now, I'm not sure if he said it but the evidence is going to show that these weren't just prisoners, they just—they weren't just detainees. They had just been involved in a riot, I think it was at Camp Ganci and they were basically apprehended and brought back to this part of the prison because of allegedly participating in a riot. But, in any event, in terms of stripping and taking their clothes off is that what the 372nd learned when they arrived in October at Abu Ghraib just a few weeks earlier was that this was a common practice in Tier 1A, that it was part of the military intelligence operation to deprive detainees of their clothes.

Furthermore, that *they were tasked in working with military intelligence, something they had never been trained to do*, they were tasked with using such techniques as sleep deprivation. And you may be saying to yourself, at this point, you know, why is this guy standing on the box? What's the point of standing on the box? And this is the risk that we face in just looking at a picture and not looking behind the picture. He was part of—the evidence is going to show it was part of the sleep deprivation duties that Specialist Harman and others were assigned to perform.

You're going to find out that they used PT and those types of exercises, holding boxes, standing on boxes, as methods to get them to remain awake so that military—they would be off balance, I guess, from a sleep standpoint that would enable successful interrogations. In fact, that goes back to the context when you have to appreciate when you look at what was going on at Abu Ghraib at that time.

The insurgency had started to attack. Abu Ghraib, the prison itself had experiences frequent mortar attacks. There was a—there was a sense of urgency in getting actionable intelligence and so the interrogators and working in concert with the guards were trying to obtain this kind of intelligence to save soldiers' lives. And so it was in that context that these events arose and occurred … which is going to give you a sense of how could something like these photos come about.

…

Now, I want to go into talk about the specific allegations … The first allegation is basically the conspiracy allegation. What this allegation means is that Specialist Harman entered an agreement with an intent to commit maltreatment along with the other people named there.

...

This is where the fight is going to be because obviously in the specification it says she posed for a thumbs up photograph with Corporal Graner behind a pyramid of naked detainees, concede, the picture is there. This is not like a picture of the UFO when you don't know if it's a UFO or not. The picture is there and we're going concede that she was behind the pyramid of detainees. This is what we do not concede, that she entered any agreement to maltreat detainees. That's where the fight is.

And what the government will be relying on in great part for their case is called circumstantial evidence and you have direct evidence and circumstantial evidence and the judge is going to define those terms for you when we get to instructions. I do not anticipate that any witness is going to come in and say, oh, we sat down with Specialist Harman and we said hey let's—tonight let's have some fun and maltreat detainees. That's not how the evidence is going to come out. The way the evidence is going to come out is that while she was there, they were there, detainees were maltreated, so by inference there must have been some agreement to maltreat detainees. The defense is going to put on evidence that, in fact, Specialist Harman was upset as early as the 20th October 2003 about some of the things that she was seeing. Some of the things that she was never trained to contemplate or anticipate and it bothered her, and she started taking pictures to document that was going on. Not because she was part of a conspiracy, but because she was offended by what she saw and she hoped to be able at some point to prove it.

...

Now the next specification, Charge II, Article 92 is a wilful dereliction of duty specification.

...

With respect to this specification, there will be evidence presented by the defense that shows that Specialist Harman actually cared about inmates and tried to help inmates. And on occasion went to limits to see that they got proper care, safeguarded, and medical treatment.

...

Now, was she there on November 4th when Gilligan, as you'll hear the name that he was called is Gilligan, and he was made to stand on the box and the wires were put on his hand? Yes, she was there, we're going to concede that. Now, we're not going to concede something that you may wonder like, well, surely Mr. Spinner has lost his mind. We're not going to concede that she put the wires on his hands. Despite the fact that—I'll concede the government had as statement that she said she put wires on his hand—on his fingers or whatever, but we're not going to concede that. And there's going to be some evidence and some testimony that's going to refute that.

Additionally, you're going to learn more about Gilligan than just this hooded man with wires standing on a box. You're going to find out that actually Specialist Harman developed somewhat of a friendship with Gilligan. That, in fact, he achieved sort of a trustee type status in that part of the prison. That you can't look at this one snapshot in time, however terrible it may look, and understand it's all about those relationships. How he got on that box? What happened on that box? And what happened after he got off the box?

The government is going to present the argument to you that that was an attempt to some form of maltreatment and/or torture. The defense is going to present evidence that, in fact, it was a joking type thing and that Gilligan was in on the joke and that this was simply a matter of sleep deprivation.

With respect to the 24/25 October incident, under Charge II, under item 9, you're going to hear conflicting statements and you're going to see some pictures of these three detainees that were suspected of raping a 15-year-old male. Three male adults suspected of raping a 15-year-old male were brought back into that Tier 1A because of the allegations of raping this boy. Now let's—what's interesting about the pictures that are going to be presented to you with respect to this specific incident is that we're going to see pictures with multiple soldiers there, male soldiers standing around these individuals who are handcuffed, the Iraqis on the ground, naked and hand cuffed together.

But what you're not going to see is any picture of Specialist Harman involved in that incident. In fact, the defense is going to present evidence that contradicts the evidence presented by the government.

We're going to be calling, to testify, and I forget his rank, I can't remember if he's a specialist, sergeant, Staff Sergeant Ken Davis. In any event he'll come before you and he's going to contradict the witnesses presented by the government. He's going to say he was there, I think, for around 45 minutes or so that the operation was being run pretty much some of the MI people along with Corporal Graner and that he didn't see Specialist Harman there but she came there for a very brief period of time and then departed So, understand, your finding on this one—the evidence will be in conflict and of course at the end of the presentation of evidence I'll be arguing that she didn't do what they alleged she did. In fact, what you're going to find out from Ken Davis is that he, in fact, reported what he observed and that nothing was done about it. Nothing was done about it. So there was someone there that night who observed these events, who reported it, and nothing was done He reported it right to an officer.

Which leaves us with November 7th ...

...

When you go through each specification you'll see the word maltreat, maltreat, maltreat, maltreat, and maltreat ... What does that mean, maltreat? How do you define maltreat? How do you know if something is maltreatment or not? So recognize that's where the fight is. Not that there were pictures taken. Not that certain things happened. Now somebody might argue like, I'm going to show you in a minute, but whatever it was that happened, is that maltreatment? That's the fight. So let's walk though these. Specification 1, what you're going to see is there's a consistency between Specification 1, Specification 2, and Specification 5 because each of these allegations of maltreatment are not that Specialist Harman assaulted somebody, stepped on their toes, otherwise abused them, slugged them, hit them, slapped them, or otherwise, the allegations of maltreatment with respect to Specialist Harman is that she took photographs and that's what constitutes the maltreatment.

With respect to Specifications 1 and 2, we're going to concede that she took photographs of those events, okay. So we're not fighting whether or not she took photographs. The fight is over whether it's maltreatment. The evidence that we're going to present is pretty much that the detainees are hooded, they don't know they're being photographed, and so therefore they're not maltreated ...

We will dispute whether or not, under Specification 2, even though it's not alleged, whether or not Specialist Harman knew that Corporal Graner hit the detainee after the photo was taken. We're further going to present evidence, as I said earlier, that Specialist Harman was taking these pictures, not as part of the conspiracy, but to document what she was going on—she saw going on. And then you're going to learn that she left two days later on leave on November 9th, which was actually a time they could have shared—it started at 1600 on the night of the 7th and ran to 0400 the next day and then approximately 24 hours plus later she goes home on leave. By the way that just—that caused me to remember one thing. With respect to the maltreatment that occurred that night, some of it was witnessed by an individual, a government witness, Specialist Wisdom and it was witnessed by him, he reported it, and nothing was done about it. So as you realize that night to The Specification that she failed to safeguard the prisoners or failed to report these things, you're going to have evidence that someone also observed what happened on November 7th, and reported it, and nothing was done about it.

Now, with respect to—since we're talking about the photographing, I'm going to skip down to Specification 5 and then come back and pick up on 3. Because Specification 5 we are not conceding that she took those photographs or that videotape or digital videotapes. Okay, so Specifications 1 and 2 we're conceding that she took the photos but we're fighting whether it was maltreatment. In Specification 5 we're saying she didn't take these pictures and we're going to present evidence to establish that those were the last pictures taken on that night on the pre—I'm not even sure the government talked about this but let me sort of educate you. You're going—there are three cameras that were in operation on the night of September—November 7th and so one of the government witnesses, Special Agent Pack is going to talk about these three cameras and he's going to talk about the sequence in which pictures were taken and which pictures were taken from which cameras to sort of show a sequence of events over the course of that evening. We're going to concede that Specialist Harman was there about the time—the same time that the seven rioters were brought back into that area of the prison and for the most part these pictures accurately depict what happened that night, but where it ends is that Specialist Ambuhl and Specialist Harman left before the last pictures were taken. They went over—they went to make some phone calls. Now, Specialist Harman's female friend, companion, back in the states, who shared—they shared an apartment together, the 7th of November was her birthday and so Specialist Harman wanted to call her and tell her Happy Birthday. And so she went over and procured a calling card so she could call Kelly Bryant, we're going to call her as a defense witness in this proceeding, and so the evidence is going to corroborate that she bought a card that night and that, in fact, she made phone calls to Kelly Bryant and that she and Specialist Ambuhl had left together and used the internet on a government computer in one of the locations over to perform these transactions. So Specialist Ambuhl is going to testify that, in fact, she did go away with Specialist Harman and there's going to be evidence to show that Specialist Harman wasn't there at Tier 1A the entire duty shift. In fact, they shouldn't have even been the runner that night so it wasn't even as though she was supposed to be there during that entire shift. So in any event, understand that the pictures that are in dispute that show the masturbating, the government is alleging in this Specification 5 that she took those and we're going to present evidence that she wasn't even there. In fact, I think Frederick who was the one who initiated the masturbating incident. In any event he's going to say—I think he's going to testify that she wasn't there to his recollection for that event. So we're contesting that you're going to get conflicting evidence on that point.

…

So we're down to two specifications that I want to talk to you about. Specification 3, this goes back to the wires, placing the wires on his fingers and then telling him that if he fell off of the box that he would be electrocuted. Here the fight isn't whether or not it is maltreatment. The government is going to present it as this was some kind of maltreatment torture where they were using him and making him think that, no kidding, you really could be electrocuted. The defense is going to present evidence that Sabrina Harman, whether or not she put the wires on his fingers is almost secondary that this was a joke, that Gilligan understood it to be a joke and that this was just part of a bigger relationship that they had with Gilligan. They still had duties to do as soldiers and guards, yeah, they had to engage in sleep deprivation and this guy was still somebody who needed to be interrogated, but even in that strange context of what—the events that occurred at Abu Ghraib there were actually relationships that developed with these inmates. In fact, what you're going to find out is some of these detainees were given—many were given enduring names, like Gilligan, Taxicab, some of them not so enduring, primary example "shit boy," you may hear about that one, why he got that one, but some of these people weren't just numbers and they all weren't, you know, suspected terrorists, but there were relationships beyond what is shown in the pictures that the government has put before you.

So that brings us to the last specification that I'm here to talk about, not the last specification in the list, but the last one to talk about Specification 4. The defense—and through cross-examination of some of the government witnesses we may show through that or through our own witnesses, that it was permissible to write on detainees, okay. Sometimes different pieces of information were written on the detainees. Now, where's the fight? We're not contesting that Specialist Harman misspelled the word rapist and wrote that on this detainee's thigh. There's no contest to that, she did that. The fight and, in fact, the evidence is going to show that he was a suspected rapist. The fight is that this wasn't maltreatment. The fight is whether or not he suffered any harm, whether or not he was degraded in anyway. I don't think the government is going to be able to present any evidence that he could read English or he knew what was written on him. He may have known that something was written on him, but it comes down to was this maltreatment.

...

Now, I have been derelict in my duty in one respect, and that is, I meant to introduce my co-counsel, Captain Patsy Takemura, she's a Reservist, she was assigned to represent Sabrina Harman in Iraq and she has continued to represent her after coming to Fort Hood. She's s a—in real life she's a public defender in the state of Hawaii. I'm a Retired Lieutenant Colonel Frank Spinner, I have an office in Colorado Springs, Colorado, and I served as a JAG in the Air Force so please forgive me for not at least introducing ourselves earlier.

Once both sides have concluded and put on all their evidence, once you receive the instructions, you're going to hear arguments. I hope that at least at this point, now that you've heard my opening statement, that it comes as no surprise that when I stand before you again, like this, based on the evidence, based on the law, I'm going to argue that the government has failed to carry their burden of proof and that you should return a finding of not guilty of all charges and specifications.

Thank You.
Civilian Defense Attorney Frank Spinner
(12 May 2005, SHCM)

Chapter 1

It was not Lucifer Achieved: Zimbardo, Women, and Abu Ghraib

Zimbardo does not fit—this was a special area of confinement and there were unique problems that existed in that kind of environment.

Civilian Defense Counsel Spinner, SHCM

Zimbardo is like the minimal starting point. I think what was at Abu Ghraib was much worse ... there was much more going on with the social disorganization at Abu Ghraib.

Dr. Stjepan Mestrovic, expert witness Harman Courts-Martial (May 2005, SHCM)

Within the social sciences, one of the important questions centers on the construction of knowledge: How does the social scientist view the world and make sense of it? How does culture seep into scientific explanations of the world, and in turn, come to shape the very world it attempts to explain? Feminists argue that any knowledge creation that does not take into consideration an analysis of gender is lacking in that it does not adequately interrogate power differentials and assumptions about sex, gender and sexuality within culture. In addition, it is sometimes the case that in scientific research, women's perspectives are not represented at all, thereby questioning the universal validity and application of scientific knowledge, objectivity and truth—and fundamentally "othering" women in the process. The non-inclusion of women in some scientific research is specifically an example of how patriarchal cultural attitudes shape science, where ideas about the world influence the actual way research is approached and structured, the kinds of questions asked, as well as other aspects. These very practices come to also shape culture in that theoretical gender constructions arise, where the masculine symbolic is once again shown to define the feminine. The mistake of foregoing gender as a central concern for critical analysis was a common shortcoming in many of the knowledge constructions and interpretations surrounding Abu Ghraib.

The iconic photographs of abuse in 2003 at Abu Ghraib prison in Iraq are explained by social scientist Philip Zimbardo (2007a, 2007b) through a narrative and analysis of group conformity, and in terms of his 1971 Stanford Prison Study. Along these same lines it would seem that an additional explanation might be informed by Stanley Milgram's study regarding obedience to an authority figure (Milgram 1963). At first sight, I was seduced by the quick and easy application of experiments such as Zimbardo's and Milgram's for explaining the abuse at Abu Ghraib, because to some extent they do provide an interpretation. However, these social psychological experiments do not address entirely the fact that there was indeed a Durkheimian *anomic absence of authority* (see Caldwell and Mestrovic 2010, Mestrovic and Caldwell 2010, Caldwell and Mestrovic 2008a, Caldwell and Mestrovic 2008b) and the lack of David Riesman's ([1961]2000) inner-directed "moral compass"—both of which were non-existent at Abu Ghraib as shown by the numerous testimonies at the courts-martial of both Lynndie England and Sabrina Harman, as well as the U.S. Government's own reports (see Mestrovic 2007, Danner 2004, Strasser 2004) regarding the lack of leadership with regard to prisoner treatment, and the lack of responsibility of those higher-up with regard to the abuse itself. These issues need to be addressed in order to fully account for the chaos of Abu Ghraib. And so, I argue that because of testimony supplied at the England and Harman courts-martial, analysis of the government's reports, as well as other evidence, that the abuse at Abu Ghraib was not simply the result of a few "rotten apples" in a volatile environment conducive to group-influenced behavior defined as torture.

I further argue, however, that abuse took place because of the gendered masculine and heterosexist nature of the American military (for the Army, like the scientist, is part and parcel of larger culture) and Zimbardo does not address any of these alternate explanations in his assessment of Abu Ghraib. For example, in *The Lucifer Effect*, Zimbardo (2007a) does not even mention the existence of female prisoners at Abu Ghraib. Instead, he writes as an extension of his famous experiment with reference to "good boys" gone bad at Abu Ghraib —but does not write about the female soldiers, prisoners, officers, lawyers, commanders, girlfriends, and other female roles. I do not believe that Zimbardo's account, given its gender biases and omissions, can be considered a full explanation, and especially since it excludes 50 percent of the human race. Much like Carol Gilligan had to "fill in other voices," namely voices of women, in relation to the exclusively male-oriented work of Lawrence Kohlberg, I "fill in" the perspective of women by adding women's experiences and women as subjects associated with Abu Ghraib as a counter to Zimbardo's exclusively male-centered analyses, from the Stanford Prison Experiment to Abu Ghraib.[1] By using a gender-sensitive analysis, which accounts for both gender and sexuality, one can come to a thicker understanding of the infamous events of this now iconic occurrence at Abu Ghraib. Thus, I argue that Zimbardo's Stanford Prison Study neither fully illuminates nor makes a substantial contribution in understanding the events and the abuses at Abu Ghraib prison, which was a real place with actual suffering that involved males *and* females as well as gender and power permutations. Instead, Zimbardo's explanation seems to lack critical

---

1 I do not mean to suggest that there exists a single or only several women's perspective(s), but that for a thorough analysis, all individuals that are a part of a system should be represented.

analysis and does not really consider complex gender relations and power as a central point of departure.[2]

Zimbardo's Prison Study

Consider Zimbardo's experiment, which provides an explanation of group conformity to social roles, which within a social context, Zimbardo argues can influence, shape, alter, and even transform human behavior (Zimbardo 1971, 1972, 2007a, 2007b, Musen and Zimbardo 1991). Zimbardo's Stanford Prison Study (1971) simulated a mock jail situation where exclusively male students were randomly assigned the role of guard or prisoner. This experiment was aimed at understanding the behavior and psychological consequences of occupying and maintaining the role of a prison guard or prisoner within an institutional environment. A realistic looking prison block was constructed in the basement of Stanford University (mimicking the highly-controlled environment of the National Guards at Attica Prison), and 70 young men were screened physically and psychologically for the experiment. The 24 healthiest men—or as Zimbardo calls them, "boys"—were selected to participate in the study, and they were given their roles as either guard or prisoner. (It is important to note that these students were psychologically screened so as to rule out any deviant personalities, so as to "prove" the environment itself was pathological enough to distort the behavior of psychologically healthy individuals.) The Palo Alto city police actually participated in the experiment and arrested publicly those previously designated to be prisoners in the study. These prisoners were taken to the police station, fingerprinted, and then transported to the Stanford University basement's mock jail.

The guards and prisoners spent the next two weeks in the prison with each other. Zimbardo, the superintendent of the prison, had instructed the guards not to physically harm the prisoners, but to create situations of boredom, frustration, fear, and arbitrariness so that the prisoners understood that the guards now controlled their lives. In this way, Zimbardo played the "role" of warden in his own experiment. It was the guards' responsibility to maintain constant surveillance of the prisoners, who in turn had no degree of privacy whatsoever, and understood through these actions their absolute helplessness. Additionally, the guards were instructed to create an atmosphere of powerlessness for the prisoners, where their identities were stripped from them in exchange for a faceless identification through numbers. Once the prisoners arrived at the mock jail, they were stripped naked, given rubber shower shoes, and chained around one leg as a constant reminder of their role

---

2   I want to make clear that Zimbardo was aware that gender was a component of his study—he did put "prisoners" in "dresses" and intended them to feel as subjugated women. However, there was no real critical analysis either in his study, his analysis or of Abu Ghraib, or of the military in terms of deep level gender theorizing or a gender-sensitive analysis.

status. Symbols were used at the prison to show status, with the guards receiving a whistle, billy club, uniform, and mirror sunglasses (to allow the guards to mask their "own" identity for that of "guard")—all symbolic of their powerful role over the prisoners and their elite status. The prisoners received identical plain potato-sack outfits with armholes, which were actually women's plain dresses, prisoner identification numbers, and headscarves—all symbolic of their subordinate status to the guards, and identical inferior status as prisoners.[3] Hence, identities were all socially constructed and in terms of power.

Incidentally, here is an instance of the "logic of emasculation," which Zimbardo does not weave directly into his theory of obedience to authority—that of femininity used as a means of subordination. By dressing men in women's clothing, this questions the association between maleness and masculinity. Although feminists and queer theorists question the association of sex and gender as neither natural nor normal, which I agree with, the cultural norm that functioned in Zimbardo's 1971 context (and still now to some extent within "normative" gender categories of dominant culture) saw these categories as intertwined. Hence, the actual treatment of sexed men as "women," or the feminization of male bodies as punishment or subordination, *functioned* to psychologically break down the "prisoners." What is more, these male "prisoners" are punished by being treated as women, or labeled as such, where prisoner is akin to female, an already subjugated group within patriarchal society itself. The punishment here is thus *forced feminization*. Although alternative identities are socially constructed with regard to power for both prisoners and guards, other reasons for these identities are to minimize actual individualities as well as to force the adherence to the arbitrary, coercive rules of the prison institution; nonetheless, the analysis of gender as a descriptor is key in drawing out some important ways to think about this oppression. In this way, the mask of the mirror sunglasses, props, outfits, numbers used for detainee identification, roles, status, and other markers—all understood and mediated through the context of gendered power relations—provides alternate identities for both prisoners and guards, and makes the prison environment a complex and diffuse social network of power.

Both guards and prisoners, soon after arriving at the "Stanford Prison," became resentful and hostile towards one another. When tactics of force were shown not to work effectively, as sometimes prisoners laughed at guards' commands, thereby not taking the situation seriously, the guards began to additionally use psychological tactics to control the prisoners. Things that ultimately led to the guard's increased power over the prisoners are as follows: guards humiliated prisoners sadistically by assigning them duties such as cleaning out toilets with their bare hands, forcing them

---

3   On Zimbardo's website www.prisonexp.org, he states that prisoners were treated "more like a woman than a man," which is the only statement that examines the activities at the Stanford Prison in terms of gender and power. However, I believe he intended to use the terms of gender "feminine and masculine." This is further proof of the unquestioned assumptions Zimbardo has about sex and gender, and the influence of power between the two.

to do pushups and repeat commands, and sing songs such as repeating "prisoner 819 did a bad thing" so as to redirect prisoner hostility away from the guards. Additionally, guards interrupted sleep to do roll calls (argued to provide regular interaction with prisoners as a means to show control), called the prisoners names thereby berating them, took away their blankets, clothing (nakedness), and beds, used sexual humiliation, and forced them at night to urinate and defecate in buckets in their cells. In some cases, the guards attempted to give some prisoners privileges such as beds, clothing, and better meals as a means to gain prisoner compliance through reward. Additionally, the guards used a storage closet as a place to put prisoners in solitary confinement for punishment. These were all actions aimed at outlining and maintaining the guard's control. As a means for preserving the environment of the prison, compliance of prisoners, and the authority of the guards, Zimbardo instructed guards to put paper bags over the prisoner's heads when they went to the restrooms or when they went to the counseling office, which was not uncommon (Gibney 2006). Not surprisingly, the prisoners resisted and insulted the guards in return.

Within a day there were signs of stress and anxiety, as prisoners were beginning to feel extreme panic, frustration and loss of control. (The prisoners who did not show anxiety became blindly obedient to the guards.) On the second day, Prisoner 8612 started to complain of stomach pains and headaches, and when he went to meet with Zimbardo (as a prisoner, and not a student), Zimbardo (in the prison supervisor "warden" role) told him that he could not leave the experiment and instead offered prisoner 8612 a deal for easy treatment if he would become a "snitch" (Musen and Zimbardo 1991). Prisoner 8612 returned to the population and told everyone that he had met with Zimbardo and that there was no way that anybody could get out of the experiment (Musen and Zimbardo 1991). Because of the reported outcome of this meeting with Zimbardo, the prison superintendent, the prisoners really began to feel like prisoners. Additionally, the guards began to think of the prisoners as dangerous. There were minimal signs of physical rebellion in the mock jail, and instead there were evidences of psychological stress. After only four days, Zimbardo had removed five of the male student-prisoners who displayed "extreme emotional depression, crying, rage, and acute anxiety" (Zimbardo 1972). For example, Prisoner 8612 began to show signs of confusion and helplessness, and began to exhibit signs of a "crazy person," which turned into uncontrollable rage (Musen and Zimbardo 1991). Before the first week ended, the situation of abuse had become so bad that Zimbardo cancelled the experiment totally. Zimbardo (1972) says that guards began to treat prisoners as "despicable animals" and those guards were taking sadistic pleasure in cruelty. Zimbardo also characterized some of the prisoners as becoming so servile, yielding, and submissive that they were said to have only been concerned with their escape, their own individual survival, and their escalating hatred of the guards (Zimbardo 1972).

It is important to note that Zimbardo "decided" to end the experiment as the result of his girlfriend, and then wife-to-be, Christina Maslach's strong protestations. Zimbardo has acknowledged her whistle blowing role throughout his writings, and in fact, he dedicates his most recent book, *The Lucifer Effect*, to her with the words: "dedicated to the serene heroine of my life: Christina Maslach Zimbardo." The significance of this fact for the present analysis is that Maslach was the only female voice, the only "different voice," in the more than 30-year-old patriarchal and exclusively male-centered narrative of the Stanford Prison Experiment and its significance. Indeed, she was primarily significant to this experiment as she was perhaps the reason that the experiment itself ended.

Zimbardo explained the abuse that flowed from the experiment as resulting from the situation and environment within which the students existed, coupled with their role identification of either guard or prisoner. In this way, behavior was explained in terms of situational forces and adherence to roles within these situations. Zimbardo thus concluded that prison violence is a behavior that is rooted in the social character of jails and prisons themselves, and not in the personalities of those either working or confined there (guards or prisoners). Zimbardo is not always consistent on this point, admitting in *The Lucifer Effect* that he was the superintendent at the mock prison, and thereby may have influenced the results. In fact, Mestrovic (2007) further argues that the prestige of both Stanford University and also the prestige of science in general all played roles in convincing students to adhere to their roles within the experiment.

Zimbardo applied this narrative to the abuse at Abu Ghraib as a way of understanding the events; however, Zimbardo's account leaves out some important factors that are imperative to consider when providing a narrative for the detainee abuse at Abu Ghraib. Specifically, Zimbardo's explanation does not account for the following: how significant authority figures can have some impact on behavior; how other, competing authorities (in Zimbardo's experiment, the police department, Stanford University, and the American Psychological Association) created chaos in the minds of abusers by apparently supporting an authority figure bent upon ordering abuse; that American troops were located in a war zone and faced daily catastrophes of war; that cultural differences were exploited and used against prisoners at Abu Ghraib as torture techniques; the anomic absence of authority at Abu Ghraib; the lack of any moral guidelines for action; and above all, how Harman and England, the women of Tier 1A actually coped and acted differently (as shown in their trials) at Abu Ghraib *vis-à-vis* the abuse and reactions to it. Zimbardo does not consider the obvious fact that any context, such as even a prison, has mitigating factors that flow from outside that context (such as culture itself), inward to the prison and effect the social climate, shape the individuals who are part of that environment, and replicate cultural power differentials (including authority, but not limited to that) within those contexts themselves. Indeed, cultural flow can even shape how torture and deviance are enacted and gendered.

Milgram and the Absence of Authority Figures

Another approach for understanding the abuse at Abu Ghraib is in terms of Stanley Milgram's 1962 social psychology experiments at Yale University, where

Milgram aimed to understand the effects of group behavior and blind obedience to an authority figure (Milgram 1963). Using this study, it is possible to account for some of the influence that those higher-up in the military had regarding prisoner abuse, for which the application of Zimbardo's experiment failed to account.

Milgram conducted conformity experiments in a controversial study that was aimed at understanding how inhumane actions can be understood with no concern for consequences, such as with Nazis in World War II. His research question was the following—*Under what conditions would a person obey authority when it goes against one's conscience?* In this experiment, Milgram explained to male recruits that they would be taking part in a study of how punishment affects learning. One by one he assigned them to the role of either 'teacher" or "learner," and placed the learner (who was also the accomplice in the study) in a connecting room. Note again that the idea of testing how women would behave under similar research conditions did not seem to occur to Milgram or any of the noted researchers in the obedience to (male) authority paradigm.[4]

The teacher watched the learner sit down in a contraption representing an electric chair, where the researcher applied electrode paste and electrodes to the learner's wrist, explaining that the paste would prevent blisters and burns. As the teacher looked on, the researcher then fastened a leather strap to prevent movement when given electrical shock. Although the shocks were to be painful, Milgram assured the teacher that there would be no permanent damage. The researcher then led the teacher into an adjoining room and showed him that the electric chair was hooked up to a generator that gives shocks; however, the "teacher" role did not know that these would be phony shocks. There was a dial that could be turned to adjust the intensity of the shocks, and once seated in front of the shock generator, the teacher is supposed to read a pair of words aloud and then repeat the first word, waiting for the learner to repeat the second word. If the learner got it incorrect, he would be shocked, with increasing intensity. The listener was supposed to moan when "shocked," and as the shocks became more intense, the learner was instructed to begin to yell and pound on the wall. After a certain level, there was silence from the learner following shocks given from the teacher. Now, even with this silence, Milgram was trying to research how many teachers would go all of the way to the highest shock level under the command of Milgram, the authority figure in the experiment. When the "teachers" expressed concern and asked Milgram how far on the shock meter they had to go, Milgram would reply "As far as necessary" (Gibney 2006).

At Milgram's urging, the "teachers" kept participating with the experiment, even though they believed that they were causing harm. The responsibility for this "harm" was deflected onto the researcher, and Milgram, the authority figure, could

---

4   I am not arguing that women would all have the same perspective, that women in general would respond in similar ways, or that male power is always analogous; however, I am arguing that women should have been included in Milgram's research so as to fully represent all human behavior for comparison.

be understood as taking the blame for the "teacher's" actions with his prodding for these actions. In this way, responsibility was removed from the "teachers" with regard to the harm they perceived that they were causing, as Milgram "the authority figure" insisted in their compliance of action, thereby forcing responsibility onto Milgram. Almost two thirds of the subjects ("teachers") went all of the way to 450 volts, even with all of the negative responses from the learners, and even after their final silence. Milgram thus reached the conclusion that pressures keep us in the roles that we accept and that behavior itself is dominated by social roles we are to play. Milgram's research into obedience suggests that people are likely to follow directions from legitimate authority figures even when it means inflicting harm on others.

Applied to Abu Ghraib, Milgram's study about compliance with authority figures provides an interpretation concerning the influence that those higher-ups in the military had regarding prisoner abuse. For example, there was some confusion about the status of the prisoners at Abu Ghraib—were they prisoners of war or enemy combatants? The President of the United States was not clear in the characterization of the status of these detainees in Iraq and there was much discussion about their relative standing. This unclear characterization of prisoner status by the Commander in Chief of the United States (and various attorneys for the White House), and within the military itself, led to uncertainty with regard to prisoner rights. Thus, it was not initially clear if the Geneva Conventions applied to prisoners at Abu Ghraib, and hence there was some confusion about proper handling of detainees. This confusion was specifically a result of the confusion between prisoner rights in Afghanistan, where the Geneva Conventions *did not* apply, versus prisoner rights in Iraq, where they *were* applicable.

Moreover, the new situation at Abu Ghraib that is different from Milgram's male-centered studies is that Brigadier General Janis Karpinski was a female commander of all the prisons in Abu Ghraib. But as she explains in her book, *One Woman's Army* (2005), her male superiors dealt with this unwelcome fact by simply bypassing her completely when it came to all decisions regarding Abu Ghraib. As she points out, she was kept "out of the loop," and she makes it clear that she believes that this is because she is a woman (Karpinski 2005). On the other hand, she was the only commander, male or female, who was demoted as punishment for what occurred at Abu Ghraib. This complex reality of Abu Ghraib in terms of command structure, obedience to authority, and gender does not flow out of Milgram's, Zimbardo's, or any other work in the obedience to authority paradigm.

Additionally, as was shown in the courts-martial of England and Harman, abuse of prisoners was again and again reported to those higher up in the chain of command (see Chapter 3). However, initially nothing was done about these reports of abuse, and only after the photographs of the abuse were leaked to the press did this maltreatment become an outright issue. Once abuse was reported and nothing was done about it, logically it follows that those who took the reports of abuse become implicated as "authority figures" acquiescing to torture tactics. Nonetheless, as of this writing, no officers or those higher-ups in the chain of command, including Donald Rumsfeld, the former Defense Secretary (who the ACLU and Human Rights Watch have filed a lawsuit against for bearing direct responsibility for the torture and abuse of detainees in U.S. Military custody in Iraq), have been charged with maltreatment of detainees. Rumsfeld has been quoted in the media as stating that he "felt bad about what happened to the detainees [at Abu Ghraib]," but he has personally approved interrogation techniques such as stress positions, nudity, and the use of dogs, which violate long standing military rules (Gibney 2006). In fact, with regard to using questionable tactics for detainee interrogation, Vice President Dick Cheney was also quoted as saying that it might be time to "take the gloves off and go to the dark side" (Gibney 2006).

Additionally, training in interrogation techniques migrated from Guantanamo Bay, Afghanistan, and to Iraq, where Major General Geoffrey Miller provided training. Miller is the officer in charge of interrogation at Guantanamo Bay, Cuba, and his instruction in Iraq evidences an authority figure as associated with the questionable treatment of prisoners. Case and point, interrogation tactics were taught to the MI's in Iraq by an authority figure, namely Major General Miller.

Moreover, at the England and Harman courts-martial, testimony was provided regarding orders given to the prison guards at Abu Ghraib specifying tactics for dealing with prisoners, and specifically the breakdown of the roles of MI and MP. The MPs were told to "soften up" detainees for interrogation, which was outside of the duties of the MPs, who were to function as guards. Former Sergeant Ken Davis stated at the England courts-martial, regarding the events of October 25, where prisoners were handcuffed together nude and after suspicion of rape, that he reported this questionable treatment of MPs abusing detainees to his platoon leader, and that he was told that the MIs were in charge and to let them do their job. Said Davis to his platoon leader after seeing naked prisoners handcuffed in sexual positions, "The MI's are doing weird things with naked detainees." Davis testified at the Harman courts-martial, "Cruz [MI] walks up to me and he looks at me and he says have we crossed the line? And I had no idea what was going on and I said I don't know, you're MI, aren't you? And he said, well you're the MP. And I said well I would have to say yes. He said well we're military intelligence, we know what we're doing, and he kind of turned around and walked away" (May 16, 2005, SHCM).

Additionally, in a 2006 Documentary shown on Sundance about Abu Ghraib (Gibney 2006), Ken Davis describes a conversation that he and Charles Graner had one evening after Graner's shift, where Davis asked Graner if he was getting sick since he was losing his voice. Graner said "no, he wasn't getting sick," but explained that MIs were pushing MPs to "soften up" detainees, and that he, as an MP, had been yelling all night. As bombs were going off outside of the prison, MIs were yelling at MPs and telling them, says Davis, "there goes another American losing their life and unless you help [soften up detainees] then their blood is on your hands too" (Gibney 2006). MIs were using the psychological tactics of guilt coupled with obligation as a means to get the MPs to "soften up" the prisoners, where the prisoners were now getting the full brunt of the MP's force, as they were being emotionally equated with the "terrorists" bombing the prison outside of the walls of Abu Ghraib. What is important to remember here is that most of the prisoners at Abu Ghraib were common criminals, if criminal at all, and that these prisoners were suffering violence at the hands of American troops because of the psychological techniques that MI was using on MP. Specifically, MIs were using the psychological technique of making the MPs paranoid and delusional, where events outside of the prison were being equated in terms of responsibility (transferring blame) onto the incarcerated detainee's. In this way, MI was applying psychological techniques on the MPs as a way of getting them to do specific "softening up" actions, and thus functioned as a kind of influential superior in that behavior was brought about because of MI urgings. These urgings, coupled with the high priority placed on "actionable intelligence," argues Danner in his book *Torture and Truth* (2004), led to the valuing of intelligence as more important than the lawful respecting of the Geneva Conventions or the various prohibitions on torture signed onto by Congress. Explicitly, in some cases, military personnel were told "do what you have to do to get confessions" (Gibney 2006). In fact, Private Frederick testified that Special Agent Romero (MI) told him, referring to "Gilligan," the hooded detainee on the MRE box, after stating that he wanted him as stressed out as possible that night, as he would be interrogated the following day—"I don't give a fuck what you do, just don't kill him, I need him to talk tomorrow" (May 13, 2005, SHCM). Hence, there is some evidence that authority figures instructed prisoner care, although this is different than exemplified in Milgram's study in that Abu Ghraib was not a controlled-for environment, there was not an authority figure continuously providing the delineations for correct behavior, and this authority figure could not be referenced continuously and over time with regard to responsibility for the actions being urged forward.

Again, missing even in these discussion of the role of MI at Abu Ghraib are the glaring facts that the general in charge of *all* military intelligence in Iraq was female, Major General Barbara Fast. Interestingly, the point person for implementing General Miller's Guantanamo techniques in both Afghanistan and Iraq was female, Captain Carolyn Wood. Fast and Wood are, for all practical purposes, invisible in discussions of this sort. Next to nothing is known about the following: their roles, whether they protested against the techniques, how they got along with their male counter-parts in the chain of command, and in general—their "voice" or "subjecthoods."

Nonetheless, Milgram's study does apply to the situation between England and Graner to some extent. One of the expert witnesses for the defense stated under oath that Graner could have been running a "class on obedience," where Graner was the scientist authority and England was the individual showing blind obedience to this authority, or "teacher" using Milgram's study as a parallel. In Xavier Amador's and Thomas Denne's expert opinion at England's courts-martial, England was compliant with Graner's wishes and orders, and showed loyalty and duty to Graner since they were in a relationship as lovers at Abu Ghraib prison. Additionally, Amador characterized Graner as acting as England's "father" when describing the level of England's compliance, evidencing a clear power/role differential.[5]

Consider for a moment Graner's testimony about the now infamous picture of England holding a leashed detainee. Graner stated under oath that he pulled the detainee he had nicknamed "Gus" out of the cell through the use of a rifle sling tether. Earlier that day, "Gus" had been violent towards the guards and so Graner thought he was using precautionary measures by not entering the cell and using an *extraction technique*. Sergeant Hydrue Joyner's testimony later that day also revealed that "Gus" was highly disruptive and would fight everyone when he was taken out of his cell, and he said that he remembered "Gus" specifically, as his personality made a lasting impression on him because he refused to wear clothing. Graner stated that both England and Meghan Ambuhl were present during this extraction in case the prisoner became violent, as cell extractions were repeatedly described in the courts-martial as dangerous situations where soldiers enter the prisoner's environment. Graner intended to yank the prisoner out of the cell by his shoulders, but the leash slipped and went up around his neck instead. Graner stated that the prisoner then got up on all fours and crawled out of the cell, at which time Graner handed the tether to England. Graner took three photographs of this detainee with England holding the tether, and stated that England was compliant with all of his orders—Stated Graner, "England trusts me, yes. She did not think I was going to maltreat the detainee." Implied in this statement is the idea that England held Graner in high esteem such that she (England) believed that his behavior could not be aimed at anything unethical or wrong—she trusted him as her lover. Actually, I doubt that England even questioned these distinctions when it came to her views of Graner, and specifically because of consideration of Xavier Amador's expert witness analysis of her psychological profile. Additionally, in another infamous photograph of England, where she is smiling and pointing to an Iraqi's genitals, Graner stated under oath that he had ordered England to get into the photograph. No doubt, England was compliant with this order, again demonstrating the kind of blind faith that she put in Grainer. Applying Milgram, in this example his notion of obedience to authority figures applies exactly in that England was described again and again through testimony as being compliant towards Graner's requests.

However, considering the previous examples—the questionable status of the prisoners, the fact that abuse was reported and ignored, and also that tactics for interrogation were trained for, evidence of authority figures as responsible for instructing some of the abuse at Abu Ghraib, and as separate from Zimbardo's claims of environmental conditions as the reason for action—there is indeed another narrative that should be considered as a reason for the abuse itself.

---

5   For the sake of completeness, it should be noted that Mestrovic did not agree with the tactic taken by the two expert witnesses in psychology, because, as a sociologist, he said that such an exclusively psychological explanation unfairly shifted all the blame onto Graner, and not the social climate that transformed Graner's behavior.

Specifically, the Zimbardo paradigm leaves out the role of influential superiors by only focusing on the power of situations and roles, and thus Zimbardo's account leaves out the power individuals have to influence others within these situations. What is also interesting is that in his own study, the Stanford Prison Study, Zimbardo himself acts as the primary "authority figure" in the experiment, as he both controlled the experiment and was also an active participant in the experiment as prison supervisor. Again, not only did Zimbardo serve as the social scientist and creator of this experiment, he was also a participant in this experiment with his role of prison supervisor.

Nevertheless, I do not argue that in these examples, total responsibility can be passed off to the authority figure, as was the case with Milgram's study. At Abu Ghraib, there was no written or agreed upon method or tactic for detainee care or interrogation that was consistently taught or put forth as procedure. Instead, prisoner care and detainee interrogation was described in testimony as "ad hoc" in nature. SGT Robert Jones even stated in his testimony that Graner, who was described by Jones as having a "strong personality," had a following of sorts, where it gave Jones the "impression" that Graner controlled and influenced the actions of others with his "ad hoc" approach to detainee care and handling. Says the Commander of the 372nd Military Police at Abu Ghraib, Captain Donald J. Reese, in his testimony about Internment Resettlement (IR) or how the 372nd had not even been trained for what they had been assigned to do at Abu Ghraib (they were a combat support and security combat escort company) and his perception of prisoner care and detainee interrogations: "In October 2003 there was no guidance put in writing for the prison standards. We were not trained in IR. This was a totally new mission for all of us. At that time no one stopped to review the Geneva Convention" (June 24, 2004, SHA32). At Abu Ghraib there was no authority figure supervising, urging appropriate and prescribed action for continued "duty," and there was no controlled for environment such as Milgram's laboratory. Nonetheless, Milgram's study thus gives some insight into the roles that authority figures played at Abu Ghraib, and where Zimbardo's experiment does not.

Yet the role of Lynndie England highlights again the fact that gender played a significant role: no male soldier was nearly as submissive to Graner as the female England was. Other male soldiers testified that they were afraid of Graner, and even feared that he would shoot and kill them (see Chapter 3); but, England testified and experts testified about her, that she complied with Graner's "authority" out of "love." Moreover, as the defense attorneys tried to argue, she was involved in this "abusive love relationship" because she was stressed, scared, and disoriented, so that Graner became her "moral compass." Graner made it very clear in his testimony that he did not love or even care for England or their baby, and especially as he walked off of the stand, past England and their child, without so much as eye contact. A straightforward application of Milgram and Zimbardo is not complete without taking into account these aspects of cross-gender relationships in authority and obedience.

Beyond Authority Figures: Back to Zimbardo and Abu Ghraib

While it is true that there are some similarities evidenced between Zimbardo's study and the events at Abu Ghraib, there was much dissimilarity given the realities of Abu Ghraib.

First, Abu Ghraib was located in a war zone where American troops were killed regularly, and mortar and rocket-propelled grenade attacks on the prison itself were made nightly. Additionally, at Abu Ghraib there was a lack of food, water, medical provisions, and even electricity, such that there were sometimes no electricity from the generators, and at night outside lighting from vehicles was used, according to the testimony of the supply officer at Abu Ghraib, Major David DiNenna. Master Sergeant Joyner testified under oath at the England trial that Abu Ghraib prison stunk, was nasty, and was possibly "the nastiest place on earth." Both DiNenna and Joyner asked out loud during their testimonies why the U.S. Army picked a prison that was in the middle of an active war zone (itself a violation of the Geneva Conventions) for handling supposedly high-security threats. Conversely, Zimbardo's study was located in the basement of Stanford University, and neither the prisoners nor the guards faced the daily atrocities of war that American troops experienced. In this way, although not emotionally safe, the prisoners in Zimbardo's study were physically safe from bodily harm, had supplies such as food, water, and electricity, had security, and had constant support from both the school and creators of the study. Additionally, Zimbardo's participants were released upon showing signs of emotional distress, while at Abu Ghraib emotional distress and chaos was evidenced in many ways as a normal part of life. Additionally, American soldiers were not given any way out of the chaos of Abu Ghraib as this was not a study with a set duration. Under oath and in his testimony, Graner called the prison "bizarro-world" in an attempt to characterize the chaotic environment at Abu Ghraib, where screaming from prisoners in painful stress positions was heard every night, he claimed, at Tier 1-A.

Another difference between Zimbardo's experiment and the events at Abu Ghraib is that cultural differences did not exist in Zimbardo's experiment. Unlike at Abu Ghraib, where prisoners were Iraqi, and where interrogation techniques were used that exploited Iraqi cultural fears. In Zimbardo's study, all of the participants were American males who were students at Stanford. This means that at Stanford, there was not the ability for guards to use different cultural values as a means and method of torture, as all of the Stanford participants basically had similar cultural and contextual experiences. (Only shared cultural gender codes could be used for torture at Zimbardo's mock prison.)

I argue that yet another dissimilarity between Zimbardo's Prison Study and the events at Abu Ghraib is that women were present at Abu Ghraib, and only men participated in Zimbardo's study. This is foundationally important when analyzing misogyny and sexism at Abu Ghraib. In the courts-martial of England and Harman, it came out in testimony that American soldiers imprisoned women and children at Abu Ghraib. Through interviews with soldiers who were witnesses at the trial, I learned that the women and children were "swept up" along with the men in disorganized arrest raids, and in some cases were kept as "hostages" to make the men talk during interrogations. What is of great interest is that the U.S. Government conceded in open trial that it kept women and children at Abu Ghraib, without charging them with any crime, but never stated the reason for their detention. (The government reports also fail to investigate the reasons for detaining women and children.) Captain Donald J. Reese, the 372nd Military Police Commander testified that women and children were detained in tier 1B, stating, "We knew it was in violation of the Geneva Convention … We did the best we could to segregate the males, females and children. It was physically impossible to keep all the detainees separated" (June 24, 2002, SHA32). Nonetheless, if the "backstage" reason stated by the soldiers is that, indeed, the women and children were held as hostages, then it seems that the U.S. Army engaged in a practice it condemns in its enemies, namely hostage-taking. But the soldiers stated they were not asked the reasons for this curious fact while they were testifying on the stand, and thus one of the hidden realities of Abu Ghraib was exposed.

Cultural Code of Masculinity

Against all of these critiques, there are indeed some similarities evidenced between Zimbardo's study and the events at Abu Ghraib. For example, both situations evidenced emblematic use of symbols for power such as uniforms, naked prisoners, and billy clubs. Similarly, both Zimbardo's prison and Abu Ghraib show similar behavior in prisoner care with the use of stress positions/situations where prisoners were hooded and chained/zip-tied, stripped naked, and the frequent restraint of bodies in an attempt to display power. Additionally, looking at abuse in Zimbardo's study and also at Abu Ghraib, the nature of abuse at both locations turned sexual. Both situations evidenced similar sexualized and homoerotic torture techniques—a mock (homosexual) wedding at Stanford, and forced masturbation and naked pyramids at Abu Ghraib. I argue that this can be understood in terms of the connections between sex and gender, power, and sexuality, and that what is missing in Zimbardo's account of the abuse during his prison study, and his application of his study to Abu Ghraib, is this specific kind of analysis.

Consider how gender is socially constructed with regard to power, where in larger cultural narratives about gender, masculinity is equated with heterosexuality, and value is given to this association. In this way, the connections between sex, gender, and sexuality function as a culturally practiced ideology. One of the characterizations of the American military is that it has been socially constructed as a masculinist and heterosexist environment. Cynthia Enloe (2000) even goes so far as to describe the military, and the process of militarization, as part and parcel of patriarchy or privileged masculinity. This means that value is given to the characterization of things that are "masculine," where cultural stereotypes of maleness and masculinity are equated and rewarded commensurately. Consider the advertisements for the Marine Corps, where what is needed are a "Few Good *Men*," or the Army's advertisement where what is sought is "An Army of One's Own," and always a male soldier's face is shown in the advertisement. Perhaps for this reason, Zimbardo's study focused on men because it was financed by a grant from the U.S. Navy. Nevertheless, since Zimbardo's 1971 study, the U.S. military has gone co-educational, and it seems that Zimbardo has not developed his analysis associated with his study with these gendered changes.

Additionally, I argue that heterosexuality is the organizing sexuality or "logic" in the American military, where gays and lesbians are not legally allowed to "openly," and thus with open and valued knowledge of their gayness, serve their country. This is obviously because of the laws regarding "Don't Ask, Don't Tell"; however, these cultural attitudes do exist in larger culture where gays and lesbians have been given second-class status in terms of rights, benefits and value within most parts of larger society. These characterizations of the military, that of masculinity and heterosexuality, culminates in what I term a "*code of cultural masculinity*," where what it means to be male and masculine is understood as heterosexual in nature. This issue became salient when Sabrina Harman was "outed" as a lesbian, along with her wife/partner Kelly, during her court-martial. Soldiers told us that the Army was "killing two birds with one stone" by prosecuting Harman—using her as a scapegoat to support its "few rotten apples" theory, and expelling her from the military because of her sexual orientation.

American cultural values underwrite this fear of homosexuality, where homosexual men and women, or those who identify as queer, have frequently been targeted with violence in American culture and have thus faced massive amounts of discrimination physically and legally. New legislation forbids the use of sexual orientation as a means for violence or the threat of violence with hate-crime legislation, where hate crimes are punished more severely than exactly similar crimes that are not driven by stated discriminatory practices. I argue that homoerotic torture can be described in kind as a hate-crime of sorts, and one that is specifically engaging of our stereotypical cultural connections between maleness, masculinity, and straightness. Additionally, these qualities have historically been powerful perspectives (ideological canopies even) in American society, and thus function as an organizing principle of our society's heterosexist patriarchal structure based on power. Interestingly, these associations are the ones that queer theory specifically questions in its recent theoretical conceptualization.

The "code of cultural masculinity," where both masculinity and heterosexuality function together as the power symbolic of the military, was evidenced in many ways at the Stanford Prison and also at Abu Ghraib prison. At Abu Ghraib and during the Stanford experiment, both situations evidenced homosexual torture techniques to exploit culturally constructed attitudes about masculinity and fears of homosexuality. Zimbardo's paradigm for analysis does not show the importance of sex, gender, and sexuality as themselves torture techniques, which were used against both Iraqi prisoners at Abu Ghraib and Zimbardo's student-prisoners. At both Abu Ghraib and also at Stanford, prisoners were made to endure humiliation and torture that can be understood as primarily homoerotic in nature. For example, naked Iraqi prisoners at Abu Ghraib were chained into painful stress positions and forced to wear women's panties on their heads.

Regarding Zimbardo's experiment, male prisoners were dressed in very plain women's dresses that went down to their knees, and were given no undergarments. This outfit symbolizes the forced feminization of the prisoners, as their clothing is actually gendered in design and revealing as a form of humiliation. The "phallus" is actually feminized given the vulnerability of the genitals themselves, where phallic power is exerted via this exposed vulnerability. Although these outfits were not "sexy" or "erotic" in the typical fashion of the adult entertainer, they did function in a pornographic way, as genitals were exposed and nakedness was evident in movement, thereby exposing the prisoner figuratively and literally.[6] In this way, masculinity was taken away through the characterization of prisoners *as* women, and since they were actually wearing what Zimbardo himself called a "dress" (Musen and Zimbardo 1991). This is an attempt to make the male prisoners feel exposed and powerless, as this image of the prisoner goes against the masculine power symbolic, and literally "strips" protective clothing away from men, thereby making them vulnerable and thus characterized as culturally feminine.

Additional humiliation of prisoners can be understood in Zimbardo's experiment, and as similar to Abu Ghraib, through the sexually humiliating punishment by the guards for prisoners to "get down and fuck the floor" (Gibney 2006). This is an example of guards toying with prisoners to establish control through the use of raw sex. Additionally, at the Stanford prison, there was a mock wedding between the bride of Frankenstein (played by one male prisoner) and Frankenstein (played by another), where these prisoners were forced to say, "I love you, Frankenstein" to his male-pseudo wife. One prisoner is depicted in this arrangement with his arms around the other prisoner's neck, and both bodies are forcibly pressed together by the guard instructing the action. This example uses drag roles and forced femininity as a means of humiliation, and questions heterosexuality and masculinity with the stated "I love you, [Prisoner] 2093" and the wedding theme itself (Gibney 2006). In this way, sex and sexuality are both exploited as torture techniques.

What is telling about how Zimbardo's Stanford Prison Study came to an end is that it had to do with Zimbardo's then girlfriend, and now wife, Christina Maslach Zimbardo. Zimbardo took Maslach to the basement of the Stanford psychology building to show her the experiment and her reaction was that of disgust and disbelief. Her response to Zimbardo was that the study had changed him somehow and she stated that "I'm not sure I want anything to do with you if you continue this study" (Gibney 2006). It was that day that Zimbardo ended the study. What is so telling about this ending is that it was affected by Zimbardo's girlfriend, a woman, who clearly demonstrated a position of power in that her reaction gave Zimbardo

---

6   I do not mean to suggest that Zimbardo's images were somehow sexually appealing.

the impetus to see the study for its unethical nature. Had Zimbardo analyzed his study in terms of gender, surely this dynamic would have been exposed, as would have other connections of gender, sex, and sexuality.

In a way, Maslach functioned as the highest member of the Stanford Prison Study's "chain of command" in that her input ended the experiment, when even Zimbardo, after hearing complaints from his student-prisoners, did not immediately end it. Mestrovic (2007) points out this fact when analyzing why the students continued to play the roles of sadists and victims, even though they were psychologically healthy. Mestrovic (2007) argues that Zimbardo's role as scientist/prison superintendent, the prestige of Stanford University, and the prestige of science in general, coupled with the students' belief that Stanford would not permit real abuse to occur, that the institution of science would not put a student in harms way, and that Zimbardo himself would not allow the abuse to become excessive, "precluded serious questioning of the abuse that occurred during the Stanford Prison Experiment" (Mestrovic 2007: 43). Mestrovic asks a question concerning the culpability and responsibility of the low level soldiers, the "rotten apples" at Abu Ghraib—Could they have quit? Could they have walked out? According to Mestrovic, and applied to Zimbardo's experiment, the student guards were "restrained" from reporting or stopping the abuse, or even quitting their roles in the experiment "by layers of competing social and cultural rationalizations that offset the reality of abuse" (Mestrovic 2007: 43). Applied to Abu Ghraib, Harman did not "walk out the door" when she witnessed abuse because the unhealthy norms that operated in the poisoned environment of the prison, which kept her a part of the "abusive relationship" that existed at Abu Ghraib. Says Mestrovic (2007),

> The soldier who witnessed or even participated in the abuse at Abu Ghraib looked up to and idealized the prestige of the U.S. Army and of the international community whose support was assumed in the war against Saddam Hussein's pariah regime. One assumes that the soldiers at Abu Ghraib felt that their mission was honorable. The soldier would probably have assumed that the U.S. Army would not put him or her in a position in which he or she would be harmed unnecessarily, cause unlawful harm to others, or engage in actions that would bring forth disgrace to the military unit or the U.S Army

Thankfully, Zimbardo's girlfriend watched the abuse during his experiment and this incident resulted in ethical correction; however, at Abu Ghraib, this kind of female voyeurism was used as a torture technique itself, as soldiers told me that female U.S. soldiers were ordered to be present during abuse, as well as by male naked showering prisoners precisely in order to add to their humiliation. Further, "The most unhealthy norms in the poisoned environment at Abu Ghraib dictated that Harman 'went along' with the abuse" (Mestrovic 2007: 42). That said, neither Zimbardo's students nor the soldiers at Abu Ghraib could have escaped the environment within which they existed because both locations had poisoned social climates.

Conclusion

Through a consideration of the testimony that was given at England's and Harman's courts-martials, what is missing in Zimbardo's paradigm for explaining the abuse at Abu Ghraib is an analysis of the connections with regard to power, gender and sexuality. This kind of analysis explains the homoerotic nature of the abuse and the evidenced sexualized and feminized torture techniques.

As I have argued, it seems initially that experiments such as Zimbardo's and Milgram's can explain the abuse at Abu Ghraib; however, I maintain that these paradigms either do not apply, or only show partly why the abuse took place. Through the use of additional perspectives such as an analysis of the gendered masculine and heterosexist nature of American culture and military, additional narratives about prisoner abuse are formed. Because the issues above are not considered by Zimbardo's paradigm, and because his analysis is built exclusively on a male-centered obedience to authority paradigm, I conclude that Zimbardo's Stanford Prison Study does neither fully elucidate nor make significant sense of the abuse at Abu Ghraib prison.

Testimony of Captain Donald J. Reese, U.S. Army, Sabrina Harman Courts-Martial

Captain Donald J. Reese, U.S. Army Company Commander for the 372nd, was called as a witness on May 16, 2005, was sworn and testified as follows:

Direct Examination by Trial Counsel

Q: Let's go to approximately 2002, is that when you became the Company Commander for the 372nd?

A: Yes, I took the command in December of 2002.

Q: Could you describe the 372nd at that time? Again, very briefly, just what their mission was, where was the unit located, that type of thing?

A: They were—they're typically a combat support company, they were located in Crescent Town, Maryland.

Q: How large was it?

A: If we're at 100 percent strength we're at typically 180 soldiers.

...

A: Basically there's two different types of MP units. You have a combat support and you have an IR, Internment Resettlement Unit. This particular unit, the 372nd, is a combat support unit and that's how their MEDL is set up and that's how they—we trained at Fort Lee, you know, in accordance to our MEDL. So we did very little IR training, you know, to be honest.

Q: Well in terms of combat support what kind of duties would that----

A: ----we were security combat escorts, MSR security.

Q: MSR, meaning?

A: Supply Routes—convoy security, that type of thing is where we focused.

...

Q: Now, with respect to Al Hillah, did you have an opportunity to observe Specialist Harman during that period of time that you were assigned there?

A: Yes, I did.

Q: And how would you characterize her performance during that time period?

A: She did a good job for me there; I had no problems with her. I would classify— if I had to give her a category I would say she probably is an average soldier. She didn't stand out superior, but she also gave me no other problems, disciplinary problems, or any other reason to think otherwise. The kids there is the one thing that sticks about me with her and they loved her. I mean, if I would come up to the sub-station in my vehicle, you know, maybe she was off that day, they would come running to my vehicle thinking that, you know, that might have been her, hoping it might have been her probably, and, you know, they—I judge a lot of things off how the kids react to people and they loved her and they looked forward to seeing her. And I believe her relationship that she built with the kids over there, you know, will do the military and, you know, the United States a lot of justice in the future because she pulled a great relationship with the kids there.

...

Q: You mentioned the term earlier "Internment Resettlement," so are their units—military police that are primarily—have that as a mission? ...In terms of Internment Resettlement, is that more related to serving guard duty over detainees?

A: That's correct, it's—they focus on correction—well, there's a 85 Charlie, which is strictly corrections, they focus more on the detainees in the POW Camps, that type of thing.

Q: So when did you first learn that your mission would change and you'd be assigned at Abu Ghraib Prison?

A: That probably would have been the end of September, early October.

Q: What training did you receive in this process of transition?

A: We conducted, I believe, there was some mandatory training that we completed prior to taking the mission. It was basically cell extraction; we went through some training there. Some riot control training. I think non-lethal; we went over that again, as far as the rounds. And there might have been one or two other things that I can't recall at this point.

Q: Did you receive any training on the Geneva Convention and handling different categories of detainees such as you subsequently experienced in Tier 1A in Abu Ghraib?

A: No, sir, we had the brief at Fort Lee during our mobilization period but it was a more generalized brief, it just covered, you know, kind of brushed over everything. The Geneva Convention is a very detailed document, it would take a rather extensive class to cover that in detail?

Q: In any event, at Fort Lee, at that time you had no idea that you would—your unit was going to be in a position of ultimately serving as prison guards?

A: That's right, sir, we didn't know at that time.

Q: And if I understand what you just said, once you knew you were going to Abu Ghraib, you received no specific training in that area?

A: That's correct.

Q: Before we get into the specific transition, can you describe the prison at the time that you arrived? What kind of condition was it in?

A: Well, less than favorable living conditions. We actually occupied an old medical area. They had—when we arrived there was debris, you know, rocks, dirt, everywhere. There was no showers, no facilities like that. A lot of medical paraphernalia, needles and things like that laying around. We had to clean all that up before we were to move in. We had to paint the walls. So, it was in pretty bad shape over all, when we moved in.

Q: What kind of quarters were your troops provided?

A: We actually lived in jail cells ...

...

Q: Right. What occurred in that October timeframe? Did you see a change in activity?

A: Sure, I mean, us—when we went to Abu Ghraib, that's in the middle of the Sunni Triangle so that's—it's a little more hostile there as opposed to where we were. So, yes, I mean it definitely was a lot more intensive up there, a whole lot more, you know, IEDs on the road, that kind of things, explosions, and so there was definitely a lot there, a lot more there.

Q: With respect to the prison itself, what did you experience in terms of the numbers of detainees that you found there and how did that change over time?

A: When we first took the missions we had roughly about 250 inmates at that point. The big thing was that they kept increasing the number of people that they brought to us and we didn't have the space to put them in. That was a big push there and they—they kept pushing me to work with the contractors to open up more space and that was the big thing. The numbers were probably, you know, 150 to 1, detainees versus 1 guard and then of course you got to throw in the fact that those Iraqi Police—Correction Officers that worked with us were also corrupt so we had a very high number of detainees verses MP and we also had to deal with the corrupt Iraqi Police Officers that were there also.

Q: Did you feel that you had adequate manning for the mission you were assigned?

A: Actually no, I mean, I had four missions going on at one time. At least we had one platoon down there and, you know, we were understaffed.

     ...

Q: And before we get into talking any more detail about what you actually did at Abu Ghraib, let's clarify who some of the people were. Who is General Karpinski?

A: She was the 89th MP Brigade Commander.

Q: And what was your relationship to her?

A: I fell underneath her—I fell under the 320th MP Battalion and the 320th fell under the 800th, so she was directly in charge of all the prisons in Iraq.

Q: And who headed up the 320th at that time, do you recall?

A: Yeah, Lieutenant Colonel Phillabaum was my battalion commander.

Q: And then who were some of the other officers that held positions at Abu Ghraib?

A: Major DiNenna was the S-3 at the battalion, and within my company the head of the—I had a couple of captains as platoon leaders, I had Captain Brinson he was the 4th Platoon Leader and he was the OIC, I put him in charge of the actual hard site, the prison so--. I had a Lieutenant Raeder who was in charge of the escort missions. I had a Captain Steva who was in charge of PSD mission. And then I had an E-8 serving as the fourth platoon leader.

Q: What was Captain Brinson's duty assignment? What was the scope of his control?

A: Yeah, when I got there I basically put him in charge of the hard site. I said to him, you know, I can't focus on this, I have too many other things going on, just—your job is to focus on the hard site, you know, give me daily reports as to what is going on, what needs to be done, and, you know, my guidance to him was, just, you know, just make sure we're doing the right stuff down there. Make sure there's no, you know, we're doing the right things.

Q: On the MI side of the house, who were the officers?

A: Colonel Pappas was the Brigade Commander. Colonel Jordan—I'm not really sure what his title was or really what his role was, but he was involved with the MI folks. Sometimes he acted like the commander, but I'm not really sure what he did there. Those were the main players that I mostly dealt with.

Q: With respect to Colonel Jordan and Colonel Pappas, who spent more time in the Tier 1A/1B area? Do you have any sense of that?

A: Definitely Colonel Jordan.

Q: At any rate though, Colonel Pappas was seen in that area as well?

A: Yes.

Q: How about on the NCO side of the house, who were the senior NCO leaders in your company?

A: I have First Sergeant Lipinski, was—is here. There was my platoon sergeant; Sergeant First Class Snider was a Platoon Sergeant for 4th Platoon. He—his platoon was mostly working in the hard site. The majority of his platoon was down there so he kind of covered the hard site also. I had some other platoon sergeants that were—I don't know if you want me to name them all?

Q: No, Sergeant Snider was the one who pretty much was placed in senior NCO leadership control over that----

A: ----that's correct----

Q: ----Tier 1A and B?

A: Right, and like I said it was mostly because it was his—a majority of the people down there were from his platoon.

… ……...

Q: What did you see in terms of how detainees were being handled and treated there as opposed to other parts of the prison when you first transitioned?

A: It was obviously different. When I first—the first or second day I was there, you know, I walked in and, you know, I seen a lot of—not a lot, but a few people that were new within the cells, you know, not outside walking around, but confined in their cells. I asked the question, you know, where's their clothes? And, you know, and they gave me the response of, you know, this is MI tact or tactic or technique that they use or, you know, it was either that or there may have a supply issue, or it may have been, you know, they were psychological, maybe suicidal, so they may have removed their clothing. But there's—they treated them a little differently down there for sure.

Q: What kind of people were being kept in that part of the prison? What was your understanding at that time?

A: I was told it was people with intelligence value, but it really was a hodge-podge of a bunch of people down in there. We had women, we had children, we had psychological patients, we had patients with, you know, diseases that were contagious, there was everything. We also had the people with the perceived intelligence value too, all mixed together.

Q: Did you have people also like on CID hold?

A: Yes, CID, MPI, you name it.

Q: OGA?

A: OGA: ..Other Government Agencies all mixed in one.

Q: Was there—did you—was there any particular written guidance posted in that area at that time that outlined the way the different groups or the categories of prisoners were supposed to be treated?

A: No. We had no—really no idea of what category they were classified in. I—we didn't—we had not idea for the most part.

Q: In terms of the—in terms of how you were able to set it up, did you set it up—did you talk to your counterpart about that, about the axis of written guidelines and about the fact that there was a Hodge Podge of individuals in there?

A: Yeah, we—you know, we obviously talked about it. At that time, you know, it wasn't as crowded, but, you know, as we went along as a few months passed, you know, as more and more people came in we had no choice but to put them there. We had no other room for them. So we tried to segregate them the best we could as far as the females, and males, you know, the best we could do. We tried to keep the people with TB off by themselves, you know, that kind of thing, but at some point, you know, there just wasn't enough room.

Q: Now, did the Coalition Provisional Authority have any people that they kept back in that area or were they in other parts of the prison, do you—if you recall?

A: I don't recall that, no I don't know.

Q: In any event what was your understanding again in this sort of transition with respect to chain of command and who had primary responsibility for Tier1A and Tier1B?

A: It was my understanding that that was under MI control and we—although I had MPs in there, but it was under control of the Military Intelligence command and we had the rest of the wings.

Q: So had you ever been trained to work with MI in that kind of environment?

A: No, sir. There's really no doctrine out there that I could even reference because it—I don't know of any other mission that has been combined like that.

…

Q: Did you go to anyone in your chain of command about the fact that you were undermanned?

A: Yes, that was a daily battle. Major DiNenna, the Battalion S-3, and he and I had almost a daily conversation, mostly one-sided, from his end. But, you know, he constantly was tasking me with things and I didn't—did not have the people to do it so, I mean, it was a constant battle.

Q: So, in terms of the hours—duty hours and the number of days a week what was the, especially in that October, early November timeframe, what kind of shifts did your soldiers have to work?

A: We all worked at least 12 hour shifts with no days off, we just didn't have the people.

Q: Based on your assessment of the number of detainees you had, the missions you were being assigned, how many soldiers would you have liked to have?

A: We needed at least another company at a minimal. It probably would have been, ideally probably two or three more companies.

Q: Did you personally ever sit down and talk to your soldiers that worked in Tier1A and 1B and make clear lines for them in terms of how detainees could be treated?

A: I probably never actually had that conversation in a group setting. We hit the ground running and we just took the mission over. There was no time to—you know, we didn't have the time to do the training aspect portion of it. There wasn't training days. It would have been great if we could have done that but no.

...

Q: But in terms of the EPW training, and trial counsel asked about care, custody, and control. Was there anything about that training that prepared your soldiers for what they faced in Tier 1A? I'm not talking about, you know, the other camps and the other places, but for the unique conditions and circumstances as you previously described?

A: No, sir, as I stated earlier there's not any doctrine out there that I could reference to get any kind of guidance for that type of mission.

...

(May 16, 2005, SHCM)

Chapter 2

Abu Ghraib and the "Rationalization" of Rationality: Uses of the Masculine and Feminine Symbolic Narrative

There was this common place tolerance of the nudity, of yelling, of arbitraries, of capriciousness, of intimidation, of uncertainty, and it applied to everybody, the detainees and soldiers alike. There was chaos, there was confusion.

Stjepan Mestrovic, expert witness Harman Courts-Martial (May 17 2005, SHCM)

The use of a narrative to tell a story becomes the basic foundation of that story—the thing we remember about that tale, the main point and basic structure of the account itself. There have been several narratives surrounding Abu Ghraib, and in this chapter I analyze rationality and chaos as descriptors to demonstrate that both have become narratives that work to obscure and repress additional gendered explanations of what occurred in Saddam Hussein's former torture chambers—later owned and operated by the American military. Although it is true that modernist binary categories are problematic when discussing gender, I use a theoretical approach informed by binaries so as to begin a discourse about the gendered deviance and sexualized abuse at Abu Ghraib Prison.

The Enlightenment Project and Rationality

Modernist theory paradigmatically rests upon a foundation of reason and rationality as the privileged locus for both objectivity and claims of universal truth. Within this theoretical canopy, ideas of justice, fairness, and liberty have been conceptualized as products of the Western Enlightenment Project. As part of this modernist paradigm, reason and rationality come to represent the basis for intellect and logic. This paradigm of modern thought, which directly informs foundational modern theoretical presuppositions, in turn comes to define notions of the "good." Furthermore, these modernist presuppositions instruct social conceptual schemes from which society is understood and organized. It is in this way that modernist notions of reason and rationality become the symbolic measure for theorizing and conceptualization. These constructions themselves come to represent and function as the standard for thought, order, and the very basis of what some consider "respectable science."

However, many have argued that modernist grand-narrative schema serve to facilitate an oppressive and privileged position that is justified with reference to only certain conceptions of reason and rationality, namely those conceptions of the socially powerful. Feminist theorists, for example, argue in different ways that the voices or perspectives of those with little social power are silenced within modernist conceptual schemes ordered around patriarchal societies. This line of argument rests upon the idea that those with social power are able to dictate the standard of reason itself, thereby delineating its benchmark. This grand-narrative of reason serves as the basis for theory construction and informs feminist examinations of how science is done or understood (Fox-Keller [1985]1995, Keller and Longino 1996, Longino 1990, Longino 1986), how knowledge is created (Abbott and Wallace 1996, Fraser and Nicholson 1990, Harding 1998, Harding 1993, Harding 1991, Harding 1987, Harding 1986a) how gender is conceptualized (Butler 1999, Butler 1993a, Butler 1993b, Beauvoir ([1949]1952), Fausto-Sterling 1992), how sex categories are understood (Oudshoorn 1991), how sexuality comes to be understood (Fausto-Sterling 2000, Rich 1980, Rubin 1984, Rubin [1975]2002, Sedgwick 1990, Terry 1999), among many other modes of feminist conjecture.

In a like manner, building on Adorno and Horkheimer (1979), some postmodernists argue that the modernist paradigm is at odds with the aims of enlightenment and liberation, thereby resulting in an invalid and contradictory logical system. Specifically, these theorists claim that through the marking of the conceptual boundaries of "reason" and "rationality," this coupling instead subtly masks modes of domination, forms of oppression, and sites of control (Ahmed 1992, Baudrillard ([1995]2002), Baudrillard ([1981]1994), Baudrillard ([1979]1990), Baudrillard ([1991]1995), Bauman 1992, Butler 1999, Butler 1993a, Butler 1993b, Derrida 1978, Foucault 1988, Foucault [1975]1977, Foucault 1972, Haraway 1991, Haraway 1997a, Haraway 1997b, Irigaray 1985a, Jameson 1991, Lyotard ([1979]1984), Lutz 1995, Mestrovic 1994, Mestrovic 1993, Mestrovic 1992, Mestrovic 1991, Rorty 1989, Rosenau 1992). In this way, modernist conceptions of reason and rationality become paradoxical and irreconcilable with the stated goals of the Enlightenment project itself, such that both actual suffering and theoretical casualties result— the seeming impotence of modern theory construction. Thus, although reason and rationality ostensibly promise order and structure, these concepts can be shown to actually produce malice and oppression instead. Indeed, it is sometimes even the case that accounts of rationality are themselves "rationalized" in an attempt to pragmatically fit the existing modernist theoretical canopy.

Gender and Modernity

One starting point for studying gender theory within modernity is this: the binary of masculine and feminine. It is the narrative from which American culture is based, and this stereotype is still used to explain the realities of the social world, identity, bodies, roles and more. This narrative functions as a cultural code, where masculinity and femininity oppose each other, even in terms of value. In modern patriarchal societies "masculinity" is associated with all that is reasonable, rational, essential, orderly, logical, controlled, predictable, calculable, active and strong. Conversely, "femininity" is associated with all that is emotional, chaotic, weak, inessential, uncontrolled, inconsistent, passive and irrational. It is this modernist theory of gender binaries that comes to function as a rational grand narrative schema. Because this system is socially constructed in terms of reward and value, and operates as a benchmark for cultural understandings for gender, it serves as ideology in that it prescribes meaning and reward, and allows for only certain cultural conceptualizations and productions of gender themselves. However, this binary code for understanding gender is problematic in that it proposes an uncritical conception of gender that is imbued with power, where dyadic conceptions of stereotypical (and sometimes essentialized) conceptions of masculinity and femininity are prescribed, where problematic heterosexualized parings of both sexual desire and identity exist. In addition, this system does not adequately make sense or room for all gender conceptions and "genderscapings," although binary systems are rationalized to do so nonetheless. What is so curious is that the U.S. military, albeit a reflection of larger culture, operates using a similar stereotype of binary gender categories, and thus reflects the military's larger culture of masculinity or "masculinized militarism" (Kaufman-Osborn 2005).

Theorizing binaries, although socially oppressive when conceiving of gender, aids in understanding the gendered deviance and sexualized abuse at Abu Ghraib, and so I use binaries to begin a conversation about gender, the abuse at the prison and the resulting courts-martials. It is this very important theoretical starting point that is used to show how complex gender and power permutations operated at Abu Ghraib, and which also helps to explain deviance within the context of the masculinist military itself.

In this chapter, I provide a discussion of the chaos associated with Abu Ghraib prison and how this chaos does not fit into modernist narratives of rationality and order, where order and rationality can be equated with the masculine symbolic code. In this way, I describe the illusory order and actual chaos at Abu Ghraib as gendered. My reading of gendered abuse is informed first by George Ritzer and his Weberian-inspired McDonaldization project, describing modernity and the Enlightenment project as focused on rationality, order, predictably, efficiency, calculability, and control (Ritzer [1993]2004). This basic notion of "modernity," I argue, is a "masculine" modernity given its links to the theoretical binary characterizations associated with "masculinity."

However, Ritzer's notion of modernity is further divided by Chris Rojek's (1995) demonstration that modernity has two contrasting faces, namely Modernity 1 and Modernity 2.[1] Rojek's modernity of order and rationality (Modernity 1) is the one that I call "masculine" modernity because of the similarities of associations

---

1   I am not arguing for an essentialist position regarding men and women; instead, I am trying to unite notions of gender with theoretical understandings of modernity.

between Rojek's descriptions and the stereotypes of masculinity.[2] By showing that the prison was not run in a rational manner (maintaining social order), with principles applied to everyday life (a clear system of law), with precision, planning and order, it can be deduced that a deviance associated with the notion of rationality, order, and ideas surrounding traditional notions of modernity ensued. The deviance at Abu Ghraib was thus evidence of Rojek's Modernity 2, or "the feminine," in that disorder and fragmentation, flux, change, uncertainty of experience, deviance and restlessness existed at Abu Ghraib (Rojek 1995: 82).[3] This is an alternate reading of modernity, which claims the rationality and order of Modernity 1 is nothing more than an illusion—a "rationality," if you will. The consequences of the theoretical gendered "feminine" deviance of Modernity 2 were harms for the body and soul of both prisoners and soldiers alike.

I also describe the built and created environment at Abu Ghraib that was portrayed in the courts-martial as further evidence of the lacking of masculine rationality, order, and control that are all part and parcel of modernity. To be clear, applying Rojek's notion of the chaos of modernity 2, it is possible to understand this deviance, in that a lack of modernity 1 "masculine" order led to the abuse. In other words, I agree in part with Kaufman-Osborn (2005), that "a logic of emasculation" informed the abuse at Abu Ghraib, where disciplinary techniques strip prisoners of masculinity and torture is through forced feminization—"emasculate in order to subjugate". However, I argue that this "logic" was itself irrational (even if the idea of "deranged logic" at first seems to be an oxymoron). In this way, the argument that I make is that the deviance itself was gendered, as was the chaos.

Additionally, I discuss Foucault's ([1977]1995) narrative of modernist power structures, and here I am especially interested in how power was used to punish *both* the body *and* soul at Abu Ghraib—which is antithesis to Foucault's position regarding punishment in modern times. Both Foucault and many feminists share the identification of the body as a site of domination, where power has been used to exert control over women's bodies and minds. This becomes an important discussion of power coupled with gender in that women's bodies and souls (both American and Iraqi) were punished at Abu Ghraib, where Iraqi women and children were held as bargaining chips at the prison. Social control is established through the identification of the prisoner's body as the primary target of power, where actually what is controlled are *both* the prisoners' bodies *and* souls/minds at Abu Ghraib, and especially in the following situations: when dogs were used to intimidate Iraqi prisoners, nakedness as a means for control, male prisoners "friendships" with female guards, male prisoners being treated as "females," female guards being forced into photographs of abuse, the torture of Iraqi males in front of American female guards, panties being put on male prisoner's heads thereby "feminizing" them (and especially given the gendered and associated sexualized nature of this

---

2   This gendered reading of Rojek is my own.

3   Although Rojek is discussing leisure and modernity, I argue that his theory regarding modernity still applies here.

torture, and the associated violation of Iraqi cultural constructions of masculinity), among many other examples. I maintain that the dehumanization and abuse of prisoners has set the stage for the physical and sexual abuse that followed, where punishment occurred in the form of gender manipulation and humiliation.

Finally in this chapter, I discuss the nicknames given to detainees as a means to display raw "masculine" power on the part of the American male guards, as well as the use of photography itself to evidence this exposed power over prisoners. Punishment coupled with power and gender can be applied to American soldiers' experiences of Abu Ghraib, where both male and female soldiers reluctantly disclosed that they were suffering from Post-Traumatic Stress Disorder (PTSD) from the abuse they suffered and witnessed.

The Prison: Abu Ghraib

Consider the Abu Ghraib prison in Iraq. First, it was built by Saddam Hussein as a modern prison to control, in Foucault's scheme, the minds and souls of the prisoners as opposed to torturing their bodies. Paradoxically, it came to serve as a site of torture of the body under Saddam Hussein's regime, as well as the American liberation and occupation. Second, the prison itself is about the size of an average airport in the United States, thus exhibiting its domination over the built and created environment. Third, the "phallic" panopticon at Abu Ghraib stands out visibly in all photos of the prison. For Foucault, the towering panopticon serves the function of controlling prisoners through surveillance such that the prisoners are never certain when they are under the gaze. Finally, despite these modernist features, Abu Ghraib during American occupation was vulnerable to attacks, defenseless, porous to Iraqis, and incapable of surveillance in Foucault's sense. It was chosen by the U.S. Army to serve as a prison, this time in the middle of an active war zone, which also contradicts Foucault.

Under the modernist paradigm, one would have expected this American run prison to exhibit all of the characteristics of a McDonaldized society: efficiency, rationality, prediction, and control (Ritzer 2004). Interestingly, these are also gendered characterizations of masculinity within modernist patriarchal paradigms, and also characteristic of Rojek's Modernity 1. Applying McDonaldized characteristics to Abu Ghraib would mean, for example, that the prison would have been well supplied with food, water, medical supplies, clothing, and other things, up to and including the rules of engagement and the rules of detention and interrogation. Instead, the U.S. government's own reports, as well as testimony at the Abu Ghraib detainee abuse trials disclosed chaos with regard to all of these phenomenon: food and water were scarce (even for the American soldiers); supposedly there was no clothing for the detainees to wear and that is why many were housed naked; the Rules of the Geneva Convention were never posted; soldiers did not know what the rules of engagement were as they were changing every day; and Military Intelligence (MI) and Military Police (MP) roles were blurred and confusing. Interestingly, the association of duties between the MI's and MP's was a failsafe system of checks and balances that was itself disregarded. All of these examples point to the irrational, barbaric, and harshness associated with the experiences of Abu Ghraib, which I argue led to cultural and emotional harms for the prisoners there, and harms also for the American soldiers.

Examining testimony, everyone who was asked about the state of the prison at Abu Ghraib testified that the conditions were appalling, and especially given the constant attacks made on the prison itself. Many stated that it was not a "normal prison," as its detainee population included a combination of women, children, "terrorists," and common criminals as prisoners. On May 16, 2005, Captain Reese, the Company Commander at Abu Ghraib and first witness for the defense at the courts-martial of Sabrina Harman stated in open court that Abu Ghraib had "less than favorable living conditions" and that soldiers sometimes "lived in jail cells" which were dirty. Says Reese, "We actually occupied an old medical area ... When we arrived there was debris, you know, rocks, dirt, everywhere. There were no showers, no facilities like that. A lot of medical paraphernalia, needles and things like that laying around" (May 16 2005, SHCM).

Also at the Harman trial, although during the sentencing phase on May 17, 2005, Major David DiNenna, who is the supply officer and in charge of prisoner operations at Abu Ghraib, also described the conditions of Abu Ghraib as appalling, with trash, debris, and evidence of looting throughout the prison. He specifically called the prison a "trash hole," and noted not only that wild dogs and rodents inhabited the compound itself, but also that the porta-johns at the prison were filthy and sometimes overflowing because they had not been pumped. Additionally, Captain Reese added, "when we arrived to Abu Ghraib it was like a warzone with rubble everywhere. There was nothing there for soldiers. It was a below average living standard" (June 24, 2002, SHA32). Major DiNenna testified that most of the soldiers at Abu Ghraib prison were sickly, where cases of vomiting and diarrhea were commonplace among them because of the filthy conditions. Additionally, Major DiNenna stated under oath that there were not enough medical personnel and that there were 2-3 medical evacuations per day. "They—we had a lot of diabetes, TB. Based on their diet change their health went down very quickly. Towards the end we were doing two to three MEDVACs a day for heart conditions, diabetics, I think, stuff as well. A lot of amputees, and wounded prisoners came in. So they had a great deal of problems." DiNenna continues, "The conditions were, for lack of a better term, deplorable" (May 17, 2005, SHCM).

Additionally, Captain Reese commented on the extreme insurgency in the area around the prison. Further explaining the environment at Abu Ghraib, DiNenna continued, "We had a very high threat external as well as internal, we'd have between 7 and 9,000 prisoners and they have a hundred soldiers per shift to watch them all. We had to deal with that as well as the constant mortar attacks and RPGs and small arms fire, and then the IEDs picked up" (May 17, 2005, SHCM). Commenting on the environment within the prison, Sergeant Cathcart, an MP assigned to the night shift at Tier 1A stated under oath "It is fair to say

Figure 2.1   The outside of Abu Ghraib at night with lights

Source: Photograph provided courtesy of the author.

that this was a dangerous environment that we worked in. We were mortared constantly and on alert a lot. We also had to worry about Iraqi Correctional Officers (ICO) because they smuggled weapons into the detainees. It was a stressful environment. Every time we did a cell search we found weapons" (June 24, 2002, SHA32).

Major DiNenna described the lack of lighting at Abu Ghraib, where nightly attacks took place in conditions with no internal lighting. The lighting used each night at Abu Ghraib consisted of military vehicles surrounding the prison and turning on their headlights for visibility inside of the prison. The lighting inside of the prison literally came from vehicle headlights located outside of the prison. Explaining the lighting situation, Major DiNenna stated in testimony, "Well obviously when you guard prisoners you need lights at night. Lightning was an issue the entire time. We—you know, generators were—or lights would go down either from mortars or just that kind of deficiencies, we couldn't get them replaced. There was an Army contract to install permanent lighting in the outside facilities but it was never finished and to this day I still don't know why. So there were times when we had to bring in vehicles around the compounds just to add enough lighting to keep it on the prisoners at night" (May 17, 2005, SHCM). This situation was "incredibly dangerous, with low morale and high stress" stated Major DiNenna. In a word, these courtroom depictions of Abu Ghraib are themselves barbaric, where masculinist reason has mutated into representations of the female symbolic of inadequacy, or narratives of a gendered Modernity 2. Regarding prisoner uprisings at the hard site of Abu Ghraib, Major DiNenna gave several reasons for these confrontations, including the mixing of Sunni and Shiites. He even claimed that some prisoners had not even been told why they were being held for six or more months after initially being detained at Abu Ghraib. Stated DiNenna, "Most of the uprisings were a result of the food, overcrowded, being detained for a lengthy periods of time where they either were not interrogated by MI or they didn't receive timely court dates. So even though they're locked down in a cell so to speak, there's six to eight prisoners per cell. We also let the Iraqi Correctional Officers, and the Iraqi Warden attempt to handle the uprisings, but the result was … you could hear it throughout the entire hard site prison so if one tier erupted then another tier would be erupt and at the time we only had 8 to 10 MPs in the entire hard site to work the facility because that was all the soldiers we had left" (May 17, 2005, SHCM). These uprisings were acts of reprisal for neglect and abandonment, and the absence of any rational system for prisoner processing that one might have expected at a U.S. military run prison.

On the topic of food and water at Abu Ghraib, the contracted food was basically inedible because it was contaminated. Furthermore, and against the military's protocol, Major DiNenna testified that sometimes military MRE's were used to feed detainees, which resulted in a long and tedious situation for guards, as they had to strip MREs of pork products for cultural reasons, and had to remove Tabasco sauce bottles because they could be used as a weapon. Stated DiNenna in the courtroom, "Initially we started with MREs for the prisoners. When a contract was set up … The food was usually undercooked, it was dirty, it had debris, the food had rodent, feces, and glass. At times for their evening meal they would receive a boiled egg and two pieces of cheese which obviously the prisoners didn't appreciate. It got to the point where they were either throwing stones or rocks at the vendors themselves or throw the food back at the MPs. We had medics, field medicine, and field surgeons and everybody evaluating, include looking on it every time it came in. So a lot of the times we would just throw the vendors out the gate, so to speak, and give the prisoners the MREs which made them very happy (May 17, 2005, SHCM). DiNenna described the water conditions at Abu Ghraib as scarce, as sometimes delivered in fuel trucks, and stated that soldiers and detainees had access to only two, two-liter bottles of water per day for all activities such as drinking and washing.

Still further evidence of *irrationality* and the *lack of prediction and control* at Abu Ghraib were evident in additional testimony that the Iraqi police officers at Abu Ghraib were corrupt. Private Ivan Frederick an MP for the 372nd at Abu Ghraib stated at Harman's courts-martial that "basically when I first got there I observed the facility as very poorly built. There was access to weapons unimaginable. The Iraqi police were very, very corrupt. They would bring in weapons, bring in pills, drugs, they would bring in maps of the facility, take maps of the facility out, give them to family members. It was just—it was a nightmare for corrections" (May 13,

2005, SHCM). Major DiNenna echoed Frederick's concerns, stating "Bribery was and shaking hands with the families of the prisoners is a big deal … They would know a prisoner who may be in a particular village, or tribe, or that correctional officer is friends with the family and then go to the family and receive money and then would assist the prisoner to escape. They smuggled in weapons to the prisoners... They also would send—would smuggle in razor blades from the Iraqi Medical Facility which was later set up. And would take them on work details and just let them go. Give them a change of clothes. We spent a lot of time watching the Iraqi Correctional Officers as well as the prisoners" (17 May 2005, SHCM).

Major DiNenna further claimed that there was a high level of internal threat to the American soldiers since there were not adequate personnel to deal with the prisoners. DiNenna even stated that there was such a low ratio of prisoners to guards that he postulated about 150 prisoners or more to each guard at Abu Ghraib, with guard's stress levels elevated by working what he thought were 12-16 hours per day. Said DiNenna, "Yes, actually overcrowding existed everywhere. You know basically our mission—entire mission we should have seven MPs on the gate so to speak for 500 prisoners and as well as the tower guards. So it would be approximately 10 or 11 MPs per 500 prisoners. You do the same ratio—in a hard site facility it's different, that's basically a corrections operation, which is entirely different than the internment resettlement operation, so the issue we ran in to at the hard site when they put a lot of the Iraqi Civilian Criminals in there is they just kept opening tiers and kept putting them in, but we didn't get an increase in soldiers." (May 17, 2005, SHCM). Additionally, Captain Reese stated that American military personnel worked 12-hour shifts with no days off, and that really 2-3 more companies were needed to ideally run the prison effectively. Says Reese, "My soldiers were subject to threats by the Iraqi prisoners. It was well known among the guards that they were at risk. Based on the ratio of guards to inmates there was a threat to my soldiers. My soldiers were not trained to handle prisoners … I discussed the ratio of detainees to guard with my chain of command … Towards the end we were probably 1 [guard] in every 100 inmate. The desired ratio is probably 10 guards per 100 detainees" (June 24, 2004, SHA32). In his testimony, Major DiNenna stated that "prisoners had nothing to do all day but come up with ways to make weapons," resulting in further threats to guards (May 17, 2005, SHCM).

There was some confusion, according to Major DiNenna, for the American guards in identifying Iraqi prisoners versus correctional officers because of the shortage of supplies, as there were no uniforms available that would signify roles and distinction—guard versus detainee. DiNenna testified, "The problem we ran in to was when the Iraqi Correctional Officers first started working there and the prisoners a lot of times you couldn't tell who was who because they didn't have the uniforms for the correctional officers yet. They then started ordering jump suits, the orange jump suits for the prisoners, but though they were prisoners, to us very quickly they weren't keeping up with the supplies we had which again created a problem. As correctional officers were trained they were sent to work right away but they didn't have—a lot of them didn't have uniforms in the beginning so it was—you had to rely on your fellow correctional officers to ensure that this guy standing next to him is not a prisoners and he's a correctional officer. So it was very—in the beginning it was very, very difficult" (17 May 2005, SHCM). Thus, American guards were responsible for monitoring Iraqi detainees, Iraqi correctional officers, and also Iraqi police given the lack of organization, shortage of supplies, and corruption of Iraqi personnel. This corruption, confusion, and lack of organization are all mutations of masculinist modernist rationality, where individuals at Abu Ghraib experienced instead chaotic conditions of Rojek's "feminine" theoretical Modernity 2.

When asked about detainee care, Captain Reese stated under oath that prisoners were kept naked in cells as part of a MI tactic. Interestingly, Captain Reese postulated that this could also be a supply issue, or maybe that the inmates had removed their own clothing because they were "psycho." Stated Reese at Harman's Article 32 hearing, "One of the first things I saw when I walked in was female underwear over the heads of the detainees. The practice was taking place before we got there. One of the inmates used an MRE carton as underwear and to cover himself. I thought it was odd to have women's underwear on their heads so I talked to the person that I was taking over for. He told me it was a humiliation tactic. We had a supply issue. We had supply issues. We did not have enough underwear. I know some of the females had to wear male boxers" (June 24, 2004, SHA32). Although clothes were at one point available it was common practice to control the body through nudity at Abu Ghraib, and it was repeated in court over and again that it was a detention technique to strip detainees naked. What is more, one only has to consider that these detainees were arrested or detained while wearing clothing, and did not all arrive at Abu Ghraib prison naked. Captain Reese testified, "I don't know where the clothes were put when taken from the detainees … I visited the hard site 100 times from mid-October to mid-December … Iraqis were hooded during those occasions. Iraqis were nude. I did raise the question of nudity to the previous company commander of the 372nd … He told me that it was a common practice to have the detainees nude. I raised the issue with … Major DiNenna. He told me it was a tactic used by MI. I assumed that since Major DiNenna told me that the tactic was acceptable, I never looked for anything in writing" (June 24, 2004, SHA32).

Social control was thus a product of power as applied to the body in gendered ways that offended cultural constructions of masculinity itself, where the very act of being naked, housed in overcrowded conditions with other naked male prisoners, and further humiliated through the use of panties on one's head implies both a kind of feminine vulnerability and a homoerotic approach to torture. It can be argued that nakedness is equated with feminine vulnerability, where prisoner control is maintained through compliance and subordination of the exposed body. Control of the detainee's "feminized" body is achieved in several ways: through the use of uncomfortable homoerotic living conditions, where naked men share small overcrowded living quarters; through the use of "drag" given the female panties worn by the male prisoners themselves, albeit on their heads in certain situations; and through the use of forced feminization, or the stripping of masculinity (power, signifier, etc.) from the prisoners, such as when male Iraqi detainees are gender humiliated through the use of forcible nakedness in front of female guards.[4]

Captain Reese also stated under oath that there was no outline at the prison about how to treat different kinds of prisoners, and hence an absence of detainee treatment guidelines. The American soldiers at Abu Ghraib were supposed to guard all types of prisoners, some considered as having especially valuable intelligence, yet the guards had no additional training to handle these special prisoners, and had no guidance of distinction for inmate control. Captain Reese stated the prisoners in Tier 1A and 1B were "people with intelligence value," although he admitted that prisoners were mixed together in a "hodge-podge" because there was little room at the prison for detainees, thereby providing a contradictory account of detainee value in Tier 1A and 1B. This becomes problematic because some of the prisoners were just common criminals, some were Iraqi prisoners that were "CID holds" (Criminal Investigative Division) (This is a fact omitted in the U.S. Government reports, namely, that not only were some prisoners "MI holds" to be interrogated, but the Criminal Investigative Division had its own separate prisoners and the reason for this has not been explored.), others were detainees that were being investigated by other government agencies (OGA) (such as the CIA, and the dozen or so other secret agencies such as the Navy, National Security Agency, etc.), and some prisoners were even "ghost detainees," or prisoners who were not accounted for by record or number as located at Abu Ghraib. These "ghost detainees" were of high value to the military and, according to Captain Reese, were brought in through "the backdoor," with no prisoner numbers assigned to them and with strict instructions to "not let anyone talk to them, MI would be back to check on them." Says Reese, "I was confused about the chain of command at Abu Ghraib because we had so many different agencies there. Other agencies that were there were Coalition Provisional Authority (CPA), MI, OGA and FBI" (June 24, 2004, SHA32). This is a chaotic system of prisoner order at Abu Ghraib, even for Reese, the prison's company commander himself!

Additionally, women and children were kept at Abu Ghraib prison in Tier 1B, which Major DiNenna described as the only place available for segregation of women and children. He stated under oath that women and children (the youngest of which were 11- or 12-years-old, said DiNenna) were brought into Abu Ghraib

---

4 I argue that relationally, this symbolic construction of power in the humiliation scenario can be read as giving phallic power to the female guards within this context, that of the masculinist military, in addition to actual power over male-bodied prisoners, simply by virtue of the female guards being present in these scenarios. Interestingly, this is not about female hatred or misogyny, or the use of this as torture, but the powerlessness of masculinity when faced with the symbolic confrontation of "phallic femininity." Kaufman-Osborn (2005) describes these practices as "emasculat[ion] in order to subjugate." Hence, this is the breaking down of masculinity as opposed to the devaluing of femininity.

if a male in their family was arrested, and under the guise of possibly offering a kind of protection. However, it came out in court later that women and children were used as a means for bargaining, where males could turn themselves in so that their female family members would be released from Abu Ghraib. This was evidenced specifically in that women and children were given no listed offense on their capture tags, which were functionally useful with regard to specifying crimes committed thereby leading to arrest and confinement at Abu Ghraib. This rationalization for keeping female prisoners thus crumbles in terms of motivation when learned that women were kept for bribery purposes. Additionally, this system of bribery uses women as objects for trade for their male family members, representing further instances of female subordination at Abu Ghraib. Consider Frederick's testimony on the stand at the Harman courts-martial:

> A [Frederick]: It was pretty much the most stress I've ever been under in my life. It was constant mortars, rockets, grenade attacks, insurgents, everything.
>
> Q: What kind of training were you given for the unique environment that you found at Abu Ghraib in October of 2003?
>
> A: None, none, sir.
>
> Q: Were you ever trained in the Laws of Warfare of Geneva Conventions, in terms of how to treat detainees in a prison type of environment?
>
> A: Not in a prison type of environment.
>
> Q: Under what theory of incarceration do you put women and juveniles and confine them next to insurgents, terrorists, potential rapists, and murders? What's the theory of confinement?
>
> A: Sometimes they thought that family members of high priority detainees, they were trying to get information about their father, or family member that's a part of Fedyeen, or a part of Sadaam's Regime, something like that, and they try to get information to where their location is.
>
> Q: So had these women and juveniles done anything wrong that you're aware of?
>
> A: Not that I'm aware of. (13 May 2005, SHCM)

Thus, prisoners were all mixed together, even sickly and contagious prisoners with outbreaks of tuberculosis, according to Captain Reese.

What is more, Major DiNenna's testimony, as well as at least five other soldier's testimony (Joyner, Wisdom, Jones, Darby, and Rivera), echoed that of Captain Reese's description of the conditions at Abu Ghraib. Thus the descriptions of Abu Ghraib were widely corroborated as inefficient, irrational, uncontrolled, and incalculable. All of the examples of irrationality, inefficiency and lack of prediction and control at Abu Ghraib are instances of mutations of masculinist rationality schema, and specifically those connected with Rojek's Modernity 1; instead, at Abu Ghraib, gendered deviance in the form of Modernity 2 chaos existed. In fact, Major DiNenna stated under oath, when asked the question:

Q: Sir, at the time that you were at Abu Ghraib going through all of these issues, what were you feeling?

A. Abandoned.

Q. Why?

A. Actually I guess the theater IG, I can't remember the colonel's name, arrived towards the end of September, beginning of October timeframe I believe and basically stated that we were forgotten, we were a forgotten mission. We were set up just to keep these prisoners and keep them out of the way. You know, when you're at a facility whether it's a hard site prison or tents on the outside, it's—you're setting up a city and you need the resources to do that, we weren't supplied. (17 May 2005, SHCM)

From the point of view of a rationally-run bureaucracy, one would have expected that Abu Ghraib would have both a reliable chain of command in place, and that they would have also followed U.S. Army protocol for responsibility. In the *myth* of American dominance and the Western Enlightenment Project, the U.S. Army *should have been* organized, efficient, responsible, and moral. Nevertheless, evidence instead shows the *lack* of this kind of bureaucratic order. For example, the officers high in the chain of command were exempted completely from all culpability and all responsibility for the abuse at Abu Ghraib, and all responsibility was shifted onto the lowest ranking soldiers. To this day, the Army has not determined who was in charge of the prison as the commanding officer: Colonel Thomas M. Pappas? Lieutenant Colonel Jerry Phillabaum? Brigadier General Janice Karpinski (now Colonel Karpinski)?

Additionally, the government's own reports substantiated the testimonial claims of the courts-martial with the indication that almost none of the paperwork required filed by protocol was actually filed. Instead, considering military reports, the Taguba Report found that any filing system was "nonexistent" and there were no "lessons learned" Army files. Moreover, there were no "interrogation plans" filed, and in general, the U.S. Army admits that the prison was run on an ad hoc, learn as you go along and on-the-job-training basis (Taguba Report).

As well, the U.S. Army protocol requires the ratio of one military guard to fifteen prisoners, but in reality the ratio at Abu Ghraib was one guard to 200 prisoners. The U.S. government reports (Jones and Fay) state that the Army knew that overcrowding was a serious issue, but failed to remedy the situation, and still failed to do so up until its closing (Strasser and Whitney 2004). Moreover, the government reports state that approximately 80 percent of the prisoners at Abu Ghraib were not insurgents, and were not "terrorists," but were ordinary Iraqis such as taxi drivers, persons mistakenly arrested during sweeps, or even hostages (Strasser et al. 2004). In addition, women and children were imprisoned at Abu Ghraib as bargaining chips for obtaining information. The absurdity of this situation is that most of the prisoners did not have the information that the Army wanted (Strasser et al. 2004). Hence, the "feminine" irrational symbolic comes to replace the organized and coherent system, which was seemingly based upon reason as its template—where irrationality comes to replace the rational itself.

To illustrate this paradox of stated Enlightenment goals versus the actual chaos at Abu Ghraib, consider the prosecuting attorney's explanation of why prisoners wore Iraqi panties on their heads. Captain Christopher Graveline (the prosecutor for both Specialist Sabrina Harman and Private Lynndie England) stated that the reason for the panties on the heads of the detainees was that there was a shortage of supplies of clothing, so that American soldiers were sent into Baghdad to purchase Iraqi women's panties as "clothing." Captain Graveline made this statement in open court on May 17th 2005, and Major DiNenna, the supply officer for AG, concurred with this statement on the stand, saying "yes sir" to the prosecuting counselor. Interestingly, this "clothing" was used as a technique for humiliating detainees, as it was placed on their heads, and was not used as a cover or barrier against the environment or as part of a prisoner uniform.

In these outlined ways, the descriptions of Abu Ghraib evidenced the lacking of "masculine" order, control and rationality associated with the modernist Enlightenment paradigm. Hence, chaos as an explanation for the disorder and abuse at Abu Ghraib can actually be understood in a gendered manner, where chaos comes to represent conceptions of the female symbolic narrative of vulnerability, disorganization, and emotionality—all theoretical binary opposite characterizations of reason and rationality, and alternative ways that "feminine" modernity is conceptualized.

Foucault and Power

On the face of it, it might seem that prisoner abuse was a means for establishing what Foucault labels as the power of the sovereign (Foucault 1988, Foucault [1975]1977). In a modernist patriarchal society, this "sovereign" is associated with masculinity such that power is aligned with the masculine symbolic or phallic power, as this is the ultimate measure for self-determination. At Abu Ghraib, punitive abuse was used as a means for the goal of creating a power relationship in a chaotic setting—the guards in control versus prisoners. For example, Major General Miller is quoted in Frontline: The Torture Question, PBS documentary (2005) as stating words to the effect "unless the detainees feel like dogs everyday, you're not doing your job properly."

Through the use of dogs as a means of disciplinary power to scare prisoners, a power relation was created that depicted the "masculine" power of the guards and the "feminine" vulnerability of prisoners—again, sovereign versus that which is controlled. It was further documented in the Fay Report that civilians employed by the military used dogs to scare prisoners, hit them, and encouraged soldiers to abuse them (Mann 2004, Strasser 2004). Likewise, a feminist application of Foucault's contention that the body is the principal site of power in modern society is also useful in explaining the social control of Iraqi prisoners in terms of how the body is used for some of the kinds of torture that were found at Abu Ghraib, namely the gendered and homoerotic torture. These are examples of raw masculine power over the body through the use of force and in an attempt to create a means for control.

Ironically, and in contra distinction to Foucault, the use of power by the American military became a disruptive force, or understood in terms of the irrational and chaotic feminine symbolic. Intended to bring apparent order in an environment of chaos, American power-tactics actually produced more chaos, which can be understood as the by-product of mutated masculinist and modernist schema of reason and rationality. Again, against Foucault, the reality of the situation at Abu Ghraib was that the sovereign was exerting *power over both the body and soul.* Moreover, the American soldiers did not present themselves as exerting the power of the sovereign in a raw and naked sense. Instead, the wolf-like power-tactics came in the sheep's clothing of democracy and rule of law, hidden in commands from officers who would never testify (because they were given immunity) that they indeed ordered and provided training for these interrogation tactics.

For example, as shown in the courts-martials, detainees arriving at Abu Ghraib were handed a fly sheet, written in English, which stated words to the effect, "Welcome, you are now at an American-run prison, you will be treated decently and humanely, and not like you were treated under Saddam Hussein's regime." The irony is that the detainees were treated as if they were detainees under Saddam Hussein's regime. Foucault's theory does not account for this subversion of the ideals of social order, democracy, and the enlightenment project.

Perhaps it is for this reason that Baudrillard wrote a book entitled *Forget Foucault* ([1977]1987). Foucault's theory can be construed as a modernist attempt to depict a mere shift in the ordering principle of the Enlightenment from the body to the soul. To be sure, prior to the leak of the abuse photographs, Americans were received as using "psychological yet humane" methods of interrogation as required by the U.S. army field manual on interrogation, FM-34-52. In reality, FM 34-52 was rendered obsolete by various memoranda from the White House and Lieutenant General Sanchez, such that the concepts of torture, interrogation, and abuse became unintelligible (see Caldwell and Mestrovic 2008a). This is an example of how a "standard" for prisoner treatment imploded in meaning such that it resulted in confusion and chaos with regard to interpretation. Nevertheless, power as depicted at Abu Ghraib was a spectacle aimed at maintaining prisoner compliance. However, the real postmodern spectacle is that Foucault's power over the soul degenerated into gendered and homoerotic abuse of the body *and* soul, and was documented for the entire world to see. It is therefore technology itself that allowed us a new, compelling, and undeniable way of seeing the hidden reality of Abu Ghraib.

There seem to be at least three separate Western discourses in play. The first is the American discourse of conquering another nation for the sake of liberation and democracy. The second seems to be the discourse of being above the law; the rest of the world must follow the Geneva conventions, but the U.S. chooses when and if the Geneva conventions apply at Guantanamo Bay, Afghanistan, and in Iraq (Mestrovic 2005). The third discourse *seems* similar to Baudrillard's notion of *seduction* (which represents mastery over the symbolic universe) (Baudrillard [1979]1990), and involves a subversion of the first by the second, namely a pretense of bringing liberation and democracy while secretly contradicting these very principles through abuse. For Baudrillard, seduction is associated with the "feminine" and the ability of the "feminine" to rule by mastery over the symbolic universe (and "the code") versus by "masculine" power.

However, although at first glance the third discourse seems similar to Baudrillard's notion of seduction, Baudrillard himself links his notion of seduction to his overall discussion of "the code" that organizes the economy of signs and symbols in society. In the case of the detainee abuse at Abu Ghraib, the "code" becomes a *false reality* that is not merely a simulacrum that has been severed from reality, but a seduction of reality itself—or at least reality's appearance. Abu Ghraib was not a hyperreality of appearances as Baudrillard's seduction might suggest (Baudrillard [1979]1990). Instead, real actual documented empirically verifiable abuse occurred at Abu Ghraib under the guise of American simulacra regarding democracy and liberation. Neither Foucault's nor Baudrillard's theories capture the complexity of the situation at Abu Ghraib and its relationship to the larger American culture.

Through this spectacle, no voice has been given to the prisoners themselves, even if some of the people in Abu Ghraib have been given faces, they are not given their real names. One of the most fascinating aspects of this situation at Abu Ghraib that came out in the trials is that the prisoners were given American nicknames such as "Gus," "Gilligan," "Shitboy," "Bigbird," "The Claw," and so on. These nicknames can be understood in terms of American pop-culture television shows such as Gilligan's Island, Sesame Street, etc. This "Disneyfication" (Mestrovic 2005) of the prisoners is in itself a form of dehumanization and abuse, and can be equated with the objectification of women in larger American society—a process of lacking autonomous identity within patriarchal culture, and a form of "othering," or in this case, the literal erasing of identity in favor of re-naming altogether. The U.S. government reports stated that the dehumanization at Abu Ghraib set the stage for the physical and sexual abuse that followed, and was based on this objectification of detainees. In this way, these pictures have become icons

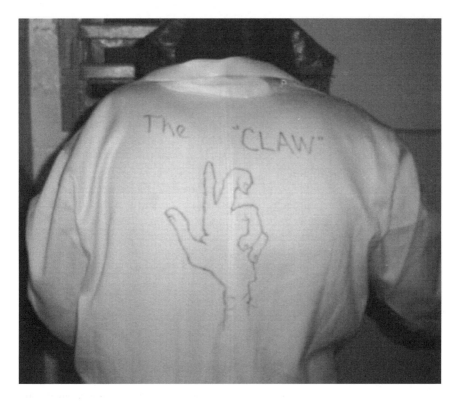

Figure 2.2   Detainee nicknamed "The Claw"

Source: Photograph provided courtesy of the author.

that blend into the violence and gratuitous sexuality of American culture, cinema, and pornography.

Reflecting on American culture, it is not surprising that there is a parallel between the objectification of women and crimes of power committed against them, and the objectification of prisoners and the associated sexualized and gendered abuses they endured. The point here is that objectification is a form of dehumanization, and at Abu Ghraib the result of these acts was the vanishing of prisoner identity and the reconceptualization of identity in a sub-human and bestial manner. (As a matter of fact, examples of treating prisoners as on par with animals have been provided above.)

If Foucault is correct about his notion of punishment of the soul, then the irony of the situation at Abu Ghraib is that punishment of the soul occurred through the taking of the pictures, which is in itself a violation of the Geneva Conventions. These pictures highlighted the homoerotic nature of the punishment, as well as the compulsory and common nudity. The homoerotic punishment evidenced in the photographs of abuse is a cultural violation of Iraqi masculinity, and places the detainees in a subordinate category of both vulnerable "female" and forced "homosexual." In a word, *the punishment of the soul has taken the form of humiliation*. It is important to understand that contrary to Foucault and Baudrillard, humiliation is not just a means of control, although it can be depicted in this way. Rather, humiliation is in itself not only a violation of the Geneva Conventions but also a form of psychological abuse and objectification. In reality, this kind of deep shame is itself savage and is not rational detainee treatment. It is on par with the medieval physical forms of torture that Foucault writes about in *Discipline and Punishment* ([1975]1977).

The photographs of abuse also function as Foucault's panopticon, since they show the abuse to the whole public consciousness. This allows the public to visit Abu Ghraib; however, too much focus on the photos negates the fact that the abuse is far-reaching and widespread in Iraq. Additionally, sometimes the photos themselves were destroyed, a fact that came out at the Fort Hood trial of Sabrina Harman in Megan Ambuhl's testimony, when she stated that she was personally ordered to remove all traces of the photos from the computer hard drive located in Tier 1A at Abu Ghraib prison. In a word, the photos themselves become a focus of masculinist power and control in that they construct and tell the "truth" of Abu Ghraib to the world. This becomes a scapegoat for reasons of insurgency and anti-American targeting, and also a rationalization for keeping the photos secret from the public eye. In the closing arguments of the Lynndie England case, the prosecution made the argument that seven soldiers (the "rotten apples"), and England especially, were to blame for the insurgencies and anti-American targeting. In the Enlightenment society, the photos would be seen as a whistle blowing tactic (see Harman's letter to Kelly, and also Mestrovic 2005), yet this meaning becomes subverted as the blame for targeting is shifted onto the lowest ranking of military soldiers. Nonetheless, in her trial, England was cited as the cause for blame for future deaths to American soldiers.

There are other forms of torturing the soul, as well as the body, yet Foucault seems to operate under an untenable principle that the body and soul are radically divided. However, psychological research has demonstrated that mental pain and cruelty has an immediate and long lasting effect on the body through stress, which in itself leads to physical symptoms. Reconceptualized in this way, other forms of abuse at Abu Ghraib can be seen: torture of the body and soul simultaneously; the desecration of the Koran; using dogs as a means of torture and control; contaminating Islamic religious prayer sessions with the presence of dogs; rape, which inherently involves torture to the psyche and body simultaneously; and religion used to torture the soul through anti-religious sentiment and actions. An additional abuse includes the hooding of detainees as an example of dehumanization, objectification, and psychological torture in that the detainees hear noise and experience physical blows, yet are fully unaware of what is going on except through sound, and therefore cannot anticipate or predict action. This is torture because it is mental abuse and capriciousness for the victim.

Additional torture of the mind is evident in the before mentioned holding of women and children prisoners, without charge and without hopes of being freed from Abu Ghraib. Feminists have applied Foucault's identification of the body as the principal target of power to analyze contemporary forms of social control over both women's bodies and minds, where femininity is policed in terms of certain juridical laws of culturally constructed gender (Bartky 1988, Bordo 1988, Sawicki 1994). In this case of women and children prisoners, the emphasis on practices through which power relations are reproduced converges with the feminist project of analyzing the politics of personal relations and altering gendered power relations. In this specific example, women prisoners do not have power over their bodies in that they are imprisoned, such as the argument goes with regard to some women's historical experiences in the institutions of marriage, motherhood and compulsory heterosexuality. Hence, at Abu Ghraib, women prisoners did not have any power over their *bodies or minds as prisoners*, and thus women's relationships to their bodies and minds are constrained by their status at Abu Ghraib as pawns and as supposedly "protected" prisoners.

However, all the while, Foucault's medieval spirit of punishment has just mutated into a new form of the same.

Moving beyond Foucault's Continuum of Punishment and Cruelty

Foucault argues that physical cruelty as a form of punishment has been replaced with notions of more humane punishment of the mind and soul in modern nations that operate under the principles of the Enlightenment project (Foucault [1975]1977). Regarding Abu Ghraib, this does not seem to be the case. Instead, the Enlightenment project, as well as postmodern notions of simulacra, are subverted by cruelty that involves *both* the body *and* the soul.

Subversion is used through the holding of "ghost detainees," which are people who are held without being formally charged. This can be seen as an example of what Foucault calls the sovereign's right to make charges against a person that they do not know about (Foucault [1975]1977). Even the notion of "rights" is itself an enlightenment ideal that is based on a masculinist narrative (see Rojek's notion of Modernity 1), which is itself a simulacra in this example.

Consider the story in *Time* magazine that reports on the murder of a ghost detainee by CIA agents at Abu Ghraib after being captured by Navy Seals November 4, 2003. Printed plainly in *Time* magazine was the following: "The death of secret detainee Manadel al-Jamadi was ruled a homicide in a Defense Department autopsy" (Zagorin 2005). It was stated in The New Yorker that a forensic pathologist testified that al-Jamadi died from asphyxiation while being shackled in a crucifixion-like pose (Mayer 2005). Indeed, no charges have yet to be leveled at the CIA, and the agent who specifically was mentioned, Mark Swanner, continues to work for the CIA. Likewise, in *The New Yorker*, reports of up to four more detainee deaths at the hands of the CIA were acknowledged, yet "US government's policies on interrogating terrorist suspects may preclude the prosecution of CIA agents who commit abuses or even kill detainees" (Mayer 2005). Where are the rights of these detainees? Are they being considered?

It is not surprising then to know that at the Sabrina Harman trial, one photograph in particular was never shown—the one with her smiling and giving the thumbs-up over a body packed in ice, the body of Manadel al-Jamadi. If this photograph were shown in court and at the trials, it can be imagined that more questions might be asked about who the dead body was that Sabrina was smiling over in the photograph, and more importantly, how did that detainee die? What is known about the photograph, however, is that Harman was ordered to smile and to pose in the picture by Graner, a male guard at Abu Ghraib. In this way, power over the body was gendered for Harman in that she was forced by a male superior to participate in the photo where she is shown smiling over al-Jamadi's corpse. Moreover, power over al-Jamadi's body and soul was evidenced in his death at the hands of the CIA.

Subversion is also used in this war when one considers current reports of "black sites," or secret prisons run by the CIA, reportedly in locations of the former Soviet Bloc Countries. This is yet another example of how the CIA operates outside of the law, thereby making the American notion of the rule of law a simulacra itself (Baudrillard [1981]1994). In many ways when Baudrillard claims that "the Gulf War did not take place" and that there has been a "perfect crime," it could now be heralded that that "American law does not exist" in the postmodern sense, and that we have now entered into the "spirit of terrorism" (Baudrillard [2002]2003, Baudrillard [1995]1996, Baudrillard [1991]1995).

For Foucault, confession (a form of subversion) is integral for punishment (Foucault [1975]1977), and perhaps this is why it was so important for the MI's to get the confession out of detainees. After all, we are seemingly looking for the truth through the punishment and control of detainees. However, the American MIs used what Foucault would term medieval methods of torture such as physical blows and physical suffering to extract these confessions, while simultaneously professing adherence to enlightenment narratives.

The trials themselves might be considered, under the common sense definition of a "trial," to be aimed at finding the truth, much like a confession of sorts. However, after attending two separate trials dealing with detainee abuse at Abu Ghraib, it became clear to me that these trials were really games of subversive strategy with revolving fictions, images, and chances for one-upmanship. If Foucault is right, and punishment is now aimed at just punishing the soul, then the "bad-apples" would not be shackled in body chains that connected at the ankles, wrists, and waist, and also surrounded by giant guards and journalists taking photos as they left the courtroom after the verdict. This kind of punishment is aimed at both the control of the body and the soul. Lynndie England and Sabrina Harman were not just handcuffed on a guarded military base, but their hands were shackled to their legs on a guarded military base— the largest Army base in the nation, and in front of the entire world view of the media who waited, leisurely camped, and strategically placed to get the best photos of this humiliating spectacle. I argue that this spectacle was really about how female soldiers, England and Harman, offended the masculinist code of the military by virtue of being female in the masculinist military itself, among other reasons.

Punishment is thus an interesting concept coupled with gender and power, and can even help explain why relationships existed between the detainees and the guards of Abu Ghraib prison. From the point of view of the detainees, there was the Stockholm Syndrome of the prisoners— laughing, joking, or complying with their abusers. This was documented in court during the Harman trial when Sabrina herself stated that "Gilligan," the man in the hood with the electrodes attached to his fingers, agreed to be hooded during the mock execution photographs. Interestingly, this was a strategy in sleep deprivation, and for a detainee that soldiers had a "friendship relationship" with. Says Sergeant William Cathcart in his testimony regarding the sleep deprivation program, "we wanted an SOP for the sleep deprivation program. There should have been a break in the sleep deprivation program after 72 hours, but there was nothing in writing" (June 24, 2004, SHA32). In Gilligan's situation, the guards created a game for their "trustee" prisoner in order to keep him awake and in response to what they saw as unfair and long MI sleep deprivation scenarios being enforced. (In this example, a simulacra of torture took place at Abu Ghraib when mock torture sessions were constructed, capturing the notion that this is torture of the soul through the mock torture of the body. This is a *simulation* of torture because no shock was delivered and only the situation was reconstructed to give the effect of the abuse. See chapter four for further explanation.) However, the Stockholm syndrome also applies to some of the abusers themselves, as a large number of soldiers (both male and female) with whom I spoke with reluctantly disclosed that they were suffering from Post-Traumatic Stress Disorder (PTSD) from the abuse they suffered and witnessed in Iraq and at Abu Ghraib. Thus, in a sense both the American soldiers and the detainees became victims of the very punishment that they exacted.

The "Rationalization" of Rationality

I have demonstrated that rationality associated with modernity has several different gendered understandings, and conceptual links to masculine and patriarchal systems, where gender can be used to understand "rationality" and "chaos" at Abu Ghraib.

Throughout this analysis, rationality itself has not been used to correct the social order; rationality has not been used to restore the legitimacy of the Geneva Conventions; instead, a gendered mutation of "masculinist" rationality has been used to rationalize torture instead of stopping it. This can be understood as a mutation of the masculinist symbolic "code" in that it is neither rational nor logical. At the Abu Ghraib prison, rationality applied should have resulted in order, control, and a safe prison. Instead, what both the detainees and military personnel of Tier 1A and

Tier 1-B at Abu Ghraib prison encountered and experienced was a prison within a prison. "Rationalization" of supposed rationality itself occurred throughout the Abu Ghraib prison, within government reports, inside of the courtroom itself, and throughout the sworn testimony of the courts-martials.

At the Abu Ghraib trials, there was the rationalization that abuse of detainees only happened specifically in Tier 1A and only at Abu Ghraib. However, in reality, abuse was happening all over the compound of Abu Ghraib (for example, when detainees were being taken out of transport trucks, when detainees were moved or searched, etc.), and abuse is still happening all over Iraq according to Captain Ian Fishback's account in the *Human Rights Watch Report*, and the more recent Levin-McCain Report (2008). This is especially important to point out because abuse was occurring before the "rotten apples" arrived in August 2003 at Tier 1A of Abu Ghraib. More importantly the abuse is still continuing after the abuse was reported in January 2004, and well into the year 2005. The abuse has been documented to extend well beyond the boundaries of the Abu Ghraib prison, and has been documented at FOB Mercury, FOB Tiger, and other bases in Iraq, not to mention at U.S. military bases in both Afghanistan and at Guantanamo Bay. But, what remains important is that much of this abuse was gendered in that it aimed at garnering power through gender humiliation and homoerotic torture over *both the body and soul.*

Within U.S. government reports, the reports themselves do admit that the chain of command set the stage for the abuse and chaos at Abu Ghraib, but rationalized that culpability fell entirely on the lower ranking soldiers, two of which were the *only women* at the hard site of Abu Ghraib, and who were shown not to have participated in abuse.

Within the courtroom, the rationalization was that these were just a "few rotten apples" doing the abuse, when even expert witnesses such as Dr. Stjepan Mestrovic testified that there was a larger "poisoned environment," and using similar terminology as within the government reports themselves, and as evidenced by the expansiveness of the abuse. Additionally, the judge had complete control of what would be admitted for evidence into the trials, thereby performing the iconic role of masculine control. Hence, the wider reasonable connection between abuse at Abu Ghraib, Guantanamo Bay, and Afghanistan was never allowed to be heard within the courtroom. Says Dr. Stjepan Mestrovic, right before the judge forcibly cleared the courtroom, sending Mestrovic out and the panel immediately back into deliberation, "connect the dots of the migration of abuse, Guantanamo Bay, Afghanistan, Abu Ghraib, Iraq." Even Captain Fishback's report on the Human Rights Watch Report web page was denied entry into the trial as evidence because of its supposed yet seemingly incorrect "non-relevance" to the abuse cases being tried at Fort Hood. Instead, the rationalizing in the courtroom was that this abuse was caused by a few "rotten apples," and seemingly continues in Iraq in part, it was argued at the courts-martial, because of their doing.

Considering the testimony heard at the trial of Lynndie England, not one officer was allowed to testify as a means to rationalize that the chain of command could not have known of the abuse. In this way, these officers could not thusly be held liable or culpable for the abuse itself. The government reports demonstrated clearly and rationally that the officers in charge of Abu Ghraib *knew or should have known* under U.S. Army protocol that the abuse was occurring. Hence, the testimony itself was skewed. The officers allowed to testify were subpoenaed and testified in exchange for not being prosecuted. Thus, a "deal" was made, and thereby a rationalization for their "acquittal" occurred.

It is through the rationalizations in each of these aspects—the prison, the government reports, the courtroom, and the testimony—that reason itself was presented as a simulacrum. "Reason" itself was not killed, as Baudrillard would have us believe ([1995]1996), but an economy of rationalization has sprung up to replace it, where at one time gendered masculine rationality and enlightenment ideals attempted to flourish.

Testimony of Major David DiNenna, U.S. Army, Sabrina Harman Courts-Martial

Major David DiNenna, U.S. Army, was called as a witness on May 16, 2005 for the defense, was sworn, and testified as follows:

Q: For the record state your rank, name, and unit of assignment?

A: Major David DiNenna, Senior, currently assigned to the 220th MP Brigade.

Q: Sir, can you tell us about the conditions that you found at Abu Ghraib when you got there?

A: The conditions were, for lack of a better term, deplorable. When we first arrived—when the 72nd MP Company was present in Abu Ghraib operating Camp Vigilant and a couple hundred prisoners, within the four walls of Abu Ghraib itself was trash, debris, glass, metal, rubble, packs of wild dogs, rodents. It had been looted by the civilian populous after the Regime released all the prisoners so it was in a—it was total disarray and trash.

Q: And, sir, can you tell us about the hygienic conditions or lack of hygienic conditions there?

A: Whenever a soldier or a unit arrived at Abu Ghraib, most of the soldiers came down with vomiting, diarrhea as a result of the—just the filth, the trash that existed. They would be like that for a couple of days and then get over it. Some would get it again, and some wouldn't. The lucky ones wouldn't get it at all, which was very few. So identically it was pretty much a trash hole, it was filthy.

Q: Did you have enough medical personal, sir, to take care of these soldiers who were getting sick?

A: We were extremely limited on medical personal throughout the entire time. Basically between battalion medics and battalion field surgeons, including the other medics from all the other units created an aide station, so to speak. But between—we had to serve the soldiers as well as the prisoners. So we—bottom line we didn't have the enough medical personal.

Q: And would the prisoners have many medical difficulties, sir.

A: Extremely. They—we had a lot of diabetes, TB. Based on their diet change their health went down very quickly. Towards the end we were doing two to three MEDVACs a day for heart conditions, diabetics, I think, stuff as well. A lot of amputees, and wounded prisoners came in. So they had a great deal of problems.

Q: And what was the danger level at Abu Ghraib in the middle of all of this, sir?

A: It was extremely high. We had a very high threat external as well as internal, we'd have between 7 and 9,000 prisoners and they have a hundred soldiers per shift to watch them all. WE had to deal with that as well as the constant mortar attacks and RPGs and small arms fire, and then the IEDs picked up.

Q: And did you have enough soldiers to deal with all of these attacks, sir?

A: No. The misconception is that when you guard soldiers you simply stand there and watch—or when you guard prisoners you stand there and just watch them. That is not the case. WE averaged probably between a 100 and 150 prisoners per soldier. We didn't have near enough military police so lots of personal were required for extra security for the MPs to run three different facilities as well as escorts, and QRF, and the list is just endless. WE were probably about a battalion and a company short of personal.

Q: And how was the stress level there then, sir, for you and other soldiers?

A: Well it was extremely high. Soldiers were probably worked between a 12 and 16 hour day. We would try to give them at least a half of day or a day off so they could do laundry. But besides that—between that and the attacks—when you guard prisoners and you're attacked you just don't seek safety for yourself, you also have to keep guarding the prisoners because they'll attempt to escape which they tried many times when we were attacked. So it's kind of two full missions when you're a soldier guarding prisoners, which made the stress level extremely high.

Q: Did you have many occasions of escape, sir?

A: We had—in the outside facilities we had 11 prisoners escape. In the outside facility we had a couple escape but they were usually aided by the Iraqi Correctional Officers would take them on a detail and then let them go. But due to the lack of lighting and soldiers it was very difficult to keep 8,000 prisoners confined.

Q: Sir, you just mentioned lack of lighting, could you tell us about that?

A: Well obviously when you guard prisoners you need lights at night. Lighting was an issue the entire time. We—you know, generators were—or lights would go down either from mortars or just that kind of deficiencies, we couldn't get them replaced. There was an Army contract to install permanent lighting in the outside facilities but it was never finished and to this day I still don't know why. So there were times when we had to bring in vehicles around the compounds just to add enough lighting to keep it on the prisoners at night.

Q: How often would say that occurred?

A: At the beginning it was quite a few times at Camp Vigilant. Ganci was a very large facility that even the truck lighting wouldn't help that much. And then the hard site prison itself, the generators just wouldn't continue to run so that becomes a very dangerous situation. The other confines themselves they have the capability of taking apart the bunks and developing—making weapons out of the metal. So the lighting for the entire times was an issue, discredited—we never resolved it.

Q: Sir, can you explain to us how the—how did—people taking apart these bunks and making weapons?

A: Prisoners had nothing to do all day but come up with ideas of how to make weapons. They—when they built the hard site prison, they didn't use proper— they didn't—well the bunks, they didn't use proper cement when they put in the bars on the windows. It was basically just a—they wanted to get it done quick. CPA wasn't really there to supervise them, they actually didn't get there until December, it was their facility to run. So when the prisoners figured out that they could just chip away at the cement on the bars, they would take them out and they could basically just bend the bunks until the metal broke which they did in quite a few of the tiers when they had uprises.

Q: And, sir, can you tell us about these uprisings in the tiers?

A: In the hard site prison?

Q: Yes, sir.

A: Most of the uprisings were a result of the food, overcrowded, being detained for a lengthy periods of time where they either were not interrogated by MI or they didn't receive timely court dates. So even though they're locked down in a cell so to speak, there's six to eight prisoners per cell. We also let the Iraqi Correctional Officers, and the Iraqi Warden attempt to handle the uprisings, but the result was—we would then take over the operation from them, bring in the internal reaction force for cell detractions. The problem was that if—you could hear it throughout the entire hard site prison so if one tier erupted then another tier would be erupt and at the time we only had 8 to 10 MPs in the entire hard site to work the facility because that was all the soldiers we had left.

Q: And how many prisoners would you have in the entire hard site with these 8 to 10 soldiers?

A: Towards the end they would bring us around 1,500 to 2,000 throughout the whole hard site.

Q: And, sir, you talked about the fact that food was a factor in the uprising. Could you tell us a little bit more about the food issues at Abu Ghraib?

A: Initially we started with MREs for the prisoners. When a contract was set up through a local Iraqi Company, it was actually subcontracted, was set up through a local Iraqi Company it was actually subcontracted to a hotel in Baghdad, and then subcontracted to another company that would deliver the food. The food was usually undercooked, it was dirty, it had debris, the food had rodent, feces, and glass. At times for their evening meal they would receive a boiled egg and two pieces of cheese which obviously the prisoners didn't appreciate. IT got to the point where they were either throwing stones or rocks at the vendors themselves or throw the food back at the MPs.

We had medics, field medicine, and field surgeons and everybody evaluating, include looking on it every time it came in. So a lot of the times we would just throw the vendors out the gate, so to speak, and give the prisoners the MREs which made them very happy.

Q: And, sir, what kind of issues did you have with giving the prisoners the MREs, did that cause issues for the soldiers?

A: Well, midway through some—around the November timeframe we were directed not to purchase any more MREs.

Q: Directly from who, sir?

A: Major General Orfakawski at the CGTS center. They wanted to use humanitarian meals which we couldn't—they couldn't give us enough because we were well over capacity. However, we did have some MREs on hand that are kept for the prisoners because we knew that the Iraqi Food Contract was going to continue, so it would be an issue. The other thing was we'd have to take out the warming products, good serving work products. We also had to take out the Tabasco sauce and a lot of things that they could use to make weapons which they would use the Tabasco sauce for. So to feed 6,000 prisoners on the outside, on the outside compounds as well as the ones on the inside of the hard site, MREs was a lengthy process because you had to sit there and trip their MREs. It took quite a bit of time which made the prisoners pretty upset which then puts more stress on the soldiers because they had to deal with that issue.

Q: And you said that there was some issue about overcrowding in the hard site. Can you tell us about that, sir?

A: Yes, actually overcrowding existed everywhere. You know basically our mission—entire mission we should have seven MPs on the gate so to speak for 500 prisoners and as well as the tower guards. So it would be approximately 10 or 11 MPs per 500 prisoners. You do the same ratio—in a hard site facility it's different, that's basically a corrections operation, which is entirely different than the internment resettlement operation, so the issue we ran in to at the hard site when they put a lot of the Iraqi Civilian Criminals in there is they just kept opening tiers and kept putting them in, but we didn't get an increase in soldiers and they did the same on the outside at Ganci and at Camp Vigilant as well.

Q: And could you tell us about the issues you had with detainees being kept in custody longer than those who were—not having court dates?

A: Well it existed both for the—well they labeled security detainees, which was attacks on coalition forces and it was the same case for the civilian detainee— the criminal detainees which was Iraqi on Iraqi violations. Every time a new sweep—or operation would come in and those who were to be interrogated would be pushed on the back burner and these new ones coming would then be interrogated. Well if you multiply this by six months you have a prisoner that was there for six months and never spoken to either by MI or the same would happen with the civilian courts, they were just standing them up. So civilian criminals that were there for—in the beginning would be there towards the end as well ----

....

Questions by the Defense Counsel Continued

Q: Sir, were there women and children kept at Tier 1 Alpha and Tier 1 Bravo at the hard site?

A: To answer the question, yes, they were in 1 Bravo.

Q: 1 Bravo. Sir, can you tell us about that? Why were women and children kept in 1 Bravo?

A: The issue was when either the Iraqi Police or the capturing unit U.S.—for the coalition units would bring a prisoner to Abu Ghraib, it didn't matter whether it was a male or female or juvenile. We could obviously not—we could not keep them in Camp Vigilant or Camp Ganci where you had 7,000 male prisoners, so we—since Tier 1 Bravo was complete we used Tier 1 Bravo for females and juveniles. And the unit there did put up—did ensure that the female prisoners had sheets, they would hang sheets so that no one could see inside their cells. 1 Alpha was not used, we had male prisoners in 1 AlphA: Then they would take the—as they started opening prisoners in Baghdad, juvenile facilities they would try to transfer some of the juveniles to those facilities.

CPA and MI came to me and said we had to empty out 1 Bravo because of a particular sweep they were doing and they needed it. Well, I did that, but it sat vacant for weeks and I was still receiving juveniles and females so I had to put them back in there which was another issue. But that's the only segregation place that we had.

Q: So you did the best that you could with what little you had, sir?

A: Correct. Sometime in January we were able to open up a tier strictly for juveniles.

Q: Sir, how young would you say was the youngest juvenile you had?

A: I think it was 12----

   …

Q: And, sir, were there ever times where women and children were brought in and they did not commit a crime or they were just brought in to Abu Ghraib because they had been with somebody who was arrested?

A: Yes.

   …

Q: Sir, can you tell us about the water conditions at Abu Ghraib? Did you have enough water for the soldiers and the prisoners?

A: That always was the direct concern. Originally when we first arrived water was rationed for the soldiers, which was two liter bottles per day. When we were finally able to—we had to run two runs to BIOP with our water trucks every day just to supply the prisoners with water as well as the soldiers. What that entails is two water trucks and then three or four HMMWVs which was a lot of personal to do trips back and forth down to the BIOP. When they finally sent up—the contracting office set up a border contract for an Iraqi company it didn't work because they delivered the water in fuel trucks, because we inspected the water and food all the time ... They later set up a ROQ unit, which is a purification unit that was trying to pump water from the outside, purify it, and then run it through to the facilities. Yet some of those hoses and water buckets were damaged by mortars which were then difficult to replace, which then made—we had to do more water runs to BIOP. So it was an issue throughout.

Q: Sir, um, you called that convoy with the water trucks and HMMWV, the security HMMWVs had to take IED Alley. Can you tell us why it was called IED Alley, sir?

A: Abu Ghraib was basically set up in the middle of the Sunni Triangle between Fallujah and Baghdad. So, to get to the BIOP, Baghdad International Airport, we had to travel down the road which was right in front of Abu Ghraib Prison which ran right down to BIOP. When IEDs, I guess for the lack of a better term, became popular as a tool to use there was so much ruble and debris on the side of the road just as well as dead animals which were used to place the bombs in so to speak and they knew it was heavily traveled. It was basically the only route to be—was actually the safest route which was going through the towns on the north side of the prison which had a lot of markets that would be congested. So they really targeted that route.

Q: So IED Alley was the safest route your soldiers could take, sir?

A: Correct, from the prison to BIAP yes.

Q: Sir, can you explain to us what the Sunni Triangle means?

A: Um, it's a—I guess we interpreted it as being the stronghold or the most support for Saddam Hussein and his Regime, and then it was three locations and it was basically just in the middle of a combat zone is where they put the facility.

...

Q: Sir, can you tell us about when the porta johns came in to Abu Ghraib?

A: Probably sometime in September and most of them went to the prisoners first and then the soldiers. Then the issue became throughout September until we got them in February, the contractor who was supposed to pump out the porta johns sometimes wouldn't show up or there was so much they had to empty it and come back and sometimes they wouldn't come back. So therefore the porta johns wouldn't be cleaned and the bays would be overflowing for both the soldiers and the prisoners which obviously created chaos.

Q: Sir, can you tell us about the supply issues at Abu Ghraib between the September/January timeframe? Or October and January timeframe … for the prisoners and the soldiers?

…

A: For the prisoners, once the prisoners were obviously captured during the summer months so when they came in they had shorts and they had no shoes, short sleeve shirts. We requested in June that we needed contracts set up for winter clothing for the prisoners. Up until sometime in December we still had not received adequate clothing and blankets. We were able to get enough Korans which were passed out to one tent—at the compound we had 20 tents so each tent received one Koran which was for the prisoners to pass around which they did. So for the prisoners themselves the clothing was probably the biggest issue. To them obviously when it gets down to 70 degrees it's very cold as it was for us as we were going through the summer. For the soldiers it ranged from everything from meals to some type of air conditioning or basic supplies, radios, we didn't have any—or enough handheld radios whatsoever to communicate at all, which was an issue the entire time. Soldiers were actually purchasing—calling home and having them sent over. Because we put in a contract for a Motorola Base Station, but it was denied and then it was approved when we left. Pretty much everything was approved when we left.

Q: Sir, can you tell us about the issues with clothing supplies to prisoners in the beginning in terms of lack of jump suits and things like that, sir?

A: That was mostly the issue in the hard site. CPA was again responsible for that facility. Tier 1 Alpha and 1 Bravo was basically given to the MI community for their, I guess, higher intelligence value prisoners. But for the rest of the facility it was CPAs responsibility. Again they actually didn't show any representation. They visited once in a while, but they weren't really there as often as they were supposed to be. The problem we ran in to was when the Iraqi Correctional Officers first started working there and the prisoners a lot of times you couldn't tell who was who because they didn't have the uniforms for the correctional officers yet. They then started ordering jump suits, the orange jump suits for the prisoners, but though they were prisoners, to us very quickly they weren't keeping up with the supplies we had which again created a problem. As correctional officers were trained they were sent to work right away but they didn't have—a lot of them didn't have uniforms in the beginning so it was—you had to rely on your fellow correctional officers to ensure that this guy standing next to him is not a prisoners and he's a correctional officer. So it was very—in the beginning it was very, very difficult.

Q: And, sir, can you just, um, verify for the record what the CPA means?

A: Coalition Provisional Authority.

Q: Thank you, sir. Sir, you—it sounds like in the beginning at least with this place we hear you had to depend a lot on the Iraqi Police or IP, did you have any issues with the Iraqi Police or--?

A: Well there's the difference between the Iraqi Police and the Iraqi Correctional Officers. But actually we had similar issues with both. Bribery was and shaking hands with the families of the prisoners is a big deal.

Q: What do you mean about that, sir?

A: They would know a prisoner who may be in a particular village, or tribe, or that correctional officer is friends with the family and then go to the family and receive money and then would assist the prisoner to escape. They smuggled in weapons to the prisoners. When the Iraqi----

Q: ----what kind of weapons, sir?

A: Well what's known is the handgun that was smuggled in around the November 24th timeframe. They also would send—would smuggle in razor blades from the Iraqi Medical Facility which was later set up. And they would take them on work details and just let them go. Give them a change of clothes. We spent a lot of time watching the Iraqi Correctional Officers as well as the prisoners.

…

Q: Sir, at the time that you were at Abu Ghraib going through all of these issues, what were you feeling?

A: Abandoned.

Q: Why?

A: Actually I guess the theater IG, I can't remember the colonel's name, arrived towards the end of September, beginning of October timeframe I believe and basically stated that we were forgotten, *we were a forgotten mission.* We were set up just to keep these prisoners and keep them out of the way.

You know, when you're at a facility whether it's a hard site prison or tents on the outside, it's—you're setting up a city and you need the resources to do that, we weren't supplied.

Q: Sir, did you ever have the opportunity to bring these issues up to your chain of command?

A: Daily. Every day from July to February we sent up a Situation Report that there was approximately 240 times just on paper that they were addressed we had visits from now Sergeant Major of the Army Preston who was a Command Sergeant Major for Lieutenant General Sanchez, September/October timeframe, it was brought to this attention. CJTF7 Staff, any general officer that—or anywhere it was brought to her attention. Obviously it went through the computer and gave them databases. There's e-mails, briefings, telephone conversations, and based on my decisions.

Q: And, sir, what would be the response to the daily e-mails for help?

A: They ranged from the contracting office to the guy that would work on it. Not much ever materialized. So I guess the response would be okay we got it, but it was the same when we had VIPs visit or anything. They'd ask who do we need, we'd tell them, and they would leave and I guess so would the request.

...

Q: Sir, have you talked about bringing—you brought these issues to them, what was his response?

A: That he was taking it back to the CJTF7 and work the issues.

Q: And how many times did you see Command Sergeant Major Preston.

A: I did personally a couple of times as well as the other Sergeant Major that escorted him around.

Q: And his response was the same?

A: Yes we'd like to receive a DFAC in December which was a pretty inadequate event. It was—the food wasn't properly prepared and so a lot of the soldiers would then go back to the MREs or fire up the MKTs so they could—during that timeframe BIAP was right down the street and soldiers knew that—what the conditions they had at BIOP were much better than ours and couldn't understand why we couldn't receive certain things which affected the morale and stress obviously.

Q: Sir, can you tell us if you spoke with General Sanchez when he came down to Abu Ghraib?

A: Yes I briefed him. We actually had a briefing for him and a lot of these issues were brought up.

Q: And what was his response, sir?

A: Basically talking to our staff and ensuring that they receive that so to speak. And I guess they took it back.

Q: Was anything ever done, sir?

A: Actually up until the story—they declared Abu Ghraib an enduring base which meant the funnel was opened up—or everything opened and we came into a very small funnel. We didn't have the resources that they were trying to put all this as well as the influx of prisoners. So that was merely in the city through the November timeframe, and then it was the MI Brigade commander was appointed as the FOB commander.

Q: When was that, sir.

A: In November of '03.

(16 May 2005, SHCM)

Chapter 3

The Abuse was Reported: Parsonian Gender Roles and Abu Ghraib Transfigurations

The social system at Abu Ghraib was not self-correcting; rather, it was self-perpetuating.

> Captain Jonathan Crisp, Defense Attorney, Lynndie England Courts-Martial

I wanted to kind of pursue a career in the military but now, after this—these incidents, you know, I'm not really going that route anymore, sir.

> Specialist Matthew Wisdom, MP [May 17, 2005, SHCM]

I would put the men and women of my company up against any active duty company. That one wing was a very small part of what we did. I saw a number of acts of courage, dignity and professionalism from my soldiers. These acts were performed under very difficult circumstances. That is what we do as soldiers.

> Captain Donald J. Reese [June 24, 2004, SHA32]

I think they were in a very abusive situation. I think that yes, not only the detainees, but they themselves [the soldiers]… there was a climate of fear and intimidation in which to various degrees they were internalized … the U.S. Government's Reports say, which with sociology say, there's a mixture of institutional responsibility and individual responsibility.

> Dr. Stjepan Mestrovic, Expert Witness, Sabrina Harman Courts-Martial

Feminist social theory is aimed at the analysis of the subordination and marginalization of women from social and cultural arenas, and is focused on understanding the fundamental inequalities between the sexes, specifically with the analysis of male power as dominant over women.[1] This kind of analysis of power associated with gender shows how our society and culture is organized in terms of attitudes and beliefs concerning gender categories. Further, these gender categories inscribe gender roles in terms of power.

Power coupled with gender informs the organization of society and thus are evidence of the effects of applied and specific gender constructions within society. Since it is the case that society is stratified in terms of power arrangements, an

---

1 As stated earlier, it is important to note that gender experiences differ between individuals, even of the same gender, and I argue that gender categories are stratified with regard to race, ethnicity, class, sexuality, and cultural value, among many other hierarchical and intersected ways.

analysis of gender constructions shows how gender roles have been conceived of as a means for establishing and sustaining social control. From these understandings of power coupled with gender, social roles emerge and social theorists have come up with many different ways to discuss these gendered roles.

In this chapter, I discuss one social theorist, Talcott Parsons, and his notion of instrumental and expressive gender roles, and argue that his gender roles served a multitude of functions simultaneously and especially given the masculinist code of the military; however, I move beyond Parsons, and argue that given the complex social situations at Abu Ghraib, Parsons' notions of "instrumental" and "expressive" are limited with regard to their explanatory power. I therefore construct new theoretical terms to illustrate the dysfunctions at Abu Ghraib and through the creative refashioning of Parsonian theory.

Parsons Instrumental and Expressive

Talcott Parsons developed his systems theory of the sexual division of labor based on biological sex roles within the family (Parsons 1937, Parsons 1951, Parsons 1954, Parsons and Bales 1955). According to Parsons, both gender roles and behaviors are informed by biological, psychological, social and cultural gender socializations, and we come to understand these associations of gender as associated with sex categories initially within the family itself. Additionally, these gender roles function in tandem toward equilibrium and assimilation with all of society's other subsystems in a structural functional manner.

In Parsonian terms, the "expressive" feminine role is associated with care giving and domestic mothering obligations, is concerned with the welfare of others, aimed at providing emotional assistance, as well as a sense of belonging or integration to the family/group. Parsons associates the "instrumental" masculine role with the man's ability to earn a wage in the public sphere, and other rational goal centered tasks. In this way, Parsons views the male as a social "agent" who thinks in terms of "rationally-linked goals and means," and is valued for such within society (Parsons and Bales 1955). The social world thus becomes organized in this gendered way, where sex categories are associated with these Parsonian gender roles, both as a means of providing social order and social solidarity for the family and larger culture as well.

I use Parsons to analyze Abu Ghraib because his theory of gender is relevant when discussing the U.S. military, as this context still works culturally on such basic gender stereotypes and prejudices.[2] In previous publications (see Caldwell

---

2   Although gender theory has developed considerably since Parsons' writings, his theory pertaining to gender seems to be the most befitting to explain the gendered dynamics at both the trials and the events at the prison itself. Feminists, gender theorists, and queer theorists have deconstructed gender roles *ad infinitum*; however, the U.S. military does not seem to have participated in this critical thinking project as of yet.

and Mestrovic 2008), applying Parsons' dichotomies to gender stereotypes of U.S. military culture was helpful when explaining the rigid typecasts of gender roles within the military. However, I expand Parsons' theorizing and show that his distinctions between instrumental and expressive are functional, even in dysfunctional social situations, and especially given the masculinist code of the military.

For example, in previous publications my colleague and I (see Caldwell and Mestrovic 2008) explain in detail the variations of instrumental-expressive distinctions that emerged at Abu Ghraib with the following thematic descriptions: *expressive abuse*, or when abuse is strategically *expressive* in nature because it will bring about an *instrumental* end (such as the *instrumental* taking of women and children as hostages or bargaining chips at Abu Ghraib, and the playing upon emotions for their release; or the *instrumental* use of women's panties on prisoner's heads as a means for *expressive* humiliation); *expressive torture* or when during torture there is an emotional bond formed, much like a Stockholm Syndrome type scenario, between the abuser and abused, and where the torture itself has no rational goals/means *instrumental* plan for interrogation (such as with "Gilligan" the hooded detainee on the box); and *the instrumental misuse of expressive functions* or when Military Intelligence manipulates emotions as part of an *instrumental*, goal-oriented strategy (such as the calculated use of dogs and also nudity to break down prisoners through the use of cultural values and social norms as torture tactics themselves).

In this additional expanded and revisited chapter on Parsons' notion of instrumental and expressive, I show how the use of these gender markers helps to explain the several circumstances where the "rotten apples" and those associated with Tier 1A and 1B actually did report the abuse that they saw and witnessed at Abu Ghraib, however without response from their chain of command. I use Parsons' theory of instrumental and expressive gender roles to discuss these reports of abuse, and show how a sociologically imagined, creative and expanded reading of Parsons helps explain further what took place at Abu Ghraib in gendered terms. New theoretical concepts such as the *instrumental perceived reporting of abuse* (where abuse is reported in the perceived belief the chain of command will respond, yet with a failed goal/means outcome), the *expressive nonreporting of abuse* (where abuse is *not* reported because of fear associated with the consequences of reporting and other expressive reasons), and the *instrumental actual reporting of abuse* (where abuse is reported with an actual means/goal or end outcome) are developed to illustrate this additional gendered interpretation. It is my aim to point out that responsibility for abuse is not only at the individual level, but also collectively at higher levels for command responsibility within the military, and that this kind of joint responsibility for abuse was non-existent at Abu Ghraib and the courts-martials.

As a functionalist, Parsons is concerned with maintaining system homeostasis, and even when that system is a prison. Abu Ghraib was characterized in court, in government reports, and in interviews as chaotic and thus "socially disorganized" in terms of the following: there was a disorganized or total lack of a filing system; confusion of standard operating procedures as well as role expectations; confusion about the leadership of the prison itself; serious supply shortages including soldiers to guard prisoners, food, water, and clothing; overcrowding; lack of due process for prisoners; lack of training and military discipline, and other things (Mestrovic and Caldwell 2010, Caldwell and Mestrovic 2008b, Karpinski 2005, Mestrovic 2007, Strasser 2004). In fact, says Seargent Hydrue Joyner (an MP in charge of the day shift at Abu Ghraib) in his testimony at the England trial regarding his orders at Abu Ghraib: "Here are the prisoners, this is how we treat them, good luck!" This statement is further evidence of the dysfunctional social system at the prison, with no established set of rules, including standard operating procedures. Nonetheless, even with these chaotic characterizations of the overall conditions at Abu Ghraib, I still argue that Parsons' instrumental and expressive dimensions, and their creative reinterpretations and applications, "functioned" with regard to understanding the reporting of abuse. *To be clear, abuse was reported. Nothing was done with those reports up the chain of command within the dysfunctional social climate of Abu Ghraib.*

The Punishing of Rapists, October 24-25, 2003

On October 24 and 25, there was a torture incident at Abu Ghraib that was captured in photographs in response to three Iraqi detainees who were thought to have raped a 15-year-old boy. (Interestingly, the prosecutor disclosed at the trials that none of these Iraqis were actually rapists.) What is known is that these prisoners were stripped naked, forced to roll around on the cement floor together, were tied together in homoerotic poses, and were verbally abused. Looking at the photos of abuse, the prisoners had abrasions and were bleeding from damage caused by the concrete flooring. The following soldiers were pictured in the photos of that evening: Rivera, Cruz, Krohl, Graner, Harman, Frederick, Adele the Iraqi translator, and two unidentified persons (labeled by the prosecutor as Unknown 1 and Unknown 2).

When Specialist Israel Rivera, a 19-year-old Military Intelligence soldier, took the stand at the Harman trial, he stated in his testimony, "SPC Cruz came to the living quarters around 1900 and told me about a rape of a 15-year-old boy. I was told that two or three detainees held him down and raped him. I asked what they were going to do with them and he asked me if I wanted to come and find out" (June 24, 2004, SHA32). (Rivera also said in his sworn statement that the purpose for him being present at this incident was to witness the show of force against the detainees.) Rivera established the heterosexist environment of the prison when he stated, "the soldier with the green BDUs [Graner] had a speaker box with a microphone attached to it. He was shouting homosexual slurs into the cell that the detainees were in" (June 24, 2004, SHA32). Further explaining the events of the night, Rivera continued, "The detainees were taken out of the cell and were shaking. They were told to get down on their stomachs and crawl, and to drag their genitals on the floor ... I questioned this behavior and I knew it was illegal. I asked SPC Cruz if we even knew if they did what they were accused of. He said that one of them came forward and recanted ... The detainees were frightened; they were shaking, begging and crying. It is terrible for an Arab to be naked with another man. They begged for us to stop" (June 24 2004, SHA32).

Then came more homoerotic abuse. Said Rivera, "After the log rolling they were gathered by the MPs into a mass of bodies. They were just—not stacked, they were placed to where they were almost hugging each other, so it seemed that they were having homosexual relations and they were chained up so that the—so they wouldn't be able to resist, and they were able to maintain style—hold on each other ... they were handcuffed in such a way that they were embraced" (May 13, 2005, SHCM). This is an example of *the instrumental misuse of expressive functions* (Caldwell and Mestrovic 2008b), although in this case, both MI and MP are using expressive torture tactics to executing the abuse. Further, Rivera testified, "Corporal Graner had the green gloves, so he was able to touch them without being contaminated—and Specialist Cruz was using his feet to push down on the buttocks of these detainees to make them seem as though they were having sex" (May 13, 2005, SHCM). The trial counsel asked Rivera how Corporal Graner would move the detainees, and Rivera responded, "He would grab arms of legs to manipulate movement ... he was manipulating their limbs in order to get that embrace" (May 13, 2005, SHCM). In Parsonian terms, Graner was instrumentally moving the detainees in a planned way, towards an end torture tactic, and using expressive means of gender and sexuality humiliation as punishment itself. Moreover, in his sworn statement, Rivera was asked if the top leadership knew about the abuse of prisoners, if they were "in the loop," "looking the other way," or "oblivious" ... and Rivera answered that they were "oblivious."

Rivera added that he was shocked at what he saw in terms of the abuse that night, claiming, "When you are there and you see this going on it has an effect on you" (June 24, 2004, SHA32). He maintained that he just stood there shocked, watching, not knowing that photographs were even being taken. Although Rivera was offered immunity for testifying against Harman, he was initially charged with dereliction of duty, or the failure to protect Iraqi detainees from abuse, cruelty, and maltreatment, as it was their duty to do so, and as if the soldiers could have stopped the abuse. So why did Rivera *not attempt to stop* the abuse?

Rivera stated in open court that he was afraid—afraid to stop the abuse that evening because he had fear of his fellow-soldiers—fear that they would retaliate against him physically. Disclosed Rivera, "I feel an obligation to step in if someone is in violation of the law. I did not step in and stop this situation because I was in fear" (June 24, 2004, SHA32). This is specifically an example of *expressive non-reporting of abuse*, where abuse is not reported because of expressive reasons, in this case, emotions of fear and also possibly the maintaining of group cohesion and unity. (Had Rivera reported abuse, he perceived the group would have turned on him.) In this example, for Rivera to display the emotion of fear within the context of the hyper-masculine U.S. military, he came across as expressive in the Parsonian sense. In the everyday language that I heard soldiers use during my research and within the trials, Rivera would have been labeled as a "pussy" had he protested the abuse.

Nonetheless, Rivera did end up telling someone—he told his female friend of the same rank, Specialist Ann Schlagel, who reported it to a superior. Stated Rivera, "As I was leaving the tier Specialist Cruz asked me if I was going to say anything and I told him that I wouldn't ... The morning after I told Specialist Ann Schlagel ... I told her of the entire incident in full ... it was someone that I could trust ... she came up to me, she said, you know, that thing you told me about, that thing with the detainees and Cruz, it has been taken care of. She said she had talked to [MP, NCOIC] Sergeant Joyner" (May 13, 2005, SHCM). Indeed, the female defense counsel Captain Takemura hammered Rivera with questions about why it was that he didn't report this incident further up the chain of command, and why he did not follow up on his report.

> Q (defense counsel Takemaura): You basically lied to him [Cruz] and told him I'm not [going to tell anyone]? ... Because you're afraid of Cruz?
>
> A: I was at the time, yes.
>
> Q: And despite the fact that this was such an emotional turmoil for you, the only person you went to was somebody that you were really close to, is that correct?
>
> A: Correct ... Schlagel.
>
> Q: And she told you that, in fact, that you both needed to talk to somebody about this? ... And yet you never did? ... because you trusted her when she told you that, in fact, she had taken care of it, is that correct? ... You never talked with Sergeant Joyner though, did you?
>
> A: No, ma'am, I didn't.
>
> Q: Ok, and as an American soldier that was at Tier 1 that night, it was your duty to make sure that these detainees were safe ... and you never stopped what was going on ...
>
> A: No, I never made any effort to make it stop.
>
> Q: And you said that Staff Sergeant Frederick was there? ... and Corporal Graner was there?... and you never asked [them] what was going on or tr[ied] to stop [them]?
>
> A: No, ma'am

Q: Because you were afraid?

A: Well I mean they were the ones—authority with the rank and they were the ones that were doing this, it seemed rather foolish of me to say, hey, what are you guys doing? It seemed like I would be compromising my own safety ... because they were willing to do this to a detainee why would they not do it to me? (May 13, 2005, SHCM)

It is clear from Rivera's testimony that he did not trust his fellow soldiers at Abu Ghraib, and the one that he did was a female. Interestingly, the phrase "don't be a pussy" was used by soldiers at the prison when fellow soldiers resisted abusing prisoners, and this very comment is a gendered statement focused on the belittling of masculinity within the hyper-masculinist context of the U.S. military itself—perhaps even the belittling of Rivera. It could be argued that Rivera's fear itself went against the unwritten "code" (Baudrillard 1983a, Lyotard [1979]1984) of constructed military masculinity, and thus his crimes can be construed as embarrassing the U.S. with his feminine-expressive and passive reactions of fear, and even though he did not participate in physical abuse.

Additionally, according to Rivera's testimony, the phrase "You didn't see shit!" was commonplace at Abu Ghraib when referring to the abuse as well. Indeed, Jeremy Sivits, a mechanic at Abu Ghraib who only witnessed a small portion of the abuse, stated that he didn't report abuse for the following reasons, "Because I was asked not to, sir ... [by] Staff Sergeant Frederick ... As I was leaving the tier that night he said, 'Hey Sivits, you didn't see shit!'"(May 13, 2005, SHCM). This was a Parsonian instrumental command using the expressive emotion of fear (from someone who outranked him, nonetheless) as a "guarantee" for the non-reporting of abuse, and in some ways, it worked. Both of the above statements have functions in terms of the *expressive non-reporting of abuse* in that they instrumentally either create a co-conspirator through the use of expressive fear ("Don't be a pussy!"), or through the use of fear keeps the fact that abuse took place concealed ("You didn't see shit!"). Again, Parsons' notion of instrumental and expressive does not fully make sense of how expressiveness can achieve an instrumental goal, and so a re-interpretation of Parsons is required.

Armin Cruz, a young MI agent testified about the events on October 24-25 and stated that another MI agent named Roman Krohl woke him up and said, "Hey we're punishing rapists!" Cruz stated at the trials that the "rules of engagement were loose so we could do what we want" and also that he "helped out" by handcuffing the "detainees" (Caldwell and Mestrovic 2008b). Although the photographs of abuse look sexual, and I argue expressive-gendered and homoerotic, Cruz insisted on the stand and to the prosecutor that the naked and tied up embrace of the prisoners was instrumental in nature aimed at their control, and "to keep them from kicking and biting." Although Cruz did not report the abuse up the MI chain of command (Caldwell and Mestrovic 2008b), he did report the abuse to a higher-up. Attorney Frank Spinner asked Cruz in court if he reported the incident to anyone, and Cruz answered, "The next day, to the day shift, MP NCOIC of the hard site, Sergeant Joyner ... the only [other] thing that I did was a little while later, I would say a week or two ... I went and asked him and he said he took care of it" (May 13, 2005, SHCM). The fact that Cruz did go back and check to see if the report had been acted upon was instrumental and focused on an end outcome—one we can never know—perhaps that of ending torture? Perhaps figuring out if he and other soldiers would be court-martialed for torture? Nonetheless, the very fact that Cruz revisited his reporting attempt, and also had a concern for its outcome, classifies Cruz's reporting attempt as an *instrumental actual report* in nature, focused on a means/end goal outcome. Says the civilian defense attorney, "to your knowledge you're not aware of any action taken as a result of that report at that time?" Replied Cruz, "No, sir." (May 13, 2005, SHCM).

Perhaps the best example of an *instrumental actual report* from the October event, where the soldier made sure that his report was heard, was seen in Ken Davis' testimony. Davis was an MP in the 372nd at Abu Ghraib, and stated that he had sought several different outlets to report the abuse from the night of October 24-25, 2003. Davis stated that he was sure that it was MI who was directing the events that night, and specifically Specialist Cruz and Specialist Krol. Trial counsel asked Davis, "And you've been pretty insistent upon that and you've sought a number of outlets to do that in, correct? ... the *Washington Post*? CNN Live with Paula Zahn? ABC News? Hardball with Chris Matthews?" He responded, "That's correct, sir" (May 16, 2005, SHCM). The civilian defense counsel Frank Spinner had the following exchange with Davis in court about his role in reporting abuse:

> Q (Frank Spinner): With respect to talking to various news programs about this case, why did you talk to those news programs?
>
> A: Because this case first broke back in December when I went to Fort Lee I tried to report it and no one was listening so I went to my congressman and I told him either you all would listen or I would tell the media.
>
> Q: And, in fact, you appeared before Congress too didn't you?
>
> A: Members of the Armed Services Committee, yes, sir.
>
> Q: So, again, were you just doing this because you wanted to be the center of attention?
>
> A: No, sir, it's because I want the truth, sir.

Q: ... Cruz or Krul, were they also talking on this program? ... and was the[ir] story ... any different than what you recall observing? ... and is that why you wanted to appear?

A: Yes, sir.

...

Q: You mentioned reporting this. When did you first report what you observed that night?

A: The next day to Lieutenant Raeder, sir ... I told him that MI was doing some pretty weird things with naked detainees. (May 16, 2005, SHCM)

Davis took instrumental command in reporting abuse, and specifically when he felt that he was not heard. He occupied the role of an active and threatening autonomous agent, both at Fort Lee and with his congresswoman, and in a creative whistleblowing attempt approached the media. Not only did this tactic serve the goal of explaining what was happening at Abu Ghraib, but it also "corrected" the story of those who attempted to explain the abuse to the media initially, yet were perpetrators of the abuse itself according to Davis and others. This was instrumental in nature given the end result aimed for, and also somewhat achieved—the abuse was now known publically.

However, the expressive consequences for Davis's instrumental role as a whistle-blower were significant: His comrades threatened him with physical injury. The prosecutor initially sought to charge him with conspiracy, and eventually dropped the charges. The prosecutor treated Davis with contempt and sought to portray him as a media-hound, not as a conscientious whistle-blower. Davis was one of the unsung heroes of the Abu Ghraib saga, but was treated contemptuously for doing the "right thing" according to Parsonian theory. Finally, his disclosures to Congress and the media had absolutely no effect on instrumentally stopping the abuse, even though the abuse was successfully instrumentally reported.

The chain of command did not correct for the deviance that was (sometimes) reported surrounding the events of October 24-25, 2003, and instead the abuse continued in this poisoned social climate, and was photographed in future events at Abu Ghraib Tier 1A and 1B.

The Pyramid Incident, November 7, 2003

On May 12, 2005, Special Agent James Boerner from the U.S Army Criminal Investigative Division took a voluntary statement from Sabrina Harman, and advised her of her rights. Boerner remembers that Harman said it was a standard operating procedure for the detainee's clothing to be removed, and that "she [Harman] did not think that this was right for the prisoners to have to do," referring to the naked pyramid and that, "she [Harman] had a problem with that" (May 12, 2005, SHCM). Additionally, according to Boerner, Harman stated "that she had not given any orders of any kind for any of the prisoners to do these sex acts" and "that she never physically abused any of the prisoners" (May 12, 2005, SHCM).

These above statements were made in reference to the iconic photographic images of the naked pyramid of abuse at Abu Ghraib on November 7, 2003, which involved all of the initial seven "rotten apples" (Harman, Frederick, Graner, Davis, Ambuhl, England and Sivits), and where naked Iraqi male bodies were piled on top of each other in a pyramid structure. This night at Abu Ghraib, there was a fight and these prisoners were brought into the hard site because, according to Charles Graner, they had supposedly hit a female MP with a brick in the face and caused a riot. In Parsonian terms, some might argue that the photographed stack of naked Iraqi men in a pyramid served a function of expressive humiliation with an end-goal, and is thus an example of *expressive abuse* (Caldwell and Mestrovic 2008b). According to Graner's testimony at the Lynndie England trial, he claimed that this was a tactic in organization to stop who they thought were dangerous prisoners from communicating and as an attempt to exercise instrumental control over the prisoners themselves, thereby confirming that expressive tactics (humiliation) were being used as a means to an end. After the pyramid, however, these prisoners were forced to masturbate and to simulate fellatio—something that was not explained as instrumental in any of the testimony.

Says Jeremy Sivits, "Specialist Harman was standing back with me looking at the pyramid with a look of disgust on her face like she could not believe this was happening. SPC Harman did not appear to approve of this behavior, but she did take photographs … Based on SPC Harman's size and nature she was not in a position to challenge CPL Graner or SSG Frederick" (June 24, 2004, SHA32). What is understood from Sivits' comments is that Harman did not orchestrate or "go along" with the sexual humiliation and gender torture of prisoners, which would have constituted an instrumental action. (In fact, in Wisdom's testimony about this night, he stated that Harman had not hit anyone.) Instead, and I will use Harman as an example here, she and the other "rotten apples" faced similar charges of conspiracy because she was present and taking photographs. According to the prosecution's theory, and because there was more than one person taking photographs of abuse, this counted as the instrumental overt act of agreement necessary for conspiracy. In other words, the act of being present at the site of abuse and taking photographs of the abuse was the same in terms of legal responsibility as was a conversation about organizing and agreeing to participate in abuse itself, and thus counted as conspiracy. For Harman, testimony shows that she had an expressive-emotive reaction to the pyramid, and further the fact that both England and Harman only took and posed for photographs rather than organized the pyramid scenario shows their ultimate expressiveness towards the situation in general (Caldwell and Mestrovic 2008b). It thus seems that female soldiers were *used* for the humiliation of Iraqi male prisoners, where the cultural constructions of masculinity are unwillingly destabilized through gender and homoerotic torture in front of females, and further these female soldiers were *framed* as objects complying with male organized torture scenarios. In fact, Graner even "ordered" Lynndie England into photographs of abuse that she felt uncomfortable posing in, as confirmed in her sworn statements. Nonetheless, she expressively complied, was described as having a compliant personality by several expert witnesses, and was also characterized by her fellow soldiers as naive and as having blind trust and faith in Graner.

When asked why he did not report the abuse he witnessed, Sivits replied, "I was trying to be friends with everyone and I did not want to get anyone in trouble" (Mestrovic 2007). What is fascinating about this response is that it exemplifies Parsons' expressive role concern with group cohesion and amalgamation, and shows an overall emotional interest with group functioning and stability, a characteristic that Parsons associates with the female role status. This gender role permutation is outside of the limits and scope of Parsons' current theories of instrumental and expressive, and thus requires a new and imaginative understanding of Parsons.

Specialist Matthew Wisdom, a Military Police officer at Abu Ghraib who worked the day shift in general population Tiers 2-4, testified that he went to Tier 1A and witnessed the pile of men on the floor on November 7 and stated "I was concerned about the pile" (June 24, 2004, SHA32). Wisdom described the situation that evening as abusive, where MPs were running prisoners into the walls with sandbags on their heads, and that these sandbags were supposedly for "security." Wisdom told the court at the England trial that Davis was stomping on toes of prisoners and that Graner was hitting prisoners in the face, but the detainees were not fighting back in any way. Wisdom further stated, "I recall Sergeant Frederick hitting one [prisoner] in the side of the chest and after he did that he looked up at me and said you have to *get some of this*, referring to hitting one of the prisoners, sir" (May 13, 2005, SHCM). In an instrumental move to report the abuse up the chain of command and in terms of formal Army regulations, Wisdom reported the first and only instance of abuse he witnessed to his superior. It can be assumed that Wisdom's *perception* was that this *instrumental report of abuse* would have an end result of terminating abuse. Says Wisdom, "I went to SGT Jones after this and I told him everything I saw. I told him because I thought it was criminal in nature. I wanted to be removed from the prison. I had a problem with everything I saw. SGT Jones said he passed the information up the chain. SGT Jones told me it was taken care of and I was moved from the prison the next day. SGT Jones told me it was taken care of so I believed him" (June 24, 2004, SHA32). Wisdom further added this statement at Harman's courts-martial, which shows expressive emotions he felt in reaction to the pyramid events with these following statements, "I just told him [Sergeant Jones] everything that I saw and told him that I was upset about it and he told me that he'd handle the situation, sir" (May 13, 2005, SHCM). Further, when asked why he reported the abuse, Wisdom stated, "I personally did not think it was right, what was going on, so I thought it was in my best interest to just report it as soon as possible" (May 13, 2005, SHCM).

Wisdom returned to Tier 1A, where Jones told him to go back to work, just as the prisoners were being forced to masturbate and to simulate fellatio. Wisdom observed these events in the hallway and stated under oath, "When I went back down [to the hard site] I saw a naked man masturbating into another man's mouth. He had his mouth open and he was on his knees. The other guards there were Graner, Davis, Fredrick, Ambuhl, Harman and England. I remember Graner posing for a photograph like he was going to hit a detainee with a sandbag on his head and then he did hit him. I saw SGT Davis walking around stomping on the toes of the detainees. I saw SSG Frederick hit a detainee in the chest. The detainees were crying out in pain ... I saw SFC Snider looking down on the pile so he did see what was going on. He was the senior NCO present at the time. He was in the position to stop it and take corrective action" (June 24, 2004, SHA32). Further, Wisdom confirmed that Sergeant Frederick turned and said, "look at what these animals do when we leave them alone for two seconds (May 13, 2005, SHCM). (As a side, Frederick stated at the England trial that he was told by MI to allow the masturbation.)

Both the prosecution and defense asked Wisdom several times about what he did when he witnessed the events of this evening, and dutifully Wisdom answered, "I immediately went back out to Tower 5, to tell my team leader what had happened ... I didn't know what to do. I was flustered, kind of sick to my stomach, kind of feeling—I didn't—I couldn't make sense of what was going on and I rushed out there to tell him what happened" (May 13, 2005, SHCM). Again, in Parsonian terms Wisdom is evidencing expressive-emotive reactions to the abuse. Frank Spinner, the civilian defense counsel for the Harman trial, confirmed that not only had Wisdom reported the abuse, but also that he thought it was handled up the chain of command:

> Q (Spinner): So you're saying that with respect to Sergeant Jones you reported all of the things that you observed and you thought were wrong that night?
>
> A: That's correct, sir.
>
> Q: And to your knowledge was any corrective action taken about that?
>
> A: *He reported back to me that the situation was handled.*

(May 13, 2005, SHCM)

Wisdom's team leader, Sergeant Robert Jones, took the stand next. Jones was a police officer in the civilian world and an MP in the U.S. Army. Jones verified that Wisdom had reported the abuse, and stated, "He [Wisdom] told me he witnessed a prisoner get his toes stepped on and some getting punched. He came back and reported to me that a detainee was masturbating into the mouth of another detainee.

He came to me twice in one hour" (June 24, 2004, SHA32). However, Jones sent Wisdom back to Tier 1 because he viewed Wisdom as inexperienced and perhaps in need of mentoring in his position as an MP—an expressive characterization of Wisdom. Said Jones, "Specialist Wisdom came to me ... he was upset. I told him to go back to work. I figured at his young age and level of inexperience he had saw a justified use of force so I sent him back to work" (May 13, 2005, SHCM). Further questioning about the incidents that evening reveled that Wisdom's instrumental whistleblowing did have some effect and served a function, as Jones was aimed at both ending abuse and "rescuing" Wisdom from the abusive situation where torture was taking place—both instrumental and expressive characteristics in Parsonian language. Says Jones, "The first report I [received] did not have much urgency because I am a police officer and know people get hit. When he [Wisdom] came back the second time about the masturbation ... I went and got in SSG Frederick's face and had a heated conversation. It was an uncomfortable position to have to get in a higher ranking soldier's face ... but I just wanted Wisdom out of there. I was not satisfied with that conversation so I went to SSG Elliot to find out what was going on. I did not hear anything about the abuse after that" (June 24, 2004, SHA32). Expanding on Frederick's response, Jones stated "Staff Sergeant Ivan Frederick ... I asked him over and over again whether it was true ... He didn't answer me, sir" (May 13, 2005, SHCM).

The trial counsel further asked how Jones tried to resolve this issue and if he wished he had handled the situation differently. Jones replied he wanted to have Wisdom work directly under him, and that "Specialist Wisdom told me—he was very excited, very angry, he told me he would not work with those guys anymore, specifically the people that were down at the prison at the time of the alleged abuses sir ... yes, sir [I wish I had handled the situation differently]) (May 13, 2005, SHCM). Indeed, at the England courts-martial, Jones claimed that Graner had a strong personality and controlled and influenced others, and preyed on those who were weak. Jones also expressed that he thought that Tier 1A and 1B was run poorly since it did not have enough military support.

Several interesting Parsonian themes are evidenced in these exchanges with Wisdom and Jones regarding reporting abuse. First, that Wisdom reported the abuse because he thought it was his "duty" is in line with an interpretation of instrumental reporting of abuse according to the rules of the military itself, and especially since it can be assumed Wisdom thought something might be done about this abuse. Second, that Wisdom had emotional reactions to this abuse can be read as expressive in Parsonian language. Third, that Jones believed Wisdom's reaction to the abuse was in terms of his "inexperience" as a Military Police Officer, and that what Wisdom really needed was a mentoring relationship of sorts, a new job position at Abu Ghraib, and to have Jones as his superior and "protector" speaks to how Jones viewed Wisdom—as expressively vulnerable and weak. This is further evidenced with Jones' actions of screaming at Frederick (an expressive emotive trait) instead of reporting the abuse up the chain of command (instrumental); however, it can be argued that this was a volatile situation of torture and so this kind of dual approach was warranted, where yelling is construed as an attempt at establishing instrumental power. After all, Jones did instrumentally report the abuse to SSG Elliott, and also instrumentally followed up on this conversation. Jones' actions can thus be understood as both expressive and instrumental in terms of how he handled the situation of November 7, and therefore Jones can be understood as acting expressively protective of a subordinate, while also instrumentally responding to and reporting abuse, and especially since he did view this part of the prison as not functioning efficiently. Parsons' theorizing does not allow for this kind of dual interpretation, and so a stretching and remolding of his theory is necessary here. What is so ironic is that Wisdom's instrumental reporting of abuse comes to be interpreted as expressive weakness and lack of ability, thereby initially negating Wisdom's entire whistleblowing function. Nonetheless, even Jones' whistleblowing did not serve its purpose—that of ending abuse at Abu Ghraib. In these ways, both soldiers at Abu Ghraib exemplified a Parsonian interpretation of *instrumental perceived reporting of abuse*, yet with a failed goal outcome.

Private Ivan Frederick, a prison guard for eight years in civilian life and also an MP at Abu Ghraib, also testified about the events of November 7, 2003. When asked why he did not report the events that he agreed he knew to be wrong he stated in court, "I was just afraid of repercussions and consequences" (May 13, 2005, SHCM). We cannot be sure who he feared ramifications from, his fellow soldiers or the military; however, in Parsonian terms this fear is described as expressive in nature. Frank Spinner, the civilian defense counsel continued to question Frederick and asked, "Did you raise questions through the chain of command ... whether or not these things were authorized (re: sleep deprivation, standing on boxes, making people do PT and trying to keep them awake)?" Frederick answered, "Yes sir. I was told that's how they do it and that's for interrogation purposes and just to go ahead and go with it" (May 13, 2005, SHCM). Spinner continued, "What kinds of practices did you raise questions about?" Says Frederick, "[In general] The prolonged nudity, the conditions of the cells, putting them in cells with no ventilation, no toilet, no window, just complete darkness, the wearing of female panties, things of that nature" (May 13, 2005, SHCM). In addition, Frederick stated under oath that his chain of command was confusing, as he was not sure who he worked for since he took orders from three different places, and was confused about who had final say regarding orders, the MI community or the regular chain of command? In this way, even if abuse was reported, it is unsure to whom these reports might have been made, and furthermore, it is unclear what counts as either abuse or a direct order. Frederick also said that he had given Harman permission to phone her partner that evening, during the abuse, such that she was not even present for the forced and homoerotic torture. In Parsonian language, and much like Wisdom is portrayed above, Frederick comes across as expressive in his fear regarding reporting the abuse he witnessed, although perhaps for different reasons. (Parsons does not seem to allow for rational, instrumental fear, such as the fear of courts-martial.) It is unclear why Frederick had fear since he did not elaborate on that in court, but fear in itself is expressive according to Parsons. (Frederick was asked "Did you draw a line in the sand? Could you control Graner?" He answered, "No." So perhaps he *was* fearful of his fellow soldiers after all.) Nonetheless, given the confusing chain of command and what seems to be a lack of clear standard operating procedures at the prison according to Frederick, it is obvious that both a rational and orderly instrumental means for prisoner care and a clear line of authority were not in place at Abu Ghraib. Although Frederick did mention fear, he also mentions disorganization and how he was told to "go ahead" with the interrogations that were taking place—all expressive actions. It thus seems that one interpretation that Frederick did not report abuse was for expressive reasons, and this is another example of *expressive non-reporting*. However, another reason could be the stated reason Frederick gave at Lynndie England's trial, which was that reporting abuse up the chain of command had no results, which made him frustrated, stressed, and angry because he had no advice or leadership from above. Frederick disclosed these expressive feelings in response to a panel member's question about why it was that he punched a prisoner in the chest.

Instrumental Females, Expressive Males, and Everything In-between

There are many stories about Abu Ghraib that have not been told because they were not depicted in the photographs of abuse that were shown to the world. Some of these stories have to do with soldiers remedying instances of abuse such as with the testimony of Megan Ambuhl, a female MP with the 372nd at Abu Ghraib, who also worked the night shift at Tier 1A and 1B.

Ambuhl stated in her testimony that in November 2003, she and Specialist Sabrina Harman reported to Sergeant Joyner that a detainee had been handcuffed for a long period of time. Both Harman and Ambuhl were concerned with the comfort of this detainee. When describing the incident to the assistant trial counsel, says Ambuhl, "Um, we—I was working on the tier with, um, Specialist Hubbard and he had—I believe he had three detainees that were on sleep management and he just decided to handcuff them above their head up to the cell door (hands above head crossed) rather than change the position of them during a time period and Specialist Harman came in to the tier and we looked at their hands and they were discolored and so we un-cuffed them and then we went and told … Sergeant Joyner at the end of the shift what happened" (May 16, 2005, SHCM). The assistant trial counsel then asked Ambuhl if she and Harman believed that they had seen inappropriate treatment of a detainee, and that by removing the handcuffs, if they were stopping maltreatment. Ambuhl answered, "yes, sir" (May 16, 2005, SHCM).

What is interesting about this exchange in Parsonian terms is that it has both expressive and instrumental qualities. Ambuhl and Harman's concern for the detainee's comfort is expressive in that it is based on empathy and a shared sense of compassion, while the understanding that they were stopping maltreatment from happening was seen as part of their job as MPs. For Parsons, however, it

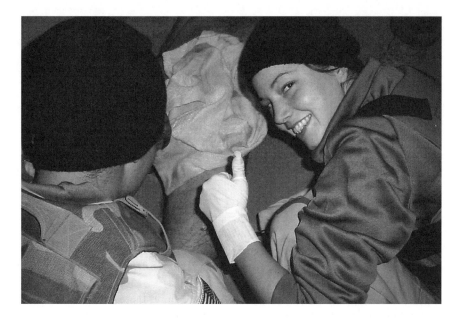

Figure 3.1   Harman giving stitches and providing instrumental care

Source: Photograph provided courtesy of the author.

is the male's role to be instrumental within the social system, and so for two female soldiers to function in this way as self-correcting mechanisms for ending abuse, and in lieu of the male soldier (Specialist Hubbard) who had fastened the prisoner to the cell door as part of a sleep management regimen, is outside the limits of Parsons' role theory. Additionally, Ambuhl and Harman did report the abuse they witnessed on the part of MI to a higher-up, namely Sergeant Joyner, which is *instrumental perceived reporting* (they thought Joyner would act on it), however, yet again this goals/ends report was made by two females, which Parsons cannot account for in terms of his gendered-role description of "instrumental." *Nonetheless, the maltreatment did cease this evening, for these detainees, and at the hands of two female soldiers—two of the Fallgirls.*

Another testimony of a soldier remedying abuse at Abu Ghraib came from Staff Sergeant Joseph Darby, also an MP with the 372nd. The civilian defense counsel, Frank Spinner, asked Darby if he turned over the photographs anonymously because he feared retribution and retaliation from some of the people involved. Darby answered in open court, "Yes sir … and some people in the unit, yes sir" (May 13, 2005, SHCM). Revealed Darby about turning the photos of abuse over to CID on January 12, 2003, "It was a hard decision, because I had served with these people for so long, some of them were my friends, and we had been in Iraq, and there was camaraderie there, and I had a really hard decision to turn them in" (May 13, 2005, SHCM).

Turning the photographs over was an instrumental action on Darby's part as it ended the torture and abuse at Abu Ghraib and can be seen as an example of the *instrumental actual reporting of abuse*. Nonetheless, Darby's fear of other soldiers, as well as the fear expressed by other male soldiers discussed in this chapter, is not accounted for with Parsons' understanding of the male's role within the social system, and is instead an expressive trait. Parsons' role theory of instrumental and expressive does not capture the kinds of experiences that took place for some of the soldiers at Abu Ghraib, which themselves allow for new interpretations of his gender roles. Further, what Abu Ghraib shows is that men can be expressive, women can be instrumental, and both of these roles can serve a multitude of functions simultaneously, and even within dysfunctional social systems.

Conclusion

I have argued that the Parsonian distinction (1954) between instrumental and expressive roles served a multitude of functions within the dysfunctional social climate at Abu Ghraib when describing how the abuse was reported by some of the soldiers there. (Indeed, some of these soldiers were the "rotten apples.") These Parsonian roles illustrated the hyper-masculine atmosphere at Abu Ghraib, where mostly male soldiers would act in stereotypical ways while abusing detainees, and would characterize those who did not go along with abuse as feminine "pussies." Additionally, when focusing on the reporting of abuse, Parsonian language is helpful in comprehending not only the motivation for the reports themselves, but also why reports were not made to those higher-up the chain of command. Likewise, the theoretical discussion in this chapter brings to light how soldiers experienced fear at Abu Ghraib, how soldiers protected each other, how female soldiers corrected maltreatment at Abu Ghraib (even ones who were court-martialed), and how power differentials flowed throughout the prison.

I always found it interesting that the only female attorney in the courtroom at the Harman trial, Captain Takemura—who outwardly wore the persona of the expressive female—was the one who elicited confessions of fear out of male soldiers during their testimony. According to the masculine military "code," the expression of fear in itself is stereotypically unmasculine; yet, she did this while wearing the masculine uniform of the military. (None of the soldiers made these confessions to any of the male attorneys or the judge.) It is for reasons such as the above example that I argue Parsonian stereotypes of gendered behavior are sometimes helpful in describing social and cultural patterns within the U.S. military, but that the events at Abu Ghraib and the surrounding courts-martials do not fit his model, because Parsons assumes that all social systems are self-correcting and functional, and especially with regard to the reporting of abuse at the prison. Thus, it is important to stretch and find creative applications to Parsons' theorizing in order to make Parsons applicable to these cultural phenomena—where dysfunctions exists.

Social theory needs to move forward and recognize that some social systems are dysfunctional and fail to self-correct, as evidenced at Abu Ghraib. We thus arrive at a new framework for understanding structural-functionalist functions in social settings, namely: Expressive and instrumental dimensions still function in dysfunctional social settings, albeit, in the dysfunctional ways described above. The results at Abu Ghraib were various permutations of instrumental-expressive torture, reporting, gender roles, and other functions, which did not result in correction. The most profound irony of the Abu Ghraib saga is that the torture and abuse continued even after the publicized courts-martial, and they continued not only at Abu Ghraib but also at Guantanamo, black-hole rendition sites, and other detention facilities related to the War on Terror.

Evidence: Sabrina Harman's Letter to Kelly Bryant, Sabrina Harman Courts-Martial

Note: In the court-martial, the government's position is that the letter applies to Harman's state of mind and emotions only, and not as evidence of Sabrina Harman as a whistle-blower.

October 20, 2003
10:40 p.m.
Kelly,

Okay I don't like that anymore. At first it was funny but these people are going too far. I ended your letter last night because it was time to wake the MI prisoners and "mess with them" but it went too far even I can't handle whats going on. I cant get it out of my head. I walk down the stairs after blowing the whistle and beating on the cells with an asp to find "the taxicab driver" handcuffed backwards to his window naked with his underwear over his head and face. He looked like Jesus Christ. At first I had to laugh so I went on and grabbed the camera and took a picture. One of the guys took my asp and started "poking" at his dick. Again I thought, okay that's funny then it hit me, that's a form of molestation. You can't do that. I took more pictures now to "record" what is going on. They started talking to this man and at first he was talking "I'm just a taxicab driver, I did nothing." He claims he'd never try to hurt US soldiers that he picked up the wrong people. Then he stopped talking. They turned the lights out and slammed the door and left him there while they went down to cell #4. This man had been so fucked that when they grabbed his foot through the cell bars he began screaming and crying. After praying to Allah he moans a constant short Ah, Ah, every few seconds for the rest of the night. I don't know what they did to this guy. The first one remained handcuffed for maybe 1 ½ -2 hours until he started yelling for Allah. So they went back in and handcuffed him to the top bunk on either side of the bed while he stood on the side. He was there for a little over an hour when he started yelling again for Allah. Not many people know this shit goes on. The only reason I want to be there is to get the pictures to prove that the US is not what they think. But I don't know if I can take it mentally. What if that was me in their shoes. These people will be our future terrorist. Kelly, it's awful and you know how fucked I am in the head— Both sides of me think its wrong. I thought I could handle anything. I was wrong.

Sabrina (May 16, 2005, SHCM)

Chapter 4

The Significance of Identity Simulacra and Gender Hyperreality: American Military and the Case of Abu Ghraib

> The simulacrum is never what hides the truth—it is truth that hides the fact that there is none. The simulacrum is true.
>
> Ecclesiastes

What does it mean to be *real*? If something is said to be *real*, then it is important, deemed to be true, seen as genuine and justifiable, and in some cases given higher levels of scientific and philosophical respect. It is believed legitimate. Many times an understanding of identity is valued on the large scale within society only if *realness* is in terms of some valued and existing citationality, such that what is aimed at being "quoted" for identity is something that larger culture has identified and named categorically. Successful cultural identity claims require the adherence to cultural and symbolic instantiation, where the claiming of invisible or culturally incomprehensible categories for existence result in the social exclusion of the identity claim itself —quite literally the non-formation of the socially valued subject (Caldwell 2009).

Both Jean Baudrillard and Judith Butler have theories that address the issue of gender "realness," and both of these perspectives outline gender as something that are on the one hand categorically simulacra in construction, but on the other hand real in their consequences—that is there are prices to pay for *doing gender* in a certain way.[1] This is an especially important perspective with regard to the experiences surrounding Abu Ghraib, as usually postmodern conjecture ends up in a theory of implosion and chaos. At Abu Ghraib, however, the imploded and deconstructed meanings surrounding gender are functional in terms of describing gendered understandings of the events at the prison, and the U.S. military in general, and specifically for understanding the consequences of gender.[2] I use the

---

1 In fact, sometimes, lives are complicated, choices are made, suffering exists, and the outcome of one's existence (what they gain, lose, reward, and authenticity) depend on how they decide to *do* their gender.

2 Understanding how power works when aligned with gender allows individuals to be critical of existing structures, and as such renders it possible to question and even destabilize existing gender schema, as the "code" for gender value can be, in this way, deconstructed and altered. Unlike some other feminists, I do not hold the opinion that deconstruction results in the meaningless and powerless platform for impossible feminism.

terms *simulacra gender code, power simulacra,* and *rule by simulacra of reality* to describe these gender processes and consequences. Examples I use here to illustrate gender and its postmodern consequences are as follows: the metrosexual soldier, that all soldiers (including Harman) wear the drag of military uniforms, the idea that "drag-techniques" were used to torture, and that gender simulacra and seduction played a role in the courtroom, among other examples.

Identity and Signification as Hyperreal *"Power-Simulacra"*: Baudrillard's Maps and the "Metrosexual Soldier"

> If once we were able to view the Borges fable in which the cartographers of the Empire draw a map so detailed that it ends up covering the territory exactly (the decline of the Empire witnesses the fraying of this map, little by little, and its fall into ruins, though some shreds are still discernible in the deserts—the metaphysical beauty of this ruined abstraction testifying to a pride equal to the Empire and rotting like a carcass, returning to the substance of the soil, a bit as the double ends by being confused with the real through aging)—as the most beautiful allegory of simulation, this fable has now come full circle for us, and possesses nothing but the discrete charm of second-order simulacra. (Jean Baudrillard, *Simulacra and Simulations*)

Jean Baudrillard, sometimes called the high priest of postmodernism, develops a theory of postmodern culture, which postulates that culture itself is now dominated by simulations. This means that objects and discourses have no firm origin, no referents, and no ground or foundation upon which to locate meaning.[3]

In Baudrillard's above citation, he concerns himself with abstractions of a map and the delineation of boundaries. He leads us to a contemplation of how lines of demarcation, even in the metaphorical and theoretical sense, are established. He suggests that these lines of demarcation are in the service of a specific conception of the "real," and therefore instigates thought about how this "real" is constructed or located. Is the map of written boundaries "real?" Is the territory itself bounded in some way that allows for the production of a map? *Simulation* is the term that Baudrillard uses to induce the project of locating the "real." However, for Baudrillard, simulation is the notion that what is referred to as "real" is without origin or reality. This means that what once might have referred to some "referential being or substance" now holds no identity apart from the actual simulation itself (Baudrillard 1983a: 169). The distinctions between object and

---

Instead, I view the process of deconstruction like an exploration, where a new venue for the insertion of perspective and voice can be found, and where the discovery of how power functions is made.

3   Specifically, according to Baudrillard, the Saussurean process of signification (signifier + signified = a meaningful sign) has failed to produce meaning.

representation, "thing and idea," according to Baudrillard, are no longer valid relationships (Baudrillard 1983a).

Consequently, for Baudrillard, locating the "real" becomes a perpetual game of referential referents, both pointing toward and away from "truth," as "truth" itself is shown to be only a phantasm or spectacle. Says Baudrillard, "Today's abstraction is no longer that of the map, the double, the mirror, or the concept. Simulation is no longer that of a territory, a referential being, or a substance. It is the generation by models of a real without origin or reality: a *hyperreal*" (Baudrillard [1981]1994). Thus, Baudrillard uses the term "hyperreal" to denote the so-called "reality" that a simulation refers, a world of self-referential signs (Baudrillard 1983a). (A simulacrum is when the distinction between representation and reality—between the signs and what they refer to—break down.) In a hyperreality, "reality" itself has collapsed, and only image, illustration, or simulation is left. Additionally, in a hyperreality, the model of "reality" is more real than the reality it supposedly represents (Rosenau 1992). In a postmodern culture, it is this hyperreality that comes to function as the "real," or a simulacrum of reality itself. Thus, for Baudrillard, "It is no longer a question of imitation, nor of reduplication, nor even of parody. It is rather a question of substituting signs of the real for the real itself" (Baudrillard 1983a: 170).

Again, considering Baudrillard's map, it is neither the territory nor the map that demarcates boundaries. Instead, it is the "real," and specifically a second-order simulacrum of the "real," that allow us to make sense of both the map's territory and the map itself. Even though the map has eroded and the territories can no longer be depicted with any exactness to that of the map, a "real" still exists for Baudrillard. Indeed, what is being made sense of is neither the map nor the land boundaries of territory. Instead, what Baudrillard seems to suggest is that notions of "real" are constructed in such a way that these notions themselves dictate "realness." In this way, the map is "real" in terms of the theory of "realness" itself.

Considering identity in a postmodern culture, it follows that realness is about signification and not about any ontologically grounded claim, but a grasping of hyperreal tags of identity such as gender. This grabbing of signs, where the signs serve as the demarcation of the self, is philosophically a radically different way to understand identity, as this conception has nothing at all to do with the individual self, creating identity from within, body versus soul or mind, etc. Instead, simulations of identity are something to be consumed and produced. This is the case with the hyperreal simulacra tags of gender identity, which exist because we as a culture have socially constructed these as correct ways for understanding and categorizing our experiences of gender—they function as Baudrillard's map, providing a theory of the "real." Nonetheless, these tags for gender identity have no reality behind their signs, and are thus hyperreal in that they function as canopies for thought—they are theoretical simulations—ultimately constructed categories themselves. Thus gender categories for Baudrillard are only phantasmic creations that do not point to any kind of natural identifications of the body, neither in terms of sex, sexuality, or any other categorical claim of coherence, and are free-floating symbols that individuals in a postmodern culture latch onto as a means for identity construction.[4] Again, these significations are simulacrum because there is no firm referent or origin to which they attach themselves with regard to meaning, and thus only have a use-value of fleeting substantiation. Indeed, gender simulations are representations of identity that are illusory, as for Baudrillard, once something is signified, this is the extent of its "realness"—its postmodern signification.

Considering both Baudrillard's map and gender, what is "real" is the construction of "reality." Both the map and gender are thus self-referentially validated in terms of some constructed theory of "realness." What is "real" in this construction is the *construction of the "real."* Within these constructions of the "real," tags of identity are fleeting, and postmodern culture only allows individuals the ability to grasp gender identity-signs. Nonetheless, these tags of identity are just that—culturally identifying claims to gender, albeit in a fleeting manner. However, the power behind these gender tags is that they function as *simulacra gender code*. Thus, the consequence for signification is that the signification becomes the "reality" through its construction, albeit a fleeting one at that. In a sense, like Baudrillard's map, simulacra gender code is thus the postmodern theory of gender "realness"—or *"power simulacra"* in that they are based on a construction of gender identity, informed by a cultural "code" for conception, and backed by this cultural conception for their very image-reality.

For some postmodernists, gender meanings have actually imploded, such that there are no stable references for gender meaning, and only free floating and interpretable fictions of gender. This means that the constructed "reality" of postmodern culture contains too many signs and significations, and where meaning itself becomes hyperreal. Reflect on the postmodern gender identity of metrosexual as an example.[5] This category for identity is something that was socially constructed to describe a sexed male who is heterosexual, but who participates in copious and conspicuous ritualistic grooming that is stereotypically (although problematically) associated with both femininity and homosexuality, such that ritualized grooming is equated with hyper-femininity and "cultural gayness." (Metrosexual is sometimes used as an insult, and is sometimes a commodified identity construct.) Now juxtapose the metrosexual image with that of the decorated war hero soldier, who is polished in presentation, shoes shined, representing the many achieved medals and ribbons, hair molded in such a certain way as to conform to a "code," and who ritually and vigorously performs the

---

4   Nonetheless, in *Seduction*, Baudrillard [1979]1990 is complicated on this point as the "feminine" is very real for him.

5   Some may argue that this example shows the ultimate implosion of gender categories specifically, what with all of the different signifiers of both gender and sexuality pointing this way and that, towards stereotypes of both gender and sexuality for the cognition of the term "metrosexual." However, this is exactly the kind of theoretical gender concept that I find interesting in deconstructing, and also functional with regard to explaining military phenomena.

identity "soldier" through production and consumption of an idealized image-sign. In this way, the military identity, like the metrosexual, can be understood as the "conforming to" of a certain characterization associated with the significations of free floating image-signs. Hence, the "metrosexual soldier" is a simulacra identity, one that is achieved through the imitation of the socially constructed code of gender itself, and specifically the gender hyperreality of pomp and circumstance surrounding the grooming rituals and uniform codes associated with the military. Indeed, the military has a rigorous standard for grooming and uniform to which all members must adhere. Again, in this way, "real" becomes a constructed simulation of reality, and is thus, according to Baudrillard, itself hyperreal given the variety of ways that the sign can be tagged. Says Baudrillard, "It is the real, and not the map, whose vestiges persist here and there in the deserts that are no longer those of the Empire, but ours" (Baudrillard [1981]1994: 1). I argue it is the simulacra gender code, or the theory (of the map) that is "real" here. That said, it is not as if the meanings of gender associated with the discussion of metrosexual have imploded and are thus meaningless; instead, I argue that there exist rich interpretable texts and narratives of gender significance, and in the true fashion of radical feminism, see this as a possible door to new thought projects about gender. Indeed, what has changed is the way that knowledge and interpretation present themselves.

Flash back to Abu Ghraib prison. Like a map, one might think that when referring to "Abu Ghraib" a reference to something that was stable in signification and demarcation was being made. However, the reality of Abu Ghraib prison is that it was not well defended from daily mortar attacks, where on a frequent basis the prison itself was bombed, thereby leading to the *actual destruction* of territorial boundaries. Additionally, a prison might be characterized as having a closed and bounded region, where the separation of prisoners and American military troops was distinct. However, the prison was itself porous, meaning that it was permeable to outsiders entering the prison grounds. One example of this that American soldiers spoke of was specifically unauthorized Iraqis who were selling cameras on the compound itself. Additionally, American military personnel actually lived in jail cells next to prisoners. In this way, like Baudrillard's map, the boundaries of the prison and its rigid instantiation were themselves simulacra, yet functioned in a rhetorical way so as to allow for reference. "Realness" was thus a product of signification, as boundaries did not exist.

Heterosexuality and the "Rule by Simulacra of Reality"

Contemporary feminist, gender theorist, and rhetorician, Judith Butler, has a theory of identity categories that can be applied to further explain Baudrillard's notion of simulacra. This coupling of Baudrillard and Butler is unique and is not something that either postmodernists or critical theorists readily expand upon. Butler's critique of identity categories, however, is important to consider when discussing notions of "realness" in that she also shows how categorical "realness" and value are relationally constructed with regard to gender categories, and in terms of sex and sexuality categories. Like most feminists and social scientists, Butler's project speaks to the separation of the categories of sex, gender, and sexuality, such that these categories are understood as distinct, and unlike stereotypical understandings of gender, where male=masculine and female=feminine, and both associations are conceptually heteronormative (or associated with heterosexuality).

Butler's discussion of relationally understood categories demonstrates two important things: the relational power that each binary has on the other, and the limiting options for identity construction given the conceived of categories for identity itself. Butler's argument is that theoretical binary pair relations (such as male/female and masculine/feminine) are both unstable and incoherent foundations upon which to construct theoretical paradigms, yet nonetheless are used in wider normative and dominant culture for gender value and instantiation. Butler considers the relationship between binary pairs, and uses the theoretical tactic of destabilizing the dominant binary in order to challenge its dominant status. This, in turn, questions not only the elevated status of the dominant binary, but also questions the entire binary relationship's categorical claim of coherence. Binary relations result in problematic understandings of gender for Butler, and as it turns out, Butler shows that it is the subordinate binary that actually challenges the status of the binary relationship. Additionally, this project is important with regard to gender categories in that it destabilizes both the association of male/ masculine and female/feminine in terms of gender and sex categories, showing its ultimate socially constructed connectedness.

Consider as an example gender constructions in the American military. One way that gender has been constructed within the U.S. military is through the masculinist system of the military itself, where masculinity functions as the dominant *power-simulacra* with regard to gender hierarchy. (Remember, for Baudrillard this "*power-simulacra*" is a fleeting attempt at signification, but for Butler this is a juridical law for gender value.) In this way, the masculinist economy functions as the "real" with regard to judging and policing gender expressions, as this "realness" allows for understanding gender value within the military context. This power simulacra, for Butler, functions as, "The cultural matrix through which gender identity has become intelligible" (Butler [1990]1999: 17). Hence, one way that the dominant simulacrum of gender has been conceptualized within the military is as masculine, and this is its hyperreality, as this description of masculinity as a standard culminates in an understanding of a "*power-simulacra*" that is constructed within this cultural context.

This is a text of gender that is socially constructed with regard to value, among other things, and therefore has no reality apart from the system within which it is pieced together. Hence, this is a discourse of gender that is simulacra at its foundations, where power can be understood as compliance with these simulacra formations. For Butler, and unlike Baudrillard, actual power is associated with this account of gender, as bodies are policed and given value in terms of legitimation with regard to the rules of this system itself.

Additionally, Butler is especially concerned with heterosexist frameworks for understanding sex and gender, such that male/masculine and female/feminine are understood in heterosexist opposition, and she calls these "exclusionary gender norms." Says Butler about gender, "Gender is the repeated stylization of the body, a set of repeated acts within a highly rigid regulatory frame that congeal over time to produce the appearance of substance, or a natural sort of being" (Butler 1990[1999]: 33). Hence, for Butler gender is something that is discursively and performatively constituted by "the very expressions that are said to be its results" (Butler 1990[1999]: 25).[6]

Consider Sabrina Harman and her military courts-martial in terms of the military's masculinist simulacra identity and also Butler's heterosexist "exclusionary gender norms." It came out in the Harman courts-martial that Harman is a lesbian soldier. The social construction of gender has historically equated both femininity and masculinity with heterosexuality in that femininity and masculinity are seen as opposite binaries, thereby mimicking assumed heterosexual lived-relations. The social-construction of the military follows this gender characterization in that it is conceptually a heterosexist institution, where homosexual individuals are not welcome per membership *as* homosexual individuals. Instead, homosexual military personnel are required in accordance with military's "exclusionary sexuality norms" to render their identities secret. This is the consequence of the "Don't Ask, Don't Tell" policy that has been implemented by law into the armed forces, thereby constructing a standard of the "real" for identity. [7]

Nonetheless, it remains that there are indeed homosexuals within the military, yet they are closeted in their identities. This is a perfect example of Baudrillard's notion of the "code" as instructing "reality" in that "reality" is not represented, and only formed through the simulation of heterosexuality, thereby culminating in the simulacra of reality in terms of the *"power-simulacra"* of heterosexuality. Harman's identity thus functions as a simulacrum identity of heterosexuality in that she is understood in terms of a military *"power-simulacra"* of heterosexuality; yet, she is also subversive of this identity given her actual status as lesbian. Additionally, this is an example of a subversive repetition of forced military heteronormativity, which subverts the very system that attempts to control the soldier's body through compulsory heterosexuality. This is exactly the kind of subversive practice that Butler is concerned with, which shows the "status" of

---

6   This term 'performatively' is to imply a culturally sustained temporal duration of gender performance.

7   As of this writing, DADT has been overturned, yet many stories exist in the news that show prejudicial attitudes against homosexual soldiers. I argue that simply because laws are overturned does not mean that long standing practices of discrimination and attitudes of prejudice will disappear within the military. Hence, the military can still be characterized as heterosexist unproblematically. Additionally, during the trials discussed within this book, DADT was for sure still in place.

heterosexuality as a discursive characteristic of militarized gender. Nonetheless, even though these signs of gender can be destabilized, homosexuality is still a crime in the U.S. Army once it is disclosed, and thus has a consequence. At Harman's courts-martial, soldiers stated privately that they thought that the Army was killing two birds with one stone at this courts-martial, Harman was being punished for the following: being a lesbian in a heterosexist military, a female within a masculinist military, and as a scapegoat for detainee abuse given her various minority statuses.

Butler's project also shows the socially constructed notion of gender itself to be a hyperreality in the sense that Baudrillard employs, as gender is shown to be a system of "realness" that is constructed and reified, and in turn functions as that which is itself "real." Remember Baudrillard's map, where what is deemed "real" is in terms of the theory of "realness" itself. For Butler, gender categories are thus "real" in that they are self-referentially validated in terms of this theory of gender "realness"—or what can be understood as Baudrillard's "code."

Butler's critique of heterosexualized identity categories thus rests on the notion that the polarities of what is included in a category and what is not included are inherently reactive, both reflecting and reflected, in the claiming of an identity category. When individuals conform and contort their identities to the hyperreal categories of gender, or when gender identities are conceived of in terms of these categories, what has taken place is the *rule by simulacra of reality*. Says Butler commenting on normative sexuality identities, "gay is to straight not as copy is to original, but, rather, as copy is to copy" (Butler [1990]1999: 41). This statement echoes Baudrillard's claim about simulacra as being "a copy of a copy, for which there is no original" (Baudrillard [1981]1994: 169). Interestingly, since gender categories are socially constructed and understood in terms of a context, there is no original understanding of gender, and only a hyperreal doctrine used to control actual bodies. Perhaps the claim should be that *gender is a simulacrum—a copy of a copy for which there is no original.*

It is important to remember that Butler thinks that the identity category that instructs heteronormativity is itself rallied against *at the site* of these identity productions and categorical power struggles through the use of parody and mimicry, "through repetition of the law [of heterosexuality] into hyperbole" (Butler 1993: 122). This is very Foucauldian with regard to understanding power, and Baudrillard argued against Foucault's theoretical conceptions of how power operated. Nonetheless, for Butler, through contesting the dominant category (the theoretical act itself) the ideal of heterosexuality is subverted, thereby culminating in the questioning of the theoretical primacy of the category heterosexual (Butler 1993: 123). Think here of Harman's lesbian identity as a member of the heterosexist army. The message about the "rule" or "code" of military heterosexuality is that it is only a simulacra code, as plenty of closeted soldiers exist within the bounds of the American military system, and thus subversion of the "law" has taken place. The heterosexual doctrine of the military is thus shown to be a *rule by simulacra of reality* in that it does not represent any reality in its conception. Again, there are after all plenty of gay and lesbian soldiers who would attest to this if sanctions would not be taken against them, and hence this is the consequence of the simulacra code. Interestingly, many former military members speak out against the "Don't Ask, Don't Tell" policy once they exit the military itself, and are currently in support of overturning DADT. For the military, then, a hyperreality exists with regard to the simulacra of heterosexuality that is required by the "code."

Seduction and Drag

Interestingly, Baudrillard develops a thesis on gender with his understanding of *seduction* as belonging to the order of sign and ritual, and as that which removes a dimension from real space (Baudrillard 1990). Baudrillard says of seduction, "The only thing truly at stake is mastery of the *strategy of appearances*, against the force of being and reality" (Baudrillard [1979]1990: 9). Baudrillard's seduction shows what Butler is concerned with making clear, namely that legitimating systems and conceptual schemes (political, libidinal, etc.) inform and provide the "code" behind ways of thinking. It is important here to point out that I read Baudrillard as attempting to get out from under theoretical canopies that instruct ways of conceptualization. But, what Baudrillard does not account for is that even his descriptions of gender seduction considers real bodies, such as transvestites, that are envisaged in terms of *power-simulacra*, or the simulacra of gender that has been reified culturally to serve as "reality," albeit a hyperreality itself.

Consider Baudrillard's account of transvestites. Baudrillard gives an example of seduction, namely that of the Barcelona drag queens, who wear women's makeup and clothing, but keep their moustaches and hairy chests in full view. Again, there is an excess of appearance for Baudrillard, as there are more signs than "reality," again pointing to the irony of too much reality or hyperreality.

> Uncertainty is the greatest in the play of femininity, such as with transvestism. With the transvestite, the signs are not duplicated with biology—they don't match up. This is the seduction of the signs themselves. Perhaps the transvestites ability to seduce comes straight from parody—a parody of sex by its over-signification. (Baudrillard 1990: 14)

Thus for Baudrillard, there are too many signs of gender, both masculine and feminine, thereby providing a dilemma with regard to categorization of either. For Baudrillard, this is not production, but the seduction of the signs themselves.

Baudrillard articulates the complexity of the relationship between production, seduction, and drag queens when he says that "The signs of the drag queens make the claim that femininity is naught but the signs with which men rig it up ... It is a challenge to the female model by way of a female game" (Baudrillard [1979]1990: 14). This is the strength of seduction, the implication that a category is actually nothing (the female is "nothing" or "nothingness" for Baudrillard), the artifice

Figure 4.1   Female soldier in Iraq with bikini and rifle

Source: Photograph provided courtesy of the author.

is greater than the reality, and that "the feminine exists in the signs but there is
no reality behind the signs" (Baudrillard [1979]1990: 14). In this way, the signs
themselves suggest a challenge in terms of integrity of the category feminine,
and for gender categories in sum. Hence seduction is an ironic, alternative form
that breaks signification and provides "a space of play and defiance" (Baudrillard
[1979]1990: 21). This is a theoretical dual of sorts, according to Baudrillard, since
seduction is above all a strategy of displacement—it is seduction that prevails in
the long term because it implies a reversible, indeterminate order (Baudrillard
[1979]1990: 22).

    Consider Sabrina Harman as an example of Baudrillard's seduction. In
numerous photographs of abuse at Abu Ghraib, she is shown displaying military
masculinity in her dress, in her membership as a military soldier, while wearing
the masculine drag of a military utilities uniform (a t-shirt and fatigues), and as not
evidencing stereotypical femininity (in keeping with Baudrillard's example) in her
appearance. In this way, Harman was wearing the "drag" of the military. Harman
was a military soldier who existed as female within the masculinist "code" of the
military itself, thereby further evidencing the use of forced "drag" for identity,
as Harman's identity was "made sense of" in terms of this code. It is through the
consideration of the below photograph, of the female in the bikini experiencing

"down time" in Iraq, with her rifle next to her, that notions of military masculinity and the drag of femininity are best juxtaposed against each other.

In fact, we can understand all soldiers as wearing the "drag" of military uniforms, as these uniforms are gendered and are forced upon the bodies of soldiers, and without choice or regard for their own gendered performance or instantiation. Further, drag can be understood when camouflage is worn because like make-up, this is meant to disguise, conceal or cover the body. Camouflage is clearly another version of the military's drag in that it hides the reality of both the body and the soldier's identity, and especially when the oil of camouflage is applied to the face. This face "make-up" is comparable to an individual wearing feminine lipstick, eye shadow and the like to "capture" her prey (male or female), yet in this case, the soldiers are out to hide, seduce and trick, etc. "the enemy." What is more, the soldiers at Abu Ghraib Prison (and at most military bases in fact) wear combat fatigues (camouflage); however, the only combat at Abu Ghraib existed beyond the prison walls, and thus it seems that the soldiers inside the prison are seducing each other with the drag of their uniforms.

Considering gender and sexuality, Harman actually existed as both a female and a lesbian within the heterosexist and masculinist "code" of the military, and this was most evident when her wife took the stand on her behalf during her courts-martial as a character witness. (As a side note, nobody said the word "wife" in Harman's entire courts-martial. It was one of the many elephants in the room.) There was a seduction (an excess of appearance) with Harman as a member of the military, as a lesbian, and as a female, and these identities rendered the military's masculinist and heterosexist "code" unintelligible, thereby showing its ultimate constructed and simulacra nature. By the very virtue of Harman being female within the masculinist military, and as a lesbian with a (semi-)closeted heterosexual identity within this military, these identities seduced the military's code of constructed masculinity and heterosexuality. Harman evidences simulacra in that she was identified in terms of all of the following: a military *"power-simulacra"* of heterosexuality, a homosexual given her lesbian identity, and a female in the masculinist military. This is a subversion of the "code" into oblivion, which makes Harman's identity a "seduction," according to Baudrillard. Additionally, by remaining under the radar of the "Don't Ask, Don't Tell" requirement of the army, Harman subverted the very system that attempted to control her by being gay and wearing the drag of the military uniform openly. This is subversive of the military's heteronormativity and is an example of troubling the gendered masculine code of the military. Hence, there are too many conflicting signs, masculine and feminine, heterosexual and homosexual, thereby leading to this seduction.

According to Baudrillard, the "feminine" is not just seduction; it also suggests a challenge to the male, in that the status of the categorical male cannot be understood as the inversion of the feminine. With this example, and in accord with Butler, Baudrillard questions the connectedness of gender and sex categories and shows their ultimate disassociation, as he did with the Barcelona drag queens example. Even so, says Baudrillard, "Every structure can adapt to its subversion or inversion, but not to the reversion of its terms. Seduction is this reversible form" (Baudrillard [1979]1990: 21). This is evidenced with Harman's inversion of the sexuality and gender signs of the American military "code," thereby showing its hyperreal nature. Hence, Baudrillard understands seduction as an ironic, alternative form, one that breaks the referentiality of sex and provides a space of play and defiance (Baudrillard 1990).

This is similar to Butler's project of destabilizing binary pairs and showing the dominant binary to be a faulty construction of power over the subordinate, yet Baudrillard takes it one step further and claims that an implosion of meaning has occurred given the displacement of symbolic referents. For Baudrillard then, seduction represents mastery over the symbolic universe, while power represents only mastery of the real universe (Baudrillard [1979]1990). Butler is concerned with this "real universe" (and the consequences for embodiment and actual bodies), where narratives of gender exist and structure reality in terms of power. Although it is true that Baudrillard renders gender meaningless via seduction and the displacement (read "implosion") of symbolic referents, Butler basically does the same with her identification of gender categories as tied to power, and as meaningless outside of these power systems, and especially since gender cannot be understood as apart from these normalizing systems themselves.

Both England and Harman seemingly offended the masculinist military collective through their actions depicted in the media of the photographs of abuse, and this was pointed out in both courts-martial cases' closing arguments. The prosecution in both cases was quick to point out that the actions observed in the photographs was offensive to the military, and this point became gendered when at the England trial the prosecuting attorney looked at the all-male panel and stated "she has tainted our army. Her actions have made us look badly, has harmed the image of the army, and it is she who is responsible for more violence done against American soldiers in Iraq because of these photographs."[8] This seems to be a clear delineation of boundaries in terms of gender such that a theoretical "us /them" rhetoric is used to distinguish between good and bad, masculine and feminine. Obviously England was not in the good-old-boys club of the military and did not count as a fellow soldier anymore. She was now evidence of the feminine irrational symbolic code. Nonetheless, this interpretation is in favor of the hyperreal rhetoric of gender simulation, as both England and Harman were shown not to have participated in the physical abuse of detainees, and thus this is an example of Baudrillard's implosion of reality itself, as these women were not part of the "them" and instead are *Fallgirls*.

The Simulacra of Gender at Abu Ghraib and the Courts-Martial

If all gender is *power-simulacra*, in that it is a self-perpetuating and reifying category of the "real," then Baudrillard and Butler would agree that gender

8   This is a paraphrase from the trials themselves.

performances are understood with regard to their socially constructed system or "code" for reference. For postmodern identities, it is this code or model of reality that is more real then the reality it is supposed to represent. In this way, I argue that gender is a simulacra identity in that it is real only as a "consequence" of its performance within contexts that have created a narrative of gender "realness," albeit ones based on image or power.

Both Baudrillard and Butler independently argue for a deconstructed understanding of gender, and one that culminates in simulacra of gender reality. I argue that it is possible that Baudrillard's notion of simulacra can come to function as a kind of postmodern policing technique, where what are being enforced are *power-simulacra* within a specific context. These *power-simulacra* are what the collective conscience has come to regard as "real," albeit this notion of "reality" is unstable and could change at any time. Hence, this notion of *"power-simulacra"* is a concept that I find helpful in understanding power associated with Baudrillard's theorizing, where "power" is understood as the legitimation of certain, yet unstable, significations within a specific cultural context. In addition, and applying Butler, it is possible to show how *power-simulacra* can be attached to the body in terms of signification and value, where the *power-simulacra* function as the policing mechanism for gender itself.

For Butler, unlike Baudrillard, gender performances have direct consequences for bodies, where gender is realized through power and the policing/surveillance of norms. On the other hand, Baudrillard would critique these norms in terms of simulacra norms, as gender for Baudrillard is only a game of seduction, and not about the production of identity in terms of power. Nonetheless, both Baudrillard and Butler show that systems of "realness" are themselves constructed, and then reified such that "realness" is obtained through mimicry of the normalizing system itself, or what I call *"power-simulacra"* and the *"rule by simulacra of reality"*—all informed by the overarching "code" of gender signs and rules.

Again, consider the gender narrative of the American military, where gender is understood in terms of *power-simulacra* based on the code of constructed masculinity. This account informs a conception of gender, where the text itself is what is deemed the standard from which to measure, thereby functioning as a decoder, translator, and informer of the "code." In this way, the code becomes the gender standard, albeit fleeting, for *"rule by simulacra of reality."* This code lies in the symbols that represent, legitimate, and celebrate the order of the code itself.

One way that gender is solidified within the military is through the use of uniforms, where bodies are given military legitimacy. Only certain dress is appropriate for certain events in the military, and options exist for women with regard to military uniforms that "feminize" them using the drag of military uniform. Not only do these uniforms control the body in terms of identity, but they actually literally control the body in their binding fit. These uniforms seem to function as drag in that they allow for a gendered understanding of identity that is in terms of a normalizing ritual and code for dress. Additionally, uniforms are worn in accordance with the "law" or rules for dress. For example, pins and medals must be worn in a certain manner and in a certain order on the uniform, specific uniforms are worn in specific situations, hats are only worn in certain occasions, and then never in buildings, etc. Hence, both identity and gender are constructed and performed through the use of uniform as well as repetition and the ritualized style of both the body and code itself.

Nonetheless, at Abu Ghraib, soldiers did not consistently wear uniforms, salute, or follow other military protocol, thereby providing evidence that this "code" is at its base conceptualized simulacra. These facts made me think that perhaps drag could be about something larger than just gender and sex—perhaps it could be about simulacra identity in general. So, I expand the notion of "drag" and include more than just imitation of masculinity and femininity, or male and female, because at Abu Ghraib it seemed that individuals were all mimicking some simulacra identity that was "drag-like." For example, testimony at the courts-martial showed that uniforms did not always function to police bodies, as prisoners were kept naked, and without any bounded identity markings. Additionally, American soldiers removed their nametags so that they could not be identified in Iraq, thereby testifying to their actual lack of functional identity. So here we have unmarked soldiers and prisoners, yet in order to mark prisoners, and because of a shortage of supplies, it was stated in numerous testimonies that Iraqi women's panties were purchased for "clothing." What is interesting is that a simulacra understanding of "clothing" appears in the images of detainee humiliation, as male prisoners were shown being shamed through the act of putting women's panties on their heads for punishment, and clearly not as clothing, as panties are not worn on the head. In fact, it could be argued that "drag-techniques" were used to humiliate prisoners, as femininity was literally disguising masculinity, where female panties were forcibly put on male prisoners faces, as shown in the photographs of abuse. Yet, this is not a traditional notion of drag in the sense that femininity or masculinity is being performed in order to instantiate the subject, and instead "drag" is used here to abuse prisoners.

I think this association of prisoners and "drag-techniques" can best be seen in Colombian artist Fernando Botero's latest works on Abu Ghraib (Botero 2006), which depicts some of the prisoners being abused at Abu Ghraib literally *in drag*. In Botero's latest works entitled "Abu Ghraib," he depicts the prisoner abuse at Abu Ghraib through a series marked 1-50 of drawings and paintings (50 oils and sketches—170 paintings total) that depict pain, degradation, and torture—and more. He shows the juxtaposition of masculinity and femininity within this series, where in some pieces the male body is hyper-muscular, yet is also wearing the *drag* of lingerie—sometimes that of a complete red bra and panty set and other times panties alone. This image can be read as making the exact point I am discussing, that prisoners were tortured through the use of "drag-techniques," which highly offends the cultural sensibilities of Iraqi constructions of masculinity. This could be Botero's point about the torture of Iraqi detainees at Abu Ghraib—that humiliation and gender were both used as weapons. There is the added humiliation for Muslim religious beliefs that forbids nudity and males dressing as females—the separating of stereotypical cultural feminine and masculine practices (although not queer ones). The very use of the term 'humiliated' has a direct link to men being treated as women, and thereby offends the socially constructed ideals of masculinity, both Iraqi and American.

Civilian contractors were also present at Abu Ghraib and they were abusing prisoners, yet they were not identified with nametags, and OGA were also at the prison imitating the military and giving orders, and some of them wore uniforms (as "fake soldiers"), yet some of them imitated civilians. In this way, there was a seduction of appearances taking place, where the strategy of both the contractors and the OGA was to master the symbols associated with their identity. I argue this is a kind of "drag," although not the kind that Butler and Baudrillard discuss with regard to gender. Additionally, we see this mimicry of identity when we consider that the MP soldiers were not doing work associated with the job of a military police person, but were being coerced by MI to assist in "softening up" detainees, and thus were imitating the torturer's assistants. In addition, MIs were surely not doing military intelligence work, as the prisoners did not have any actionable intelligence to give them. Instead, MI was imitating some NCIS (Naval Criminal Investigative Service) simulacra of what it means to be in an intelligence position within the military. In these above ways, it seems like everyone was doing a form of drag at Abu Ghraib, although not completely and always in the ways that Butler and Baudrillard understand. In reality, even the prisoners were supposed to be terrorists, yet most were common criminals arrested in street sweeps. So what was "real" in these situations? I argue the consequences of abuse, the fact that the blame for this abuse fell onto the shoulders of low-ranking soldiers, as well as the gendered and homoerotic interpretation of abuse.

Using the narrative that couples the military and masculinity as a frame for conceptualization, an analysis of gender and power within the Fort Hood courtroom emerges. Interestingly, during the England trial, an expert witness for the defense makes this point about gender identity and military uniform clear. This expert was a female who testified as an expert witness in child and adolescent psychology for the prosecution. Her name was Lang, and she argued that England was not suffering from depression, even though England had been on Zoloft (and anti-depressant) for 10 months now. It immediately seemed logical to me that England was not suffering depression or anxiety at the moment because of this medication, as the purpose of the medication is to alleviate these symptoms. Lang gave England a mental status exam and claimed that England displayed below-average intelligence, and labeled England a "follower." What is interesting is that Lang did not give England any objective tests for measurement of either intelligence or depression and anxiety, and argued that England had adjustment disorder with mixed anxiety and depression. Additionally, Lang did not consider any family history or context for England's previous diagnosis of anxiety and depression, which is typical in psychiatric diagnostics.

Although her testimony was interesting, her gender was made clear in the courtroom and in terms of an oppositional relationship to the masculinist economy of the military symbolic. Lang was the only female (other than the defense attorney during the Harman trial) who wore a skirt version of the army uniform, in a room filled with men and women of the military wearing pants. This was noticed as the expert walked to the stand, in front of the filled room, and took her oath. Additionally, as Lang explained her findings as an expert, she repeatedly referenced her male mentor that she worked with as a legitimating tool for her findings. Lang stated that she had just graduated two years prior with a psychology degree and was new to Fort Hood. In this way, she was evidencing (feminine) weakness as an expert (her role at the trials) by referring to another male expert in the field to justify her professional position and psychological findings. Possibly the greatest evidencing of femininity made by this expert was her act of knitting a long yarn project in the middle of the courtroom, and in full view of the panel (jury) and other military peers. (Literally, her yarn project was unrolled into the isle of the courtroom for display.) This is an important, if not genius move, by the prosecution because it served to legitimate and reify the masculinist code of the military through an oppositional subordinate relationship of femininity. Additionally, it was an all-out statement that this expert knew her place and would happily occupy the subordinate feminine role through her actions, or use of craft as a feminine symbolic narrative. In this way, the prosecution expert was succumbing to *rule by simulacra of reality.*

These actions can be read as making the following claim: "The military accepts femininity so long as it is subordinate to masculinity." After all, this was the courts-martial of a female soldier, and the gender message here is that this "rotten apple" was "rotten" because of her lack of ability to interpret and reify the code of military constructed masculinity correctly. After all, this is the hyperreal code that England was being judged in terms of, and even though this code of gender simulacra was itself constructed, it indeed functioned as power-simulacra in that it was considered to be "real" with regard to understanding gender within the military.

This interpretation reifies without critical questioning the separate spheres doctrine of gender division, namely the association of masculinity and the public sphere and femininity and the private sphere. As one can imagine it to be difficult to be a female expert witness in a room of alpha military males, the performance of femininity that Lang gave served to comfort masculinist positions in the room by bowing to the law of the father or phallus. Specifically, to be heard in a room full of masculine subjectivities, it might have been the best legal strategy to legitimize the phallus so that the phallic order was not questioned. Consequently, this interpretation is about the authority of the *power-simulacra* of masculinity within the military, functioning as the policing mechanism for gender itself and the hyperreality of gender category simulations.

Another example of gender performance (at the Harman trial this time) that can be understood in terms of the masculinist code of the military was that of Captain Takemura. Consider both defense attorneys, the female and soft-spoken Takemura versus the tough, rational, and hard-edged civilian attorney Frank Spinner. Repeatedly, when Harman was described as a maternal caregiver it was by Takemura in a soft voice and through the use of photographs showing Harman doing service activities and making friends with Iraqi families and children. During closing arguments it was again Takemura who pled with the panel in her soft voice, sometimes so soft one could not be sure what she said, as she motioned to maternal-Sabrina and the pictures from Iraq that showed Sabrina performing stereotypical feminine roles.

In the courtroom, it was a telling site that the only female attorney in the Harman trial was the one who elicited confessions of being afraid out of the male soldiers. In this way, Takemura wore the persona of the motherly caregiver who could empathize with fear, and who could make it a safe place to address this fear, even in the courtroom which was itself doused plentifully with the military's simulacra code of masculinity. I argue that she could elicit these confessions because she understood the military code, and inserted herself as a role acceptable with regard to this masculine symbolic narrative. According to the code itself, the expression of fear is stereotypically understood as unmasculine. Interestingly, Takemura elicited these confessions while wearing the masculine uniform of the military. What is telling here is that none of the male soldiers made these confessions to any of the male attorneys or the judge, and only to the "mother figure" in the courtroom. Thus, the policing technique associated with gender and power is evidenced in the form of a code that sets up *power-simulacra* as the self-reifying standard of the code itself, and namely masculinity. Interestingly, with regard to gendering Takemura, she is both feminine and masculine in this example, thereby showing gender constructions to be simulacra identities because of their constructed and fleeting nature of identification. Regarding the male soldiers who testified that they experienced fear, their claims do not match up with masculinity, and this is Baudrillard's point about the simulacra nature of postmodern identity categories—they cannot signify themselves in any stable and meaningful way. Hence, masculinity as a category for identification is fleeting with regard to coherence.

Consider the above example in terms of Baudrillard's seduction. Male soldiers admitted under oath that they were scared to stop the abusiveness of other American soldiers towards the Iraqi detainees because they were in fear of retaliation. The male soldiers admitting to being scared in a military court shows the seduction of gender identity in that these males are shown to evidence both military masculinity and feminine fear. This was an important point in the courts-martial with regard to gender identity, as these admissions of fear were being made to the only female attorney associated with the trial, and to one who embodied femininity as she was wearing the skirt-version of the military uniform, or exhibiting the feminine persona-*fascia* while in military "drag." As a further testimony of Takemura's performance of femininity, every day in court, Takemura showed up in full make-up and with her hair immaculately styled. She even was concerned with re-applying make-up throughout the day, and visibly during court recesses. Takemura's gender performance was thus the seduction of gender signs, as Takemura displayed the signs of both masculine power and femininity

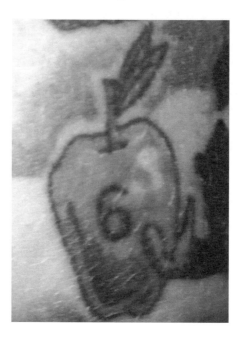

Figure 4.2   Harman tattoo, "rotten apple 6"

Note: Some of the soldiers charged with abuses at Abu Ghraib marked their bodies with variations of the "rotten apple" tattoo as a means literally to embody resistance.

Source: Photograph provided courtesy of the author.

in the courtroom as well as within the masculinist military. Likewise, the male soldiers who displayed fear in their testimonies evidenced both the masculinity associated with the military by virtue of being a soldier, but also the vulnerability of femininity in their claims of fear. Takemura thus both displays the powerful masculine subjectivity while also wearing her feminine persona identity, and the soldiers display femininity while also maintaining their roles as soldiers within the masculinist military.

This same use of gender simulacra was further evident in the Harman trials when Harman was sold to the panel as a maternal caregiver. The archetype of "maternal Sabrina" was vivid in the life-sized photographs of Harman at Al Hilla, another military compound in Iraq. Again, Harman was not seen as a soldier in the courtroom or in Iraq, and instead was repeatedly described as a caregiver, motherly individual, and even a social worker who cared about the experiences of Iraqi children.[9] Instead of being an equal soldier in the courtroom to other

9   Interestingly, the job of social worker can be understood as a caregiver occupation and thus symbolic of femininity itself and allowable instances of femininity in the public sphere.

male soldiers, Harman was cast into the role of the female symbolic narrative that defines women as caregivers and nurturers, even though she was a member of the masculinist military itself. Unlike Takemura, however, Harman was not inserted into the code of masculinity because she did not evidence the simulacra gender of masculinity. Instead, her identity as a soldier was stripped from her, and possibly given her characterizations as a feminine soldier, which subverted masculinist military ideals.

Perhaps this is why she, and other soldiers who faced courts-martial, obtained the tattoo depicting a rotten apple and their trial number. (Most of the "seven rotten-apples" had tattoos of rotten apples on their bodies with their courts-martial number.) In an attempt to claim an identity in a postmodern culture, where identity is fleeting, and in a situation aimed at stripping important distinctions such as rank, job, and sense of worth, these soldiers forever solidified not only their bonds to each other, but also their bond to the military. Nonetheless, and per Baudrillard's account of postmodern culture, these identities are fleeting and ungrounded. However, given the permanence of a tattoo, I argue that Harman embodied in a lasting way her identity as part of the masculinist military, and despite her gendered descriptions in her courts-martial as a "feminine" and "care giving" soldier. In this way, Harman subverts her gendered characterizations in the courts-martial, and reifies through the use of tattoo her identity as a female lesbian soldier within a heterosexist military, and as accused in the Abu Ghraib scandal.

Conclusion

In conclusion, I have shown that what is considered theoretically "real" instructs the formation of conceptual and organizational paradigms with regard to sex and gender categories. I use the theories of both Baudrillard and Butler to discuss gender "realness," and argue that gender is a simulacra category for identity. Although the categories of gender are simulacrum in their construction, there are real consequences for offending the "code" of gender with regard to conceptualization.

One way that Baudrillard and Butler are different is that Baudrillard thrives on chaos, hyperreality, and simulacra, and sees a "sea" of circulating fictions as existing in "reality." For Baudrillard, this gendering of reality serves as reality itself—a hyperreality indeed—simulations and free floating imaginary. It is this hyperreality that comes to function as the "real," or a simulacrum of reality, as signs have been substituted for the real itself, and gender identity in this case. Although for Baudrillard, there is no reality apart from the signs, he provides a way to discuss gender as hyperreal simulations that are self-referentially reified within their very definitions.

Additionally, Butler points out that gender is under surveillance and can only be understood with regard to its very own policing practices based in power itself. In this way, gender performativities within the military can be understood with the concept of gender *power-simulacra*, where masculinity becomes the regulatory frame and policing technique for understanding legitimate citations of gender and value. Says Butler, gender is thus an act of "doing," where the socially constructed standard is neither a representation of reality, nor a description of reality, as "reality" can only be found in its simulation, or the code for surveillance itself. This means that "realness" is constructed in the military through the conformity and surveillance of norms, such that the actual space of the military is characterized in terms of this code. Apart from this code there is no understanding of "realness," and only the *rule by simulacra of reality*. Through the continual performance of gender within the military, the "doing" of gender becomes a means to naturalize the self in terms of the conformity to and surveillance of "masculinity." Thus, the sustained performance of masculinity becomes a means for military cultural citation, value, and signification.

Throughout this section, I have been concerned with gender and what was "real" at Abu Ghraib and the associated courts-martial. At a private dinner, one soldier told me, with tears in his eyes, that he pleaded with his wife to leave him and to take their children. This pleading was in an attempt to "protect" his family from his continued experiences of the "realities" of Abu Ghraib, which still violently run through his mind and dreams, manifesting themselves in physical outbursts and emotional distress. Although this tearful confession was made by a male soldier who was still clearly feeling vulnerable given his experiences of Abu Ghraib, and was thus a violation of the code of military masculinity showing the ultimate simulacra nature of gender constructions, this confession evidences both the trauma and symptoms of post-traumatic stress disorder that were the "realities" of Abu Ghraib. Daily destruction, followed by post-traumatic stress disorder, is how soldiers described in interview and in testimony their experiences at Abu Ghraib, as well as their current state of existence. There was chaos at Abu Ghraib, and this was real.

Testimony of Stjepan G. Mestrovic, Expert Witness in Sociology, Sabrina Harman Courts-Martial

Stjepan G. Mestrovic, civilian, was called as witness on May 17, 2005 for the defense, was sworn, and testified as follows:

Questions by the Civilian Defense Counsel:

...

A: I specialize in what is known as structural functionalism, it's the dominant paradigm within sociology. It talks about how society is held together, and our obedience, the breaking of norms also occurs. ...

Q: ... First of all, what investigative types of reports have you read regarding the Abu Ghraib incident?

A: I read the Taguba Report, the Schlesinger Report, the Faye Report, the Herrington Report, and the Church Report. I read a number of the sworn statements, for example, all the material pertaining to the Article 32 for—in the England case. Um, I read Field Manual 34-52, both the 1987 and the 1992 versions----

Q: ----what—I mean, when you reference that number, tell the members what that is?

A: It's the Authoritative Army Doctrine on Interrogation Methods.

Q: Have you observed these proceedings?

A: Yes, I have.

...

Q: Now, did you already—were you provided a copy of any kind of Psychological Evaluation that Specialist Harman underwent?

A: Yes I was.

Q: And what were you provided and what all did you read in that regard?

A: I was provided the psychiatric report by Dr. Donovan and I was provided the MCMI, which is one of the many psychological tests, a very authoritative one, psychological test on her personality and profile.

Q: About how much time have you spent with Specialist Harman preparing?

A: I interviewed her twice. The first time three and a half hours and the second time one hour.

Q: So is there anything that we've missed that you've either read or looked at or considered in forming the opinions that you are willing to express here today?

A: Well there was more material, for example, there is a sociological study about the disaster of the Space Shuttle Challenger at NASA, which blew up, which I think is directly relevant to this case. I've read the sociological study of that, which won an award in sociology. And I read Akbar Ahmed, who was a well-known Muslim Scholar about Islamic culture because that's one of the issues that was raised in the Schlesinger Report, the insensitivity to Islamic Culture. So I've prepared on that. And I also read Mark Daniels book *Torture and Truth*, which includes a number of documents pertaining to Abu Ghraib. Among other material that was relevant.

Q: Okay. Let's then begin by looking at some of the terms that you used before we get into your actual opinions. You referenced Functional Sociology?

A: Yes.

Q: Could you define that term for the court members?

A: It's an assumption that society, rather you're talking about a family unit, whether we're talking about a courtroom, an Army unit, school, whatever, has a certain component that are called norms, beliefs, values, and sanctions which have to synchronize together for it to work in a safe, healthy way. And also an implication, when those norms, sanctions, values, and beliefs are sync, then you have deviance, then you have a break in the norms which can include anything from being late, dirty looks, to suicide, murder, and the most extreme sort of things.

Q: How does that relate to social disorganization?

A: The way that it relates is that every social system has always operating within a certain expectation, certain preferences, certain ways to enforce those. Every class, every courtroom, every school, every hospital there are norms and expectations about what will be done, how it will be done. So that when a system is disorganized it means that those expectations, the ways of the force, and all the beliefs and structures that go into that are out of sync and we call that deviance.

Q: Are you familiar with the term Normalization of Deviance?

A: Yes I think that's an extremely important concept. I mentioned that book about the disaster of the—of Challenger. The sociologist who studied it found that NASA knew ahead of time that the o-rings, which eventually led to that disaster, were eroding, there were problems. By normative of standards, and deviance was occurring because the Engineering Standards, the Aerospace Standards, the other Normative standards that NASA was supposed to be using were ignored. Instead of NASA saying the o-rings are not deforming, the standards were changed. The parallel that I see here very directly is that the standards for interrogation and also in FM 34-52, which is Authoritative, and also the standard to keep MI and MP functions separate, which all the U.S. Government Reports type, they were merged. That was a breaking of norms. That was a breaking of expectation and I think that the explosion, if you will, at Abu Ghraib is as inevitable as the explosion of Challenger.

Q: Okay, well we're going to go into more detail in that regard. How long have you studied sociology and worked in this field?

A: 25 years.

Q: So as an expert, given the length of time that you spent in this field and all the things that you have viewed and you have examined, do you have an expert opinion pertaining to how social disorganization relates to the Abu Ghraib Prison situation and in particular as it relates to Specialist Sabrina Harman?

A: Yes. It's right in the United States Government's own reports, they cite the fact that nobody was certain who was, in fact, in charge of that prison. Was it Colonel Pappas, was it Colonel Phillabaum. They cite that the filing system was inadequate. They cite that the low expectations, what people were supposed to do were confusing. They cite the fact that MI roles and MP roles, which used to be kept distinct, were, in fact, merged. They cite tremendous problems with just the basics of knowing when the prisoners would be released. They cite of numerous problems with social chaos which the reports directly call, in fact, a "poisonous atmosphere," that's a direct verbatim quote from the Faye Report at Abu Ghraib and an unhealthy mystic. So that is the equivalent of that sociological state of social disorganization that I spoke about which results to deviance.

Now the second part of your question, how that relates to Sabrina Harman? Is that I think any person who is caught in a situation which was that disorganized in which rules are not clear, which has got confusing, is going to be disoriented. That they will be—it will be difficult for them to validate what is expected, what is right and what is wrong. And that's for the healthiest a person be.

Q: This—how does this relate to the term Role Confusion?

A: While most of the time we know what's expected of us. As a professor I know what my role expectations are, to prepare for lectures, to give my lectures, to give examines. The students know what's expected of them, be on time, listen, take notes, don't party too much, so forth. When those role expectations become confused, when, you know, you're doing a job that you're not trained for, that you're not prepared for, when you don't know who your boss is, when you don't, let's say, enforce the fact that people shouldn't come late to class or can't turn in papers, you're going to have disorganization and you're going to have deviance. Well, like I said the government's reports decided a number of confusing, disorganized aspects to Abu Ghraib and this will have an effect on performance, on what a person feels is expected of him.

Q: Well you just used the term deviance and you may have defined that a moment ago, but what is the deviance that occurred or existed at Abu Ghraib?

A: Well, deviance is sociologically as the breaking of norms. Now, what the government reports say very clearly are words to the affect that the nudity and the humiliation, and I'm paraphrasing here, but it's almost verbatim, led to or condoned or opened the door to more serious abuse. In other words, that's that normalization of deviance. If you don't stop the breaking of norms early on, if it becomes normal, like the eroded o-rings. You say oh, it's just a nudity thing, it's no big deal and that makes the next breaking of norms easier and the next breaking norms easier. Another way we put it is, sociology we speak about primary deviance versus secondary deviance. Now, sometimes in their youth almost everybody has played hooky in school or may have gotten drunk or may have sexually been promiscuous, once, you stop there okay you broke a norm, you learned your lesson. But, if you continue like that then it's easier to do the next thing and the next thing and the next thing, I mean that's the principal here of the normalization of deviance and then you have somebody who ends up as a drug addict or as a criminal, as a kind of quote, career. So in that sense it's very important sociologically that when deviance first occurs that it is identified, that it is sanctioned, and that is corrected.

Q: Well, as you look at the Abu Ghraib situation and what happened there, weren't there safeguards in place to keep this deviance from coming about?

A: No, I mean, the Taguba Report especially is crystal clear Geneva Conventions were not posted. The Schlesinger Report is even more critical and says that there was confusion about whether Geneva Conventions applied. In principal they were supposed to apply in Iraq, but they did not apply in Afghanistan and some of the people who were at Abu Ghraib, the MI, were coming from the----

...

A: ----the Schlesinger Report explicitly states just that, that practices which were called folk or unofficial practices were brought in to Abu Ghraib from Afghanistan.

Q: And did you see evidence of these practices at Abu Ghraib based on the reports that you seen?

A: Yes.

Q: Now, can you identify what some of those things were that were—are these violations of the norms that existed in the Army?

A: Yes, and here I have to go in to FM 34-52, which is the Authoritative Normative Standard still for the Army----

Q: ----okay----

A: ----that's the thing that's interesting about this?

Q: Please explain?

A: Well, FM 34-52, the Geneva Convention apply. It tries to establish report between the interrogator and the detainee. And it works on willing cooperation. Practices were put in place in Afghanistan where the Geneva Conventions did not apply and the Schlesinger Report says the problem—the confusion stemmed from the fact that these practices migrated, that's exactly what they used, into Iraq, and therefore caused confusion for the soldiers. The other sources of confusion was the merging of the MI and the MP functions. This created this climate, this poison atmosphere, which led to further abuse.

Q: So let me ask you specifically about nudity, how does that relate to what you just said? Nudity of detainees in Tier 1A?

A: Nudity is a violation of Geneva Conventions. It was not seen as such as the reports themselves state. It was seen as routine, common place, and accepted. Now I can take that statement from the government reports and put it in the sociological language, deviance became normalized. When you have a situation in which deviance is normalized, the normalization of deviance, then like I said any other further deviance is not going to seem that deviant because they've already broken so many norms along the way, it makes further deviance easier.

Q: How does this balneology—you mentioned NASA before, can you relate this question of nudity to the NASA situation?

A: Very specifically NASA has certain standards about lowering performance which are tied into the Engineering Community, the Aerospace Community, and NASA's own Bureaucratic Community. They have certain standards, you know, there must not be so much erosion, there must not be so much burning. Those things are violated and instead of NASA saying let's get new o-rings, let's fix them, let's go back to our standard, they just changed the standards. They just kept making deviant standards until it got so bad that it led inevitably to the disaster. So that's the parallel that I'm drawing here. FM 34-52, Authoritative Version, keep the roles distinct. Authoritative Version, the government's reports are saying those two roles were mixed which already broke a norm and interrogation techniques that you will have put in with our safeguards which went beyond FM 34-52. Instead of seeing that as deviant, it led to the fact—it became normalized and led to further deviance.

Q: So with respect to nudity and the MPs when you talk about this blurring of MI/MP roles, what evidence did you see that the MPs knew what the norm was?

A: I don't think they did know, but they were put into a situation—it's the same thing as the NASA situation. They didn't know, but they did know that the stuff was going on and that it was common place and it was accepted, it became organized, that's the thing. It became origination of deviance. So when you see nudity, when you see humiliation, when you see yelling, when you see coercion, when you see intimidation, all of which are violations and these things are accepted as normal, then I agree sociologically with the reports by the U.S. Government that this leads to further abuse. It opens the door to it.

...

Q: ... There are signs up in one part of the prison that say treat detainees with respect or words to that affect. And then a guard, forget who—you know, any guard—a guard goes and works in Tier 1A and sees that detainees are being put in stress positions while they're nude with women's underwear over their head, do those things appear to be treating people with dignity and respect in terms of the Geneva Convention as you understand it?

A: No.

Q: Okay, so what problem would that create for a guard who sees a posting in one part of the prison and this kind of treatment in another part of the prison?

A: The sociological term we use for that in any situation is cognitive dissidence. Dissidence being that the mind has to reconcile the two opposites. One can be like a father, whom you respect and love, who beat you mercilessly and abuses you, that will create cognitive dissidence in a child. So I can get out of the Abu Ghraib situation and use this as a metaphor. It will create cognitive dissidence, it will create a child who will feel helpless, it will create somebody who feels invalidated, and again opens the door to further abuse. Cognitive dissidence is what it would cause.

...

Q: What safeguards did you see that were in place at Abu Ghraib to keep something like what happened at Abu Ghraib from happening?

[Pause]

Q: Did you see any safeguards in place?

A: I'm thinking, that's why I'm pausing. It's like—first of all, the first thought that comes to mind is the U.S. Government reports did not talk about safeguards, in fact, the Taguba Report is very critical about the lack of safeguards, in fact, the Taguba Report is very critical about the lack of safeguards, the lack of standard operating procedures. That the Geneva Conventions were not posted. That the filing system was inadequate. That lessons learned were not being done. I mean they had a long list of criticisms of failure to safeguard. So your questions throws me off, I cannot think of anything immediately that reports say here are the safeguards.

Q: Well let's look at another aspect of this. I mean we had testimony from Ken Davis on the 25th of October he basically shows up in Tier 1A, he sees some abuse, and he says—he reports it to a lieutenant the next day. On the night of November 7th a Specialist now, he sees abuse and he immediately reports, I think it was to Sergeant Jones, I'm not sure his rank, but—and of course we now have Specialist Sabrina Harman who was in this environment, saw these abuses, and she has now been found guilty by the court members of dereliction of duty and of maltreating detainees. From a sociological standpoint is there an explanation as to why those two individuals would report what they saw, but someone like Sabrina Harman who was in the midst of this for a number of weeks would not report what she saw?

A: Yes, it's the concept of learned helplessness. With the—in the case of Sergeant [Kenn] Davis, he was not actually assigned to Tier 1A, he was doing transportation----

…

A: ----yes, Kenn Davis, it's my understanding his primary duty was transporting prisoners to Baghdad from Abu Ghraib. He was outside the situation. So coming in from the outside situation which is more normative, coming into a deviant situation, yes, you're going to see the deviance and you're going to do something about it. Similarly in the other—with Wisdom's case, but when you're immersed in it it's kind of like, you know, if I could use a metaphor an analogy, if you're seeing a fight occur at a high school and you're there right from the beginning, I mean there's sociological studies in this, you're less likely to get the coach or somebody to break it up than if you come in from the outside and see it. I mean there's many cases of this and one of the most famous cases is the Kitty Genovese Case, which is often used in sociology, where this woman was screaming for help because she was being attacked. It was an apartment building, it was full of people, nobody called the police. Subsequent studies show that everyone in the apartment building thought somebody else would call the police. The responsibility is diffused. People are helpless in that situation, it's a kind of conical thing. But when you come in from the outside and are fresh to it, the deviance hits you in the face and you're more likely to do something.

Q: And focusing then a little more closely on Specialist Harman and given that you've had access to her psychological evaluation, apart form what you've described from a sociological standpoint, what can you say as an expert about her particular psychological make-up and whether or not that was a factor here?

A: Sure. Well first I want to say that it's striking to me in reviewing her case that on the 23rd of October she did report along with Megan Ambuhl a case of the person who was handcuffed so tight, but she was still at that point fresh into this situation, so the learned helplessness had not set in. So going to the other part of your question about the psychological report, the diagnosis that she was given by Dr. Donovan is Post-Traumatic----

Q: ----and Dr. Donovan is a military doctor?

A: Yes. It's Post-Traumatic Stress Syndrome and also she has what are known as dependency personality traits. Dependency personality, I want to explain and this is confirmed by the psychological tests so I confirmed Dr. Donovan's opinion, it's a kind of personality which is the opposite of sadistic. The opposite of a person without a conscience. The opposite of a person who is aggressive. In other words, in psychology we have what are called character or personality disorders, Narcissism, Sociopath, Sadists, she scored way below the norm of those. There's just no way that she's any of that. Those are the people who we in ordinary language refer to as morally corrupt. Instead she scored above the norm in anxiety, dependency, and depression. So in terms of her profile if she were thrust in a situation like that she would have a more difficult time than the average person in standing up and defying authority because basically she goes along with whatever else is going on. In a good way sometimes too, because one of the other interesting things about dependency personality and I think this jives with everything I seen about her helping with children and so forth. In a good social environment they are very helpful because they want to make people happy.

Q: And did you—does that—how does that relate to the testimony, I think someone testified in the findings case that she was more suitable in being a relief worker than a soldier?

A: Yes, that struck me very powerfully when Sergeant Jones said that because I agree with that. In the psychiatric literature somebody with a dependency personality traits, because they want to please others, because they want to make people happy, because they basically go along with things, I mean they would be perfectly suited for trying to bring joy and happiness to others. But they're unsuited when the situation is deviant because they don't have that something inner that makes them be able to stand up and say—well this is very difficult for them. I think it was easier for her in the beginning, but then becomes even more difficulty for an average person to stand up to.

Q: As an expert then you are able to give any insight to the court members with respect to the picture, which they have in evidence that shows the pyramid with naked bodies and Sabrina Harman smiling in that situation?

A: Yes. Basically it's not a sadistic smile. It is not the smile of somebody without a conscience who is enjoying it and I'm basing this on my knowledge of psychology. It is a smile of somebody who is pretending to go along because they are afraid.

...

A: ... based on my knowledge, based on the test, based on the circumstances interpret that smile as one of learned helplessness and dependency ...

...

Q: Dr. Mestrovic, I want to go back and rephrase some of the questions that I asked you a moment ago.

A: Okay.

Q: First of all, as an expert—can an expert—based on—can as psychological test of a particular individual whether it was Sabrina Harman or not and then having the type of photo that we have, that existed with this pyramid and the context of what happened at Abu Ghraib, what are the range of possibilities to explain why a person might be smiling such as Sabrina Harman is smiling in that picture?

A: There's a full range, ranging from sadism to random smiling, to feeling helpless to other possibilities.

Q: Based on the psychological test that you've examined would that smile be consistent with sadism?

A: No.

Q: Why?

A: Because those test results are unambiguously clear that she does not have the character disorder of sadism.

Q: Now as an expert you can't sit before these members and say what—in fact, why she was smiling or what was going on in her head at that time, can you?

A: Correct, I cannot.

Q: Could it be consistent also with this learned helplessness that you described earlier from a sociological standpoint?

A: Yes.

Q: And why do you say that?

A: Because what, again, what those tests showed is that she scores very high in anxiety, depression, and dependency, all of which would be consistent with —whether we're talking about her or anybody else, with somebody smiling in a situation that is very uncomfortable as a way to try to please others or to just get along.

Q: And in terms of this concept of learned helplessness you—I mean we're talking about a very short timeframe. And you talked about how she did report something on the 23rd of October and now we're down to the—just the 7th of

November. Is it possible for something like learned helplessness to develop in such a short period of time?

A: Yes, learned helplessness can occur almost immediately and it can sometimes take months or years depending on the situations and also depending on the personality and temperament of the individual.

...

(May 17, 2005, SHCM)

Chapter 5

The Fallgirls of Abu Ghraib:
Feminist Analyses and the
Importance of Context

I believe that SPC Harman is in one photo. It is more serious to kill someone than to take a picture.

> Civilian Defense Attorney, Frank Spinner, June 24, 2004, SHA32

Numerous credible witnesses have testified that SPC Harman at no time physically assaulted any detainees.[1]

> Major Gary L. Carson, 89th Military Police Brigade, Victory Base, Iraq,
> appointed as Article 32 Investigating Officer

Fall.girl (noun . slang)
1. A fallgirl is a person of feminine gender who is used as a scapegoat or easy victim to take the blame for someone else's actions. **2.** An individual said to "take the fall" in terms of responsibility for someone else's actions.

Some of the resent feminist scholarship surrounding the abuse at Abu Ghraib is really exciting to read, while other analyses I find problematic in that their examination unfairly and without evidence, and only mere speculation, blame and scapegoat the women of Abu Ghraib, and specifically Sabrina Harman and Lynndie England. We are all familiar with the now infamous photographs of abuse of prisoners under the care of American soldiers at Abu Ghraib prison in Iraq of 2003. Some of these photographs did indeed show both Harman and England. Given these images, it is easy to jump to conclusion and to assume that these women are guilty of prisoner abuse, which is what much of the larger culture did, as well as the military, which leads to additional cover-ups of power structures and forces at work here. However, it is always best to remember that images themselves have *contexts* within which they are taken, and rarely do photographs capture entire settings and situations.

When preparing for the separate trials of England and Harman, I read many reports and one of them was the Fay report. In this report there was mention of gender as a means for analysis, and this is the only government report that

---

1   This was stated in response to the government's attempt to charge Harman with assault by battery in the report by the investigating officer (MEMORANDUM AFVP-S3-OPS, July 7, 2004)

does make this a descriptor for examination. In fact, there are several places where it is pointed out that gender is used as torture when certain acts of interrogation take place in front of females, or that female soldiers did certain acts to prisoners. Sjoberg (2007) rightly points out that the Fay Report does show that gender matters when discussing sexual torture and this is evidence that our government considers gender partially important when analyzing war crimes—a connection that I think is both relevant and critically important when discussing and understanding the events associated with Abu Ghraib. Indeed, "The absence of gender in the policy response to the torture at Abu Ghraib is in itself a gendering of international policy" (Sjoberg 2007). I have been perplexed about this same lack of concern about gender within government reports as well. However, I am worried that many are quick to judge both England and Harman in terms of the Fay report, forgetting that this report was written before the trials as a means of "looking into" what was going on at Abu Ghraib. Wording such as "may have been involved" and "could have been involved" are used, and it is possible that some viewed these as *fact*, immediately making the leap that these women are *guilty*, or that the reports were referring to *England and Harman* simply because they mention the word '*woman.*'

Additionally, all of the pictures of abuse were shown at the trials and made available to the defense council, and under no circumstance were there any photographs of abuse showing either of these women physically abusing prisoners (jumping on, forcing masturbation, hitting, etc.) as the Fay Report seems to indicate with the conjectures "may" or "could." Furthermore, if this were the case, as the Fay Report maintains, then surely the prosecutor would have mentioned this in his arguments in either of these trials, as he was the same prosecutor (Christopher Graveline) for both Lynndie England's and Sabrina Harman's separate courts-martial. He did not mention this report in terms of either of these women abusing prisoners, nor did he refer to any photographs of abuse that this report mentions. Additionally, reading through the entire court transcript, the prosecutor did not refer to the Fay Report as evidence for his case at all.

Some of the feminist analyses of abuse claim that *most of the leaked abuse photographs* were taken on Sabrina Harman's camera (Sjoberg 2007), and that this somehow vilifies Harman to a greater extent. However, this line of argument fails to consider the fact that many of the images of abuse from Harman's camera and from other cameras at Abu Ghraib were not and have not been released to the public. Indeed, after viewing the images from the cameras at the trials, many of the cameras captured *exactly the same images* of abuse and at the same identical times, as explained and shown in the courts-martials by an expert military forensic analyst. What is more, this could have been part of Harman's plan given her letter to her wife, a trial exhibit, which disclosed that she was documenting everything she could of her experiences at Abu Ghraib so as to be a whistle-blower to this abuse. Additionally, the images on all of these cameras confiscated at Abu Ghraib contained images of things that were far-reaching and opposed to abuse at all—things such as pictures of children in the

Figure 5.1   Graffiti in Iraq

Source: Photograph provided courtesy of the author.

city of Al Hilla, towns and houses, regular life in Iraq, countryside, graffiti, and everyday functioning—not just torture, and not just Tier 1A and 1B.

Many do not know that Harman and some of her fellow soldiers demanded that they took photographs at Abu Ghraib in order to document the abuse that they were experiencing and also to protect themselves (see Harman's letter to Kelly, an exhibit in her courts-martial). In this way, the act of photographing abuse constituted whistle blowing, and even though the media and prosecution framed this as abuse and torture. Although it is true that the very act of taking photographs of prisoners violates the Geneva Conventions, this human rights standard was not used at the trials to understand the deviance. Instead, prisoners were considered PUCs (persons under control) or called "detainees" at both Abu Ghraib and the courtroom at Fort Hood, and were not called prisoners of war, who would be protected by law under the Geneva Conventions. The Army, as an alternative, used the Uniform Code of Military Justice (UCMJ) as the standard by which to interpret the abuse legally, and thus "framed" the photography and other prosecuted acts at Abu Ghraib in the following ways: dereliction of duty, maltreatment, and conspiracy.

What is more, the government did not use the word "torture" at the courts-martials, most of all because various memoranda defined torture in ways that contradicted both the Geneva Conventions and also the Convention Against Torture, effectively making the concept of torture a postmodern fiction, or at the very least problematic, confusing and inconsistent as a concept (see Falk,

Figure 5.2   Harman with Iraqi family

Source: Photograph provided courtesy of the author.

Figure 5.3   Children in Iraq

Source: Photograph provided courtesy of the author.

Figure 5.4   Harman with women and children

Source: Photograph provided courtesy of the author.

Genzier and Lifton 2006). Instead, there was a social construction of reality (Berger and Luckmann 1966) with regard to the deviance, crimes, etc. that took place at Abu Ghraib, and the government used the term 'abuse' to capture what others might term "torture" (Caldwell and Mestrovic 2008).

Maternal Sabrina and Friendships

Reflecting on the courts-martial of Sabrina Harman, she was described to the panel (jury) as a *maternal caregiver*. According to all of the sworn affidavits and testimony, she had not hit anyone, she did not yell at anyone, she did not engage in any behavior that was termed "sexual and physical abuse" (forced masturbation, forced sexual positions, assault, etc.) at Abu Ghraib. (In fact, she pled not guilty to all charges at her courts-martial.) Instead, she made sure that prisoners had their eyeglasses and medicine, she got some of them blankets and food, and she reported some of the abuse she saw, albeit to no avail (Caldwell and Mestrovic 2008). Many people do not know these facts about Sabrina Harman.

Within the courtroom, the archetype of "maternal Sabrina" was vivid in the life-sized photographs of Harman at Al Hilla, another military compound in Iraq,

Figure 5.5   "Sabrina! Sabrina!"

Source: Photograph provided courtesy of the author.

where she was shown with families drinking chai tea and always surrounded by Iraqi children.

Says Captain Reese, Commander of the 372nd Military Police, "A lot of the Iraqi kids liked her and she was very well known by the Iraqis. We would go to the substation that she was working at and I would see her with the kids. She had a good relationship with the Iraqi national. The locals would be happy to see her, yelling 'Sabrina, Sabrina, Sabrina.' If she was not there, they (Iraqis) would ask where she was" (June 24, 2004, SHA32).

Harman was not seen as a soldier in the courtroom or in Iraq. Testimony revealed that her "job" at Abu Ghraib was to be a "gofer"—to get coffee and sandwiches for male soldiers, and to carry out menial tasks with regard to prisoners. Instead, Harman was repeatedly described as a caregiver, a motherly individual, and even by her commanding officer. Said Sergeant Robert Jones, "She would have been better suited as a relief worker as opposed to being a soldier … because she was exceptionally nice to the Iraqis … put them first above us, I mean she was just very concerned with the children and their living conditions and getting along with them as opposed to being a soldier" (May 13, 2005 SHCM).

Master Sergeant Bryan Lipinski echoed Jones' sentiment regarding Harman and stated that the local Iraqis would "never forget Sabrina." Lipinski spent quite a lot of time with Harman when she was a gunner driver at Al Hillah, and further claimed in testimony, "It kind of surprises you how, you know, certain individuals really made a significant impact on the community … and no matter where you went … people knew her, they recognized her, they called her by name. She would, you

Figure 5.6   Harman and Iraqi female friend

Source: Photograph provided courtesy of the author.

know, stop the truck or if she was to stop the truck children always come around her and she'd give them candy or stuff and it was just—you could tell that she had been in the community quite a bit … If they saw Army trucks … you'd hear them holler *Sabrina, Sabrina*, just when they saw trucks going by … She helped out, you know, families and I know she would take like some of them, you know, health and supplies we had from care packages that came in, she was distributing them to the families. You know, there's, you know, lots of pictures with her with, you know, poor families, Iraqi families, just trying to do what she can make life a little more blessing … It was a very credible impact. She presented a very positive impact, a very caring image, one that I'm sure that, you know, they were a country in need and they still are in need, but they were a country in need at that time and she really filled a lot of the gaps to say this is, you know, I'm an individual that is here to help you and I'm sure she did whatever she could" (May 17, 2005, SHCM).

Even Megan Ambuhl, another MP in the 372nd, commented about this theme of "maternal Sabrina" within her testimonies:

Figure 5.7   "Maternal Sabrina"

Source: Photograph provided courtesy of the author.

> any time we'd stop the kids would come just—you wouldn't see anybody on the streets and then they come like from I don't know where, just the people, the adults, anywhere from the smallest kids to the oldest person. If it was a time when she wasn't around they would be *Sabrina, Sabrina* from the—you know the farthest stretches of our area that we … know. They were wondering how she was doing or why she wasn't with us, you know, where she was and how she was doing (May 17, 2005, SHCM).

In fact, referring to a family that lived right outside of the substation that Harman was close to, Ambuhl stated, "It was a great relationship. Their family would make her food even though they had nothing. Their house was like clay—something you'd see from ancient history books or something, it was almost like a clay hut with holes—their windows was like holes in the wall and there was no window just to speak of. They had virtually nothing, but they would make food to bring to Sabrina for lunch and whatnot and they just loved her. They adore her and, uh, they would bring their infant to her to hold and they would even try to drag her to the house to visit with their family … they just loved her. They always wanted to be around her and spend time with her. Just it was great to watch her play with the kids. When everybody else was tired and just wanted to sit in the shade she was out chasing them, you know, buying them sodas and buying them candy and just having a great time with them … she got with the interpreter that worked with us every day and found out through him what exactly their family needed because they were so poor and she went out with her own money she bought them a refrigerator and food, [crying] clothing. She bought them beds, beds for the kids and clothing for the kids, all with her own money" (May 17, 2005, SHCM).

As stated, there was no testimony at all during Harman's trial that linked her to physical or verbal abuse of detainees in any way, whatsoever. All testimony at Harman's trial substantiated the fact that at no time did Harman kick, yell at, punch, hit, or physically harm any Iraqi detainees. Consider the following samples of testimony as proof:

> I did not witness Harman hit any detainees at any time. (SPC Matthew K. Wisdom, June 24, 2004, SHA32)

> I never saw SPC Harman put a hand on a detainee. (SPC Israel Rivera, B Company, June 24, 2004, SHA32)

> I did not see Harman strike anyone. (PV1 Jeremy Sivits, June 24, 2004, SHA32)

> **Kenneth Davis, May 16, 2005, SHCM**
> **Regarding October 25th event—Questions by the Civilian Defense Counsel**

> Q: Did she [Harman] yell at the detainee? Shout at them? Handcuff them?

> A (Davis): Not while I was there

> **Megan Ambuhl, May 16, 2005, SHCM**
> **Questions by the Civilian Defense Counsel**

> Q: In the timeframe of October to the first week of November of 2003, did you ever hear her [Harman] yell or scream at any detainees?

> A (Ambuhl): Not that I recall, sir.

Instead, some detainees at Abu Ghraib said Sabrina was their sister and friend.

The translated deposition of Mr. Amjad Ismail Khail Kjalil al-Taie was presented at Harman's courts-martial in Fort Hood, Texas in open court. There were connection problems with Iraq via telephone, and so there were several attempts at questioning and translation. Mr. al-Taie (via the translator) claimed that he saw Harman five times weekly and that he had witnessed her with other detainees. Stated Mr. al-Taie, "It was good contact between Sabrina and the prisoners. It was a good relationship. She was very kind to them ... the contact with Sabrina seems to be a good relationship between a guard and detainee ... we have a view of peacefulness of this woman ... [she] did good things. They [prisoners] respect her and, in right, she respects them as well ... one thing is the surgery. He must be taken care of ... they used to give him two doses of medicine and two meals, but she used to help them in giving more doses for the cure and more meals for him. She helps him. She gives him aid—she gave him aid. This is one of the facts that proved her peacefulness with him ... for all detainees not only for him ... she had such behavior for all detainees, yes" (A translated deposition of Mr. Amjad Ismail Khail Kjalil al-Taie, May 17, 2005, SHCM).

Additionally, a second translated deposition from a detainee that Harman interacted with shows the same kind of relationship, namely a *friendship*, existed with detainees at Abu Ghraib. Mr. Al-Habasi Thame Abed Salah stated that he was in prison from October 2003 through January 2004, and that he knew Harman. Says Mr. Abed Salah, "She was good with me and other detainees ... she didn't abuse them in speech or talking to us rudely ... She was a peaceful woman. She didn't abuse any of us ... I tried to express her goodness with us because she has really good things with us. She used to treat us peacefully, kindly, and whenever we ask her for her to do us further, she did it with kind and with gratitude. For example, we asked her, you have somebody who is ill and in need of a doctor, she talked to them to call a doctor. If they are in need of medical, she helps them. If they have need of food or something, she helps them always. So this proves her kindness for us, being a peaceful woman ... She used to talk with us ... she starts to laugh with us, makes jokes with us ... I feel relief, me and other detainees when she had her duty because she's the only one who can hear—listen to us and she can do things for us. Really relief—we feel relief at that time ... During her duties we can sleep ... the reason behind this is because she's the only one that had quiet treatment. She was quiet with us so we feel relaxed and we could sleep after ... other guards do no[t] have such features, they do not have such kindly treatment ... We [the prisoners] refuse any involved for her or any accusation or something because she is the only good woman or good guard with us in many things of her treatment. So I appreciate her treatment with us during that time. We refuse any accusing or any offense to her because she is a good woman" (A translated deposition of Mr. Al-Habasi Thame Abed Salah, May 17, 2005 SHCM).

Further take into account the detainee nicknamed by American guards "Gilligan," who was photographed with the bag over his head and was standing on a supply box naked, with electrical wires coming from his hands, as if waiting to be electrocuted. Defense Attorney Frank Spinner asked in open court, in an attempt to establish this *friendship* to the panel, and to further characterize the nature of the relationships that Sabrina Harman had with Iraqis, "Why was Gilligan standing on the box?"

Spinner then made claims in court that at first glance might sound absolutely absurd, and especially since we were at a military trial that was looking into abuse of detainees. Spinner argued that Harman had struck up a "*friendship*" with "Gilligan" and that he was a trustee of sorts who was cooperative, and helped American soldiers clean the prison, among other things. Spinner stated in court that "Gilligan" and Harman were joking and being silly when he was standing on the box, and that because of the jovial nature of this "*friendship*," there was no way to conclude that this incident constituted maltreatment on Harman's part. Spinner argued that this was a "game" of torture, and was Harman's attempt at complying with instructions to keep the detainee awake all night because he was to be interrogated in the morning. Indeed, Gilligan received no electric shocks that evening, as the wires were not connected to electricity, and this entire tactic was aimed at sleep deprivation. What is more, Private Frederick claimed that he, and not Harman, put the wires on "Gilligan." These were his responses when asked by the civilian defense counsel, Frank Spinner, about that event:

Q (Frank Spinner): I believe in your direct examination you said that you put wire—or wires on Gilligan?

A: yes, sir.

Q: But you did not see Sabrina Harman put wires on him correct?

A: No, sir.

…

Q: The primary point of that was sleep deprivation, correct?

A: yes, sir.

…

Q: … With respect to Gilligan, he was a CID detainee, why was CID telling you to use sleep deprivation type procedures since this wasn't MI?

A: I guess they wanted him stressed out so he could—he just wanted him stressed out so he could speak to him the next day.

Q: So CID felt that they could use these types of activities along with MI?

A: yes, sir (May 13, 2005, SHCM).

Nonetheless, the photo of the hooded detainee was described in the courtroom as a "joke" between friends, as Harman tried to make the situation as pleasant as possible under the circumstances for her friend, and under MI orders.

Overly Compliant England

It is important to know about the initial trial of Lynndie England that took place in August 2005. At this trial, Lynndie England pled guilty to prisoner abuse at Abu Ghraib. In a dramatic move, Judge Colonel James Pohl, the same judge who would preside over all of the Abu Ghraib trials and who is now a judge at Guantanamo Bay, declared a mistrial in August, in the midst of ongoing proceedings. This was due to the fact that England's ex-boyfriend and convicted soldier, Charles Graner, testified that England was following his orders at Abu Ghraib, and thus could not be responsible for her actions of charged abuse. According to the judge, England could not plead guilty and have testimony that she was following unlawful orders at the same time. It was at this first trial that the now infamous images of Lynndie England came into question. Among others of importance was the photo of England holding a leashed detainee who had been supposedly dragged out of the cell with a belt around his neck. This detainee was nicknamed by American soldiers Gus.

Several soldiers described "Gus" as a prisoner. At England's trial Sergeant Joyner stated that "Gus" made a long lasting impression on him as he was a difficult detainee in that he refused to wear clothing, and was complicated to take out of his cell since he would fight everyone who would try to remove him. Additionally, Joyner stated that he was highly disruptive and that he "just ain't right."

Graner testified at England's second trial as well, arguing this time that the use of the belt to extract prisoners from cells was a legitimate technique for detainee handling, stating that it was *he* who used the belt to extract "Gus" from his cell. Graner stated under oath that "Gus" was laying on the floor of the isolation cell with his head by the cell door and that he wanted to get "Gus" out of the cell without entering the cell. (It was known by the soldiers that entering detainee cells was dangerous, as this was their environment. "Control, secure, and move." This is how a soldier safely relocates a detainee, and MI needed Gus' cell.) Additionally, Graner claimed that he made England and Ambuhl wait there with him incase "Gus" became violent and as back up. Graner confirmed that *he, not England*, had actually looped the leash around Gus' shoulders and body in an attempt to "coax" him out of the cell, and that it slipped up around the prisoner's neck as *he, not England*, attempted to remove "Gus" from the cell. After the tether, which was actually a rifle strap or sling, moved to "Gus'" neck, "Gus" actually crawled out of the cell on all fours and once out of the cell collapsed onto the ground. Graner then confirmed in his testimony that he handed the tether to England to hold—only after "Gus" was out of the cell, acting calm, and after he exited on his own accord.

Graner, the reputed ringleader of the abuse, testified at England's sentencing hearing that pictures he took of England holding a naked prisoner on a leash at Abu Ghraib were meant to be used as training aids for other guards. In this way, Graner wanted to document *his* use of the leash as an extraction tool (using the least amount of force possible) and means for controlling detainees in a chaotic environment. Graner stated at the England trial, as he cracked a smile, that as junior soldiers they "were on their own" and that "cell extraction was one of the things supposed to be covered in training"—training for MPs which they never received at Abu Ghraib.

One of the important aspects of this situation is how Graner used England as a witness to his abuse. Looking at the Abu Ghraib photographs, *everyone thinks England* was abusing prisoners, but *really* Graner was abusing England. Graner said in his testimony that he asked England to hold the strap while *he* took photos. In typical expressive fashion, England "went along" with Graner's request in order to please him—as this was her boyfriend at the time.

Additionally, England described the events of that evening as follows: "CPL Graner and SPC Ambuhl had said that there was a prisoner named "Gus" in solitude. He was arrested for attacks on Coalition Forces and was telling the soldiers working at the Hardsite that he "hated Americans and wanted to kills us." … CPL Graner then got out a tiedown strap and went downstairs to solitude. He opened the door got "Gus" out. "Gus" was not handcuffed, but he was naked. CPL Graner had "Gus" lay down on the floor and he made a big loop in the tiedown strap. He then placed the tiedown strap loosely around Gus' head and neck. He gave me the end of the strap and took a picture. At any time, I did not drag or pull on the leash. I simply stood with the strap in my hand. "Gus" started to crawl on the floor and CPL Graner took another picture. We then took the strap off of him and placed back in his cell" (January 14, 2004, Sworn Statement of Lynndie England).

Two expert witnesses, Dr. Thomas Denne and Dr. Xavier Amador, regarding this interpretation of England's role in the infamous leash photograph, presented extensive testimony. The gist of this testimony, which considered the context at Abu Ghraib and also England's psychological and social history, was that England had an overly compliant personality and that she looked for power figures to dictate behavior. In this way, she behaved in ways that others wanted her to and did what she is told. Both Dr. Denne and Dr. Amador claimed England had language-processing deficits, and that in interviews with her, she had difficulties ascertaining the meaning of questions. Additionally, Dr. Amador stated that England was clinically depressed and that the environment of Abu Ghraib would further trigger these kinds of depressed thoughts, such as worthlessness, depressed moods, suicidal thoughts, among other problems. Dr. Amador further compared England's relationship with Graner to that of a battered wife or an abused child. Thus, the overly compliant and overly reliant England was a victim of Graner's abuse, *but not a perpetrator, and not even a co-abuser*. Again, England was compliant with her boyfriend's request because she viewed him with legitimacy and as an authority figure. Said Dr. Amador at the England trial, "The result of England's personality trait made her incapable of agreeing to conspire with Graner. She always looked to the social compass for direction … A compliant personality in a context of a relationship with Graner led to her to agree with a sadistic and abusive person." It is this exact importance of social context that makes a difference here in that it exacerbates England's deficits, and also provides an additional interpretation of the photographs of abuse.

When Lynndie England took the stand at her courts-martial, she described feeling grown up, experienced and older around Graner. "He started smoking for me," she said, "He made me feel good about myself." She claimed that she felt that he would lead her to the right things. For instance, she never felt like she wanted to go out and that she had a social phobia; but with him, he wanted her to drink and socialize and so she would go out to dinner. In fact, England told the panel that she had never travelled at all, and that going to Iraq was the first time that she had been on a plane, and that Abu Ghraib was a much bigger prison than she had expected—she had never been in a prison before. Said England, "I hung out there [Tier 1A] because I felt safe around Graner." Once England became pregnant with Graner's child, and even though Graner had all but forgotten her and moved on with his life and married someone else, England stated in her testimony that, "it made her feel good again because he [Graner] was taking care of her again." This shows England's ultimate and deep emotional dependency upon Graner, which experts testified to, and that is visible in her own testimony.

Interestingly, in a recent analysis of the abuse at Abu Ghraib, Barbara Ehrenreich, in the book *One of the Guys: Women as Aggressors and Torturers*, uses an image of Lynndie England at Abu Ghraib to argue *against* the stereotypical characterization of women as caregivers, and instead for a conception of women, England in this case, as able to perform aggressive acts (Ehrenreich 2007: 2). However, what Ehrenreich did not realize is the situation under which the photograph was taken, and thus mistakenly vilified England as acting aggressively instead of as simply going along with Graner's instructions. (In fact the irony of Ehrenreich's statement is that England *does act stereotypically* as a "female" in this situation with Graner, and as stereotypically helpless and dependent.) Moreover, Ehrenreich seems to assume, along with most journalists, that the act of holding the leash in order to please her boyfriend is on the same order of aggressive abuse that England's boyfriend exhibited by punching blindfolded prisoners. Ehrenreich and others jump to unsubstantiated conclusions based upon prejudgments made on the basis of photographs, without considering the social context that was explained by four separate expert witnesses at the trial.

Feminist writer and activist Barbara Ehrenreich argues that the certain naive view of feminism, where women are depicted as caregivers and men as associated with cruelty and violence, has been challenged with the role that women have played regarding abuse at Abu Ghraib prison (Ehrenreich 2007: 4). I agree that this naive view that characterizes women as good and men as evil is shallow and needs revision, especially in feminist theory. Stereotypes are basically generalizations lacking in descriptive power and exactness. But, I might remind Ehrenreich (and other feminists) that what we see in photographs is not always the entire reality. Images have a context, and much like it is important to understand the context women face when formulating feminist and activist agendas, it is important to understand the context of a photograph to really know the truth of the matter. During the courts-martial, what was said in numerous testimony and deposition was that neither England not Harman were the abusers at Abu Ghraib. I agree with Ehrenreich that women can indeed be abusers, and in very small ways in comparison abuse did take place at the hands of women at Abu Ghraib. Nonetheless, this abuse cannot be equated with the perception of abuse given the photographs of detainee treatment at Abu Ghraib.

When England pled guilty on the stand, she told the judge she knew that the pictures were being taken purely for the amusement of the guards. She took responsibility for the photographs that pictured her smiling and thumbs-up, which basically made her *the face* of the Abu Ghraib scandal. Inside information from the defense attorneys was that she made these "admissions" in the hope of getting a lighter sentence, and that by pleading guilty the trial might be over sooner because of the immense stress it was causing to herself, her baby, and her mother. Although England did not abuse the detainee in the photo that shows her with the leash in her hand, and did not pile detainees naked or into pyramids, she *was* pictured alongside these detainees. She *appeared* to be guilty of these actions, but simply appeared in the photos themselves.

Judge Pohl threw out England's plea of guilty and declared a mistrial, and instead entered a plea of not guilty for England regarding a charge of conspiring with Private Charles Graner to maltreat detainees at the Baghdad-area prison. This first trial thus resulted in the scheduling of a second trial in September 2005 for Lynndie England. Conspiracy[2] is one of the most serious charges in the Uniform Code of Military Justice and carries the more severe sentences in contrast to dereliction of duty and maltreatment.[3]

Captain Crisp, the lead defense attorney, expressed strongly his opinion that the judge declared a mistrial so that England would be charged with conspiracy. Captain Crisp was also frustrated by the fact that "conspiracy" is relatively easy for the government to prove—any action that involves the actions of two or more persons can be interpreted as a conspiracy, even if one of the actors *did not intend* what the other or others in the group intended—and extremely difficult for the defense to disprove. To put it another way, "conspiracy" colors the commission of other crimes carried out during the "conspiracy" as being performed deliberately in terms of rationally chosen goals and means (Caldwell and Mestrovic 2008).

---

2   One might argue that the notion of conspiracy to commit an offense requires an agreement (formal or otherwise), or an overt act, to show the covenant of conspiracy. The government must prove an agreement to commit an illegal act in an overt act in the furtherance of that agreement by one of the co-conspirators. The government's theory was that if you were present you were part of this and that the notion of agreement is the joint maltreating of prisoners, which shows the common purpose agreement. According to the government, because there was more than one person taking pictures, this goes to show conspiracy, and an agreement ("overt act of conspiracy") amongst various people, and not just one person.

3   The notion of dereliction is described as failure to protect the detainees from abuse. Dereliction is defined as a failure in duty, a shortcoming, or delinquency. Judge Pohl defined maltreatment in the Harman court martial, saying "Maltreated refers to treatment that, when viewed objectively, under all the circumstances is abusive or otherwise unwarranted, unjustified, and unnecessary for any lawful purpose and that results in physical or mental harm or suffering or reasonably could have caused physical or mental harm or suffering. Assault or improper punishment may constitute this offense. The alleged victim of maltreatment need not be aware of the acts allegedly causing the maltreatment."

Figure 5.8   Military Intelligence Interrogation Shed, Abu Ghraib, Iraq

Source: Photograph provided courtesy of the author.

On the first early September morning of the actual second trial for England, and the day after jury selection, there was much discussion about whether England participated in a *conspiracy* to maltreat detainees. The prosecution argued that she had stepped on detainee's fingers and toes and that with these actions, England was to be understood as *culpable to this conspiracy*. However, as the defense pointed out, England was not bound in any previous agreements to treat detainees in this manner (Caldwell and Mestrovic 2008). For moral responsibility, it was argued by the defense that she did not have this previous agreement for action, also known as "intention" or "motive." So how do we understand England's actions? The answer is *context*. On November 7, 2003, a riot had just taken place and a detainee had just thrown a brick in the face of a female soldier. In fact, live ammo was used to quell this riot because of the lack of rubber bullets. What were assumed to be the instigators of this riot were brought to Tier 1A, and England and the rest of the soldiers were heated, vengeful, and in a word—vengeful!

So how does context play a part in these events? Well, England did not make it a habit of walking up to prisoners and randomly stomping on fingers and toes. This does not excuse what she did—at all—but it does make it comprehensible within a context of events. The only other soldier who stepped on fingers and toes was Javal Davis—and it was not a finger stomping orgy. The stomping lasted 30 seconds at most (that came out in Davis's trial), and Davis and England did not do anything else abusive except lose it for 30 seconds, and out of revenge. (Note: this was *the only* event of physical abuse that England participated in actively at Abu Ghraib.) An additional context of these events is that this group of "detainees" was later abused seriously by Graner and Frederick with the masturbation, nakedness, homoerotic abuse, etc., and England neither gave these orders nor participated in this kind of abuse. The final context of these events of abuse at Abu Ghraib actually have nothing to do with this night of abuse, but with the fact that MPs at Abu Ghraib were ordered to "soften up" detainees for further interrogation purposes. This is nothing compared to the real, brutal, premeditated torture techniques the CIA, OGA and civilian contractors were using daily at Abu Ghraib, not at Tier 1A or 1B, but in the wooden sheds outside the main building.

After a lengthy discussion, Judge Pohl upheld his previous ruling that England had not made an agreement prior to these overt acts, and therefore could not have entered a plea of guilty, although she could still be tried for conspiracy to commit these acts. In this way, England's "going along" with the actions of abuse led to her charge of conspiracy. Many journalists at the England trial found these lengthy, intricate legal arguments concerning responsibility and conspiracy boring and incomprehensible, and on many days of the trial were gone by lunch. As a rule, the journalists did not see England as a "conspirator," or truly capable in this regard. However, journalists disliked her intensely—and made no effort to hide this fact—they labeled her privately as a "slut," "bad girl," "tomboy," and other emotionally-based stereotypes (Caldwell and Mestrovic 2008).

I am sure that these same kinds of stereotypes were used by the panel (jury) to describe England, although either behind closed doors or even within their own heads perhaps, as many of the photos that the panel saw of England and Graner depicted them in compromising sexual positions. Many photographs that were not leaked to the public included naked photos of England posing for Graner or of both of them actually having sex together. It could be for this "offensive" reason that England was given more time in prison than Harman, as the UCMJ rule of no sex in the military (something England was not charges with) was broken. England was not seen as a soldier, and instead was viewed as a sexualized object. (England was given three years and Harman six months, reduced to three months.)

However, it was not only England and Graner, and the prisoners themselves, who were photographed in sexualized positions in the unleaked photographs of Abu Ghraib. In reality, other male and female soldiers were also shown in sexualized poses, although not actually having sex and fully clothed, and joking around. Many unseen photographs depict soldiers humping each other, posing in positions similar to the ones the prisoners were forced into, with female guards simulating fellatio with male guards using fruit, or male guards simulating anal sex with other male guards. Other photographs show male and female guards in sexual position, or sleeping soldiers with other soldiers exposing their penises in silly pictures over them, as if to shock them once they are awake. The point of even mentioning these photographs is to show that the environment at Abu Ghraib, and I argue the larger social environment of the U.S. military, is hyper-sexualized in nature with more of the same kind of masculinist and homoerotic behavior throughout. I have even see this kind of behavior in other trials I have worked on, for example Jeremy Morlock's trial out of Afghanistan, where photographs of men "tea-bagging" each other were prevalent, or where the use of guns pointed at each other mimicking the phallus/power was seen in photos of soldiers. Hence, this kind of behavior seems to be widespread within the military and not just at Abu Ghraib.

Just the Facts, Ma'am

What is interesting when considering the torture at Abu Ghraib is that this torture was ordered and orchestrated by male soldiers in an attempt to reify the masculine role of power. The pyramid, simulated fellatio, nakedness, and the leash—all of these abuses can be understood as means to create the masculine position of power over detainees. In his testimony, expert witness Stjepan Mestrovic distinguished sharply between the "passive" abuse committed by England and Harman, who did not hit anyone and were guilty primarily of posing in photos and taking photos, versus the "active" kicking, punching, organizing of and physical violence exerted by male soldiers upon prisoners. In the one case where a female (Harman) wrote on a male, it was the misspelled word "rapist," which in our culture mostly denotes the perpetration of male violence against women (although male rape is underreported, and lesbian rape is on the rise). This can be understood as a cultural message or symbolic, where war itself can be understood as an extension of rape—a theme that an American woman can easily identify with, given the nature of the crime against women.

However, at Abu Ghraib, there was some confusion about if writing on bodies constituted a crime. What is now known because of sworn testimony in the court cases concerning the detainee abuse is that the written on detainee actually did not commit the crime of rape, and was subsequently beaten as a result of this label. The defense counsel claimed, "Again the detainee was hooded, he didn't know what was being written on his leg. Detainees were written on all the time, Your Honor, this was common practice. Detainees were written on—numbers were written on them, their acts or their convictions or allegations were written on them too ... because it, in fact, could go to the protection of the female MPs ... I would submit that because it was done for a legal reason it's not maltreatment" (December 4, 2004, SHCM). Private Ivan Frederick also agreed that the use of writing on the body was common for identifying crimes in his testimony, and stated that seven prisoners were identified once for having a "shank" through the marking of their bodies with the word "knife" on their hands. Megan Ambuhl also stated that, "MI had written on different detainees to separate them so that we wouldn't confuse them from each other" (May 16, 2005, SHCM). Finally, Jeremy Sivits stated that, "SPC Harman told me that she did not think it was bad to write rapist on the leg of the detainee. The detainee was identified as a rapist on his processing sheet ... When we were coming back from leave SPC Harman told me that she was taking pictures of the detainees to document the abuse" (June 24, 2004, SHA32). In this way, the defense as well as the testimony at the trials established the commonplace marking on prisoners as a way of identification within the prison itself, regardless if it was "rapist" that was being written or not. In fact, one reason the defense attorney claimed that it might be necessary to mark on a detainee was to protect female MPs from violent criminals, and thus for legal reasons, and hence Harman's actions would not count as a crime.

However, some feminists outright claim, "At Abu Ghraib, there were three women soldiers who sexually abused prisoners, and who appeared to take great joy out of that abuse" (Sjoberg 2007: 96). Further, that "*these women* are the prisoners' enemy from whom they (men) need protection" and that it is "undeniable that they had some agency in their actions. At the very least, they chose to allow their pictures to be taken, to smile for the camera, and not to report the abuse" (Sjoberg 2007). Again, this interpretation of the abuse at Abu Ghraib does not match the facts of the numerous testimonies at the trials of England and Harman, where these women were not characterized as sexual and sadistic abusers (in reality Harman did not abuse at all), and what's more England and Harman did not ever participate in the homoerotic physical and gender/sexualized torture of prisoners. Case in point, there was no testimony at England's or Harman's trials that linked them to the abuse that many suppose they participated in because they see photographs of abuse in which they are photographed. *This means, they were never linked to organizing a conspiracy to torture or orchestrating the forced masturbation, the pyramid, forcing naked men to roll around with each other on the ground, dragging prisoners on a leash, none of it.* Now, this does not mean that they were not charged with abuse or found guilty of abuse. What I came to understand in the courtroom was that social-construction is alive and well, and that "facts" can be manipulated easily in a trial so as to "win." In fact, even the judge was capable of allowing or disallowing certain ways that truth could be constructed given what was allowed as evidence and what was not. So in a way, this discussion is not about changing some stereotyped essentialized notion of women or men by looking at soldiers smiling in a photograph and deducing what happened without asking, well what happened ten minutes before?; instead it is a discussion of facts, pure and simple. (And mostly a discussion about the facts pertaining to questions about context.) Clearly, any feminist analysis of these events needs to take into consideration situational power permutations, facts surrounding the events, and not make speculations about behavior to the point of assigning moral and ethical agency. What is important here, again, is context.

I am also surprised that feminist, activist, and playwright Eve Ensler bought into the "reality" of the photograph of Lynndie England holding a leash that was tethered around a detainee's neck without asking about the context of the picture. Ensler posits that England must have been sexually abused in her childhood and that this abuse must have hurt her in some fundamental manner to make her act this way now. Ensler states "She's been robbed of her self-esteem and went into the military to get some of it back" (Ensler 2007: 18). Ensler argues that within this military, England was able to achieve some level of power and prestige, and that England felt that she had to prove herself within this masculinist atmosphere. Ensler even goes so far as to say, "women's ability to empathize has been so tragically damaged that we [women] are capable of torture" (Ensler 2007: 18). Ensler does not bother with the testimony of numerous expert witnesses who interpreted the leash incident in terms of England's desire to expressively please Graner, and also the fact that she posed for a photo in which she held the leash for a few seconds, and that she did not drag "Gus." Ensler asks the question "I still don't get how you could put a leash on a human being ... I still don't see how putting a leash on someone and dragging them around and humiliating them could ever be right in your brain" (Ensler 2007: 18). First, England was not dragging the prisoner around, and second, the military doctor at Abu Ghraib testified (through a written affidavit admitted into evidence) that the leash was used to control this prisoner under the doctor's orders because the prisoner was psychotic, and the medical staff had no medications or other means to normatively control the psychosis. Ensler sees England's actions aimed at proving herself within the masculinist military cultural atmosphere and states, "She had to out-macho the most macho in order to prove that she was 'one of the guys'" (Ensler 2007: 19). Ensler speculates widely, without investigating, facts, evidence, or testimony regarding this incident.

Regarding the sexual nature of the abuse, Ensler argues that England and the women of Abu Ghraib were acting out their aggressions with regard to abuse that *must have* happened to them. What is ironic is that only men were shown in the courts-martials to be the abusers with regard to the sexual and homoerotic nature of abuse, and thus Ensler's analysis should be instead focused on the men doing abuse, and thus conversely, and according to Ensler, these male guards as having a history of sexual abuse. Moreover, there was no evidence at all that England or Harman had been sexually abused—and this is something the four expert witnesses in psychology and psychiatry automatically considered, and rejected as an explanation.

What is more, Harman repeatedly reported the abuse she saw and to no avail. In this case, a woman did say "no," it is just that her voice was not heard given the masculinist system of value within the military. In this sense, Harman and the other female soldiers at Abu Ghraib were *not* just passive "torture devices" as argued by Kelly Oliver (2007).

What is important to remember is that assumptions regarding single images are dangerous and that images occur within contexts and should be understood in these terms. I was surprised to find these feminists missed this contextual analysis given that most of their own work provides this kind of pedagogical approach.[4] What the problem here may be is that women are being shown in photographs doing things that are out of our conceptual association of women as caregivers—some feminists seem concerned with that issue. However, this is about power, and specifically the power of image, and as feminists we are taught to know about the importance regarding frames of reference and how these are necessary for interpretation of the "facts" of women's lives. Actions take place in contexts and interpretations of the photographs

---

4   American feminists learned the importance of context from the first international United Nations Decade for Women conference in 1975, where feminists around the world gathered and shared their varied contextual experiences.

of Abu Ghraib should not be made without all of the contextualized facts. Otherwise, this is not responsible theorizing or feminist sociological imagining.

The Drive Home

I remember the drive home after both the trials at Fort Hood, Texas. At that point in my life I lived in College Station, Texas and the drive took about two and a half hours, so I had a lot of time to think about and process the events of the courts-martials themselves. I was drained to say the least.

One of the main concerns that I had after the trials was that it seemed that the military was placing all of the blame onto low level soldiers at Abu Ghraib—all of the blame for the chaos of prisoner care at the prison, for detainee "softening up" practices, for things that the soldiers had told me that they were ordered to do, in fact. After sitting in court and hearing that things like The Human Rights Watch Reports, Captain Ian Fishback's famous whistleblowing attempt, and anything going on at Guantanamo (including how their head of interrogations had come to train in interrogation techniques at Abu Ghraib) or Afghanistan was not relevant to these trials, the truth about Abu Ghraib seemed so controlled. In addition, when I saw that no officers were being brought to trial or even called as witnesses, and after listening to expert witnesses speak, well I was concerned that the abuse at Abu Ghraib was not fully being investigated, and especially in terms of the chain of command and command responsibility. I mean, thinking about gender and power, some of the most powerful women in the Army were basically "in charge" of Iraq, and their names were not even mentioned at the trials. I kept thinking that these women surely knew something, or should be at the very least questioned at the trials about what happened at Abu Ghraib in terms of command responsibility: Lieutenant General Barbara Fast, Chief of all Interrogations in Iraq; Lieutenant General Dianne Beaver, Chief JAG Officer in the U.S. Army; Brigadier General Janis Karpinski, Chief of all Prisons in Iraq. All I could think of was Voltaire's quote, "With great power comes great responsibility." What had happened to the responsibility that these women had given their command roles and responsibilities for overseeing the training and running of Abu Ghraib? Didn't the doctrine of command responsibility require that these women know what was going on, and require that these women were also responsible for the actions of soldiers below them? Weren't these generals somehow "in charge" of overseeing the functioning of Abu Ghraib? I mean, especially given their job titles?

It was not until the Levin-McCain Report came out in December 2008 that I was sure that I was correct of my hunch. Basically, the Executive summary report on the treatment of detainees in U.S. custody by the Senate Armed Services Committee, headed by Carl Levin and John McCain stated the following:

Senator McCain said: "The committee's report details the inexcusable link between abusive interrogation techniques used by our enemies who ignored the Geneva Conventions and interrogation policy for detainees in U.S. custody. These policies are wrong and must never be repeated."

Chairman Levin also said: "The abuses at Abu Ghraib, GTMO and elsewhere cannot be chalked up to the actions of a few bad apples. Attempts by senior officials to pass the buck to low ranking soldiers while avoiding any responsibility for abuses are unconscionable. The message from top officials was clear; it was acceptable to use degrading and abusive techniques against detainees. Our investigation is an effort to set the record straight on this chapter in our history that has so damaged both America's standing and our security. America needs to own up to its mistakes so that we can rebuild some of the good will that we have lost."

In addition, Part One of this Committee's Inquiry into the Treatment of Detainees in U.S. Custody was completed on June 17, 2008, and one very interesting section about Lieutenant General Sanchez and the Secretary of Defense became apparent:

> On September 14, 2003, Lieutenant General Sanchez issued the first Combined Joint Task Force 7 interrogation SOP. That SOP authorized interrogators in Iraq to use stress positions, environmental manipulation, sleep management, and military working dogs to exploit detainee's fears in interrogations. In the report of his investigation into Abu Ghraib, Major General George Fay said that interrogation techniques developed for GTMO became confused and were implemented at Abu Ghraib. Major General Fay said that removal of clothing, while not included in CJTF-7s SOP, was imported to Abu Ghraib, could be traced through Afghanistan and GTMO, and contributed to an environment at Abu Ghraib that appeared to condone depravity and degradation rather than humane treatment of detainees. Following a September 9, 2004 Committee hearing on his report, I asked Major General Fay whether the policy approved by the Secretary of Defense on December 2, 2002 contributed to the use of aggressive interrogation techniques at Abu Ghraib, and he responded, *Yes.*

Yes to what, indeed? After reading the Senate Report, things finally made sense. I knew that abuse had happened at Abu Ghraib. Obviously, that was clear. I am not trying to make excuses. But I am trying to show the importance of context, of taking a step back and seeing the bigger picture, of asking questions about things like the following: Who orchestrated the abuse? (What were the standard operating procedures and the rules of engagement?) Who gave orders and within what context? How does power operate within certain environments? How does obedience work within large institutions such as the military? What does a command structure look like? And additional questions about free-choice, and other important considerations, which include context when making analysis.

Conclusion

I want to point to two final quotes as a way of understanding that there was some doubt by even the prosecuting attorney and also the judge regarding the primary guilt of the "rotten apples."

The first quote is made at the Harman case and by the lead prosecutor, Christopher Gravelin in his opening statements. Gravelin states, "It was a difficult mission, these were soldiers who were not specifically trained as correction officers or to work in a prison, *there were certainly leadership problems* and other issues that you would expect to have—that you would expect to create problems in as far as a combat area" (May 12, 2005, SHCM). With this statement prosecuting attorney Gravelin seems to predict the outcome of the Levin-McCain report in that he basically argues for the defense by pointing to the fact that there was a lack of leadership at Abu Ghraib, as well as a lack of training.

The second telling quote comes from Judge Colonel Pohl, and was made as he was giving the panel instructions right before sentencing, and also at the Harman trial. Judge Colonel Pohl says, "Concerning all the charged offenses, *there is some evidence the accused was acting under the orders of a superior.* This evidence has raised an issue of these orders in relation to the offenses I just told you about. *Such an order to treat detainees as outlined in the specification, if you find such an order was given, would be an unlawful order.* Obedience to an unlawful order does not necessarily result in the criminal responsibility of the person obeying the order" (May 16, 2005, SHCM). Even Judge Colonel Pohl seems to be arguing for the defense here with his statement, and by pointing out for the panel that Harman was following illegal orders, and orders from a superior. In this way, Harman was not a rogue soldier who came up with torture techniques on her own, who was conspiring with others to persecute detainees. In fact, looking at the Judge's statement, even he seems to view at least some of Harman's actions as *under the direct orders of a superior*, as the Levin-McCain Report conclusively determined.

This narrative about "seven rotten apples" seems to be one of a plot—a conspiracy so to speak—to scapegoat the low-level soldiers of Abu Ghraib. Sure, some of them did commit torture, and they are serving lengthy prison sentences. But the women of Abu Ghraib, the low-ranking soldiers, England, Harman, Ambuhl, these soldiers were hardly the masterminds behind prisoner interrogation, sexualized torture, homoerotic abuse, and gendered punishment. In fact, court-martial testimony further substantiates these claims. Moreover, the Levin-McCain Report exposes the U.S. government of conspiracy, and even though they were successful in charging both England and Harman with crimes surrounding the prisoner abuse at Abu Ghraib. What is more, even after the Levin-McCain Report, in appeals court these charges have not been overturned, as the Levin-McCain Report has been deemed "irrelevant" within the courtroom and thus not admissible in court as evidence for appeals trial. In this way, and as an attempt to maintain this fiction that the "rotten apples" are solely responsible for abuse at Abu Ghraib, the *Fallgirls* continue to be framed as scapegoats by the U.S. government, media, and some feminists.

Chapter 6
Conversations with Sabrina Harman, Summer 2007

These conversations between Sabrina Harman and myself took place during the summer of 2007.

Did you ever experience sexism or homophobia in the army?

When I was sworn in I remember a large poster about homosexuals not being allowed to serve. I kept thinking I should back out now.

How did you feel when you saw that poster about homosexuals?

Very nervous. I knew I was lying by signing the paperwork saying I was not gay but I really needed to join if I wanted to be a police officer.

In basic training I found I wasn't the only one, in fact there were a number of females that were gay so I didn't feel too out of place.

The commander in my unit came up to me one day and told me my girlfriend was hot. I think this was the first time I had ever spoken with him. He let me know that a soldier, gay or straight, it didn't matter as long as they did their job. I was "outed" by him coming to me. I was not openly gay at first … I'm sure I looked very gay but kept quiet about it.

How did you feel about a commanding officer commenting on your girlfriend like that? Especially the first time speaking to him?

I felt sick because I thought I was going to be in trouble but he quickly made it into a positive conversation.

In Iraq I was out. I only had one soldier look down on me but it didn't bother me.

Can you tell me about this? How did this soldier treat you?

He would tell me his views on homosexuals and why the bible says it's wrong. It's funny how people always turn to that when they can't think for themselves.

In basic training, were there any rituals that used sex or the idea that men are masculine or women are fragile or feminine to describe things? What about the opposite, that women are tough and men are fragile? How were men and women, gays and straights described in everyday life? What were the words and language used? What about in Iraq? Any experiences at all that you can describe?

Not that I can think of. I'm not very PC so stuff like this wouldn't stick in my head. I do remember in the prison that the female MPs were watched and looked over. If I worked in 1A or 1B the handlers would go straight to the male soldier working. If I was to remove an inmate from the cell, I noticed SGT Snider or SGT Cathcart watching from the top tier.

Ok, so would you say this is because females were seen as needing protection? Or as incapable? Or something else?

Yes, it's because males feel they need to protect the females. I really believe in a war zone females become a distraction and can be dangerous.

Were you ever asked about your sexual orientation in the military? Did other soldiers know, for instance, about Kelly? Did you ever face discrimination from any soldiers or leadership for being gay? Were you openly gay to some and not others? If homosexual slurs were made in the military, how did you handle these?

Just by my commander, but he really didn't ask anything he just made a statement. He was a good guy.

I had a very small amount of soldiers that I was around all day long and yes they knew. No issues there.

Gay slurs are always made and sexual comments and actions but it never bothered me.

So what kind of gay slurs or sexual comments? Were there cadences or anything like that which were sexist that you can think of? Anything like that?

Oh no cadence that I can remember. All the drill sergeants were VERY careful about anything sexual including touching on the gay subject. Before I came in there was a drill sergeant under investigation for some kind of relationship with a female recruit (wanted or unwanted … not sure) but the drill sergeants were very cautious what they said or even being around us. I remember getting in trouble, almost daily because I showed "my grill" to one of my drill sergeants it was considered fraternization but I wasn't smiling at him I was breathing out of my mouth. After two months of being put down I found it funny, it was like a game and he became my personal trainer.

Can you tell me the nicknames that prisoners were given at Abu Ghraib and why? Did you have any special relationships with any of the prisoners? Did you like some of them more than others? Why?

Nicknames were given to the prisoners from different soldiers. Graner and Joyner gave them most of the names. Why? Good question. Looking back I now think it was stupid.

Gilligan (Saad) was awesome, he was the prisoner on the box who was NOT electrocuted. He was my age and was involved in a mix up over a soldier's death. He was just really funny. He was let out a lot to help around, just to get out of the cell.

Taxicab driver (Waleed) I favored him from the beginning. He was the first prisoner I saw being softened up so I think in my head I was helping him by giving him things without his handler knowing. I'm glad he turned out innocent!

Shitboy, I think he was not crazy but wanted people to believe he was so he could get sent out of Abu Ghraib. He would smear poop on everything. Poop sculptures. Poop art on the mattress. Poop in bottles. Throw poop at prisoners. I caught him one day making a picture on his mattress with a turd and he looked at me and smiled and had it in his hand. He heard SGT Snider coming and he motioned like he was going to throw it at him when he got to his cell. I said, "No, he will kill you please don't do it." Snider got to the cell and he put the turd down and smiled at me. That's the day I knew he was acting. He knew better.

Did any women prisoners or children have nicknames? What were these? Were any women prisoners raped that you know of? Or have sexual relations with soldiers that you know of?

I only remember one females name, which was Zarah and neither females nor children had nicknames that I recall. I remember being told when we took over and were following the unit we were taking over for that there was an incident with a female prisoner and a soldier in that area (1A/1B). She didn't go into details about what had happened so I don't know if it was rape or consensual. For our unit rape, not that I am aware of and consensual, only what I found out at trial about Frederick and that girl.

Figure 6.1   Harman with family

Source: Photograph provided courtesy of the author.

Can you tell me about your relationships with the prisoners in Tier 1B, the women and children? Can you describe some of these prisoners in detail for me?

I had a few that I favored, I would slip them food and cigarettes. Candy for the kids. Medicine for the sick. In detail, we had females. I didn't really interact with them too much but they were allowed out of their cells and they sat in chairs and talked. The kids in the beginning were allowed out to play games until the prisoners with mental issues and prisoners who were to be interrogated piled into the tier. For the [women's] safety they were not allowed out any more.

What about special relationships outside of the prison, in the city near Abu Ghraib, and what was the name of that city or town? Kids? Families? What did they mean to you? Can you tell me about some of your experiences with them? What do the words Abu Ghraib mean, and who chose them?

Al Hillah. It was about 45 minutes from Abu Ghraib. The people there were amazing! The kids were awesome. They families would give the shirt off their back if you had asked them too.

Figure 6.2   Harman with family and children

Source: Photograph provided courtesy of the author.

There was a family near the Iraqi police substation. The mother made me a lunch that was the best. I sat down with two of her boys and we shared that and the MRE I had. After we were done I walked them home to return the dishes and saw the house had a dirt floor, open windows, no kitchen and there was a chicken living indoors with them. They all slept in a tiny room with almost nothing. I saw no other signs of food, no refrigerator, oven, nothing. She had made me lunch and it looked as if she had nothing else to eat, and she had given it all to me. This is the type of people that lived around there.

What do the words Abu Ghraib mean? It was the name of the town.

In Al Hilla, did you purchase a family mattresses and a refrigerator? Why? What did this family mean to you?

Yes, because she made me that lunch and I wanted to return the favor. They were important to me and I was around them almost everyday for almost three months. I don't know, it's hard to explain without coming off as anti-American. They had nothing and were still happy because they had each other. Their situation seemed horrible but they made it work and never complained about it to me. If I got their kids clothes and small toys like a soccer ball they were so happy while kids in

Figure 6.3   Children in Iraq

Source: Photograph provided courtesy of the author.

the U.S. would be so pissed if they didn't get an Xbox. I don't know, they were just amazing people that I learned a lot from.

What did the children mean to you? Did they stand for something in Iraq?

They made me want to wake up and go to work (in Al Hillah). All I did was play with the kids. No matter where we patrolled I filled my pockets with whatever I could find (candy, toothbrushes, toys) and was surrounded my whole shift. Stand for something? All the kids felt different for us. Not all liked us, so we had to win them over. When we were in the market parked and this kid threw a rock at me and hit me in the side (they have *very* good aim!), before I knew it one of the Sergeants had a bat and was pushing his way towards this kid through the crowd. I jumped down and got to him first and grabbed his hand and filled it with candy and said *sadiki* (friend) and pushed him away into the crowd and he ran. The next time we were there he was the first one I noticed when I got down, and he grabbed my hand and walked me into the market. *My little protector once assaulter*. I think that they stand for what they believe or have been told by adults or how perhaps they are treated by the soldiers. They will be the future of Iraq, good or bad.

Why in the world were there so many women's panties at Abu Ghraib? I mean, they are in so many photos and they are continually referred to at the trials. What is going on here with women's panties?

The panties were there when we got there so I have no idea. Getting supplies for the prisoners was not easy. Soap, shoes, towels, Korans, you name it, it was hard to have the amount needed for all the prisoners that kept piling up. I don't think they ordered them just to put on the heads of prisoners, but then again you never know.

What about animals? Kelly said at your trial … "She is the type of person that won't let you step on an ant, or kill a spider. If there's a spider in the car she will make sure it goes outside the car and let it out. There's several instances where I've been yelled at for wanting to kill the ants or fly, she can't hurt an animal, she takes it in, any stray dogs, cats, anything." What is your relationship with pets? And animals? Dogs? And now?

Just because you are bigger does not give you the right to take its life. Pets are a form of therapy. I think they are much better to be around than people.

What does photography mean to you? Other than capturing images as a means to document and as a whistle-blowing strategy at Abu Ghraib … what other ways do you use photography?

I think photography helps me remember. It forces me to remember. I use photography to help others now.

What about tattoos? What do they mean to you? And, the rotten apple tattoo?

My arm is a half sleeve of Iraq memories. Labeled a bad apple by Bush, I thought it was fitting with my luck number and trial order in the middle.

Can you describe some of the memories of Iraq that are depicted on your sleeve tattoos? Why did you choose these memories to have tattooed? Why are they important to you?

Well... my first one was when I came home on leave in November 2003 and it's of me in a straitjacket with tape over my mouth and eyes wide open, meaning I can't talk about what I was seeing. The next one I got was during my trial was the bad apple. Thanks Bush! A skull with tape over the eyes, means trying to forget what I saw. Another is two girls facing each other hiding knifes behind their backs, meaning don't trust. And two angels, one protecting the other, it's not finished yet. Also a puppet (me) in a prison suit with my jail number hanging from a string controlled by a hand, which is the government. And a peace dove riding a missile with the Iraq colors. Oh, and I did have a tattoo of Saad (Gilligan) on a box but I just had it covered with a gas mask because I didn't want people asking what it was.

Have you experienced stress or depression since the trials and because of the events at Abu Ghraib? How have you dealt with this? How have you been sleeping? How have you been eating? How do you handle flashbacks? Do you have nightmares? Do you have anxiety attacks? Have you seen a doctor for anything like PTSD?

Oh god ... yes. Depression, yes, but mostly fear. Stupid thunder, loud noise, car doors slam ... crowds. I used to be a heavy drinker before I joined and it always made me feel better. I came home got drunk and tried to walk into traffic because I was upset at all the rich houses around me and that it wasn't fair that the kids in Iraq were sleeping on dirt.

I went a few months without drinking then went to a club. Crowds equal fear so I loaded up, I was doing good until some girl came up to me and said you know what, those prisoners got what they deserved. I lost it! Uncontrollable crying. I couldn't breathe and trying to talk to her and make her realize she was wrong ... Poor Kelly had to drag me out of there. Damn PTSD. I can't even be a functional alcoholic anymore!

I sleep like crap. I wake up easily. If there is going to be thunder at night I take sleeping pills so I don't wake up shaking and crying thinking it was a mortar. I've woken up with my gun in my hand before. For this reason I keep it unloaded and pray my dogs will do the dirty work if someone breaks in.

Anxiety attacks ... yes. I have seen a doctor and have gone to group. I have been diagnosed with PTSD. I was on meds for a very short time. They made it worst. Now I deal with it. No drugs. Some days I'm good, others not so good. Hoping one day it will just go away.

How have you made sense of your life since 2004?

I haven't. I'm still trying to find the purpose.

What are some things that give you purpose now? Even if you think they are silly, like unicorns and stuff.

I used to love unicorns. I will have to get back to you on this one.

How has your relationship handled all of this? Seems like a strong couple.

It almost didn't make it. I am 100% different than when I left. Somehow we made it. We're going on 8.5 years married.

What do you perceive your public image to be? Have you had any difficulties with your life since the trials? Like in public or anything like that??

I don't know what people think of me and I think I stopped wondering a while ago. I know what is true, I know the things I witnessed and what the press said about me. I know the truth. The prisoners know the truth. That's all that matters.

What do you think that the army is doing in Iraq? Have you kept in touch with anyone that would lead you to believe that prisoner care is different? What is the situation that you know?

Fucking ridiculous! My unit was sent to Bucca and the big thing now is no cameras or recording devices. You will be courts-martialed. I doubt anything has changed. What went on was policy. It was leaked to the public. Now they are trying to keep it so that will not happen again.

What is interesting is that in some of the cases that I am now working on out of Afghanistan, soldiers are given cameras to document "kills"—as in for what is called a storyboard for reporting to their unit the day's events. This seems out of sync with what is going on in Iraq and the use of cameras.

How do you feel about the recent repeal of "Don't Ask, Don't Tell"? Do you think this changes anything in the military for gays?

Funny, I signed the paper when I went to pride to lift the ban. Do I agree with it? I'm not sure. I should send you some Facebook gay bashing I see all over one of my old Sergeants page. I mean, gay men will never be welcome in the military. My views on gays in the military and females in the military are not what you would agree with. But you know that, we think differently.

Do you ever march in pride parades?

I did my junior year of high school for SMYLE and the next day someone came up to me and said they saw me on the news marching in the parade. I told them I must have a twin! No more marching for me. When I got back I have been kind of anti-gay, not into the whole gay scene like I was before ... I'm not sure why.

How did you handle prison? What was that like?

I did better than I thought I would. Everyone was on my side. The guards and inmates were nice.

Well, what was an average day like?

I was lucky and was chosen to pair up with one of the older inmates and sew nametags on uniforms.

Wake up. PT for 15 minutes. Eat. Go to work. Free time (this is where my obsession for law and order started). One hour free outdoor time. Hello volleyball. Then indoors until it was time to sleep, so we would play games. This is also when I found out I was dyslexic, so no more making fun of Bush.

What do you think about Spinner and Takemura? Captain Graveline? The military?

Takemura is the greatest person alive! I love her to death. I see her once a year. Spinner did a great job. Now, Major Graveline ... I refuse so say anything negative about someone ... he did his job. I wish he did it a bit more professionally.

The military ... I'm glad I'm out. It's not the place for me.

How did people handle sex in your unit? How does the army deal with that or respond to it? What about adultery?

HA! Really! Very funny question. Sex. It is all the time happening with everyone. This is my main reason I think females should not be in the military really.

Adultery, well this is basically a different zip code thing. The wife or husband doesn't have to know.

I was one of the few that did not have sex with someone over there.

What does the Army do about either adultery or sex in the Army?

Nothing, unless they don't like the soldier.

I found it a lot like high school.

Figure 6.4   Harman and some of her friends in Iraq

Source: Photograph provided courtesy of the author.

I know at one time you wanted to work with children, and that there was even a boy in Iraq that you wanted to adopt, yes? Who was he? Has this career goal changed for you?

I wanted to be a cop. Yes this has changed, I never want to have a chain of command again.

His name is Abdella, the greatest little man in the world! He was the cousin of the family that made me that lunch, he lived next door to them. I wanted to adopt him but his family was there. His dad wanted me to and I wish I could have.

I started volunteering with a group that helps children with cancer, so I am kind of working with children.

Did you personally feel violated in any way while witnessing the abuse that was committed in front of you at Abu Ghraib? Like emotionally?

Seeing what went on was draining. I remember laying down at night and tears would pour out until I fell asleep, but I wasn't crying. It was weird. When I would wake up everything I saw and felt the day before was gone.

How do you feel when you look at the photos from Abu Ghraib. Any of them. What is the first thing that comes to mind, or even the first feeling or memory?

Regret. I googled my name one day and I saw an image of a woman and a young boy holding a picture. It was me over the body of Al Jamadi, the prisoner who died in the shower. I started crying. I didn't stop to think this man had a family and now this little boy has this picture of me over his dad's dead body. It was a horrible feeling. I still feel sick when I see that image.

Why were you over Al Jamadi's body? Did you have anything to do with his death?

I didn't realize he had just been murdered until after I was in the photo with him. I was curious at the time, and looking back I find it more on the line of me being an idiot. I don't regret going in there but I regret not being more respectful. No, I did not have anything to do with his death.

After the experiences of Abu Ghraib, do you feel the same level of trust of the soldiers that were in your unit? Has that trust stayed the same or changed?

There are only a few I still trust.

Do you find it difficult to trust people you meet now? Are you more closed off?

I force myself to trust.

If I had it my way I would shut down and live somewhere with no one around.

Closing Statement of the Defense Counsel, Sabrina Harman Courts-Martial, Captain Patsy Takemura, May 17, 2005, Fort Hood, Texas

Colonel Lynn, members of the panel, thank you for your attention over these last few days. I can imagine it has been very difficult for you. And I also ask you to judge this case by Specialist Harman and not by the acts of everybody in those photos and everybody in this case.

The government would like you to say that this case is based on these few photos, but there are many other incidents, many other photos that are involved in this case that the public hasn't seen, that nobody else has seen, that speaks volumes rather who Specialist Sabrina Harman really is.

You heard from Dr. Mestrovic, he explained to you the sociological conditions that existed for how a situation like this could have occurred.

When I first looked at these photos I thought to myself, how could something like this happen---

...

And many other people would have thought that also. You, yourself, might have thought that, how could something like this happen? Well Dr. Mestrovic today gave information as to how something like this could happen. It's not pretty, it's not something that we would like to admit, we don't like to think that something like this could happen to any of us at a detention facility, but it did. We ask you to consider and carefully consider Dr. Mestrovic's explanation. The government would like you to take part of his testimony and say yes punishment is necessary and yet they would like you to throw away all of this other testimony to you and not to consider that and do not consider that. Well we ask you to consider everything.

As Specialist Sabrina Harman sits before you this afternoon, she offers you no excuses. She has read her unsworn statement. To her—it was very difficult for her, this has been an emotional nightmare for her over the last year. That is part of the punishment that she has received in this case. What she has told herself, what she has been feeling the past year is unimaginable. That is part of the punishment that you should consider. She offers you no excuses. She doesn't blame anybody. She has no hatred, no ill feelings towards her chain of command. This is a young lady that just joined the Army and was sent into a war zone. Imagine the fear. Imagine the uncertainty. Imagine the danger that she had to experience every day. Yes she had a great time in Al Hillah. Yes, things were good there. But if the government wants you to, in fact, compare her behavior in Al Hillah and tell you that it was, in fact, the same conditions that dictated her behavior in Abu Ghraib, you know that's not true. Conditions in Abu Ghraib were very, very different than the conditions at Al Hillah. The government wants you to look at these photos and just blame her for everything that occurred in this scandal.

Well we'd like to share with you some other photos that we think really expresses who Sabrina Harman is. Obviously she went to basic training, this is a picture from her basic training . I'm going to share with you photos that she happily posed for and took at Al Hillah with the local Iraqis there.

This is a photos of her and another soldier in her unit and two of the men, the local men that she got to know very well that—who made tea for her and she's particularly fond of chai tea now because of the relationship that she had with those two men. Two men that she impacted greatly. Two men that—who still think of her still as Sabrina, and who had not changed. There are dozens and perhaps hundreds of photos we can share with you, but could only print up a few. Again, the impact she had as she went out on patrol, as she went out into the community. People flocked to her, people asked her—for her by name and that was her reason, that was because of the warmth and love that she has, that she still has for the Iraqi people. You heard from Megan Ambuhl, you heard from First Sergeant Lipinski, she could not go out into the Al Hillah community without dozens of people flocking to her. Without dozens of people flocking to the car and this is the kind of impact Specialist Sabrina Harman, an American soldier, made on the Iraqi people. The Iraqi people that she came to know and love and whom came to know and love her. The pictures in Abu Ghraib are not the only impact that she had in Iraq. They are not the only impact that she made with the Iraqi people and we ask you to remember that.

She had a particular fondness for children because frankly in a lot of ways she's childlike herself in naïveness, in her innocence, in her love, and she wanting to give to people in her innocence and this is why children flock to her. This is why the parents and the families of these children flock to her.

For four months, five months, Sabrina Harman and her unit was in Al Hillah. She got more and more involved with the local Iraqis and more and more involved with the local children and this was, in fact, a peace keeping mission for her. And in fact a good image of the American soldier for her.

Do you see all the smiles on these children's faces, this is how she impacted them. And rather than only judging her for those pictures in Abu Ghraib, we ask you also to judge her with these pictures. Imagine the kind of impact she had over these children who will always think of her the same way no matter what.

She was often invited into the local Iraqis' homes because they trusted her. They trusted her with their safety. They trusted her with their children's safety. They embraced her because she embraced them.

We all know about gypsies, gypsies existed and still exist everywhere, well there's gypsies in Iraq. She again being nonjudgmental, being open-hearted, even embraced the gypsies and they embraced her back ...

We all know how horrid conditions are in Iraq. These children, these families have nothing. She tried to give back, not in terms—not only in terms of material things, but of her heart and that's what we Americans are. That's what the American soldiers are.

Again you see these young, bright faces, it tells you exactly what they're thinking. It tells you exactly what they're feeling for Sabrina Harman.

At times it was difficult for her to even move around because these children just flocked to her as she—as they grew to know her by name. And they may not be able to pronounce Sabrina, but they all knew Sabrina.

Sergeant Jones said before you that, in fact, perhaps she was not such a soldier, that, in fact, she should have been a relief worker instead and that's exactly her personality, a relief worker wanting to care for the underprivileged, the poor.

A sense of play with the children, which is why they responded so much to her and then her childlike innocence.

And in a lot of sense, a sense of maternalism. This is the true Sabrina Harman.

Specialist or Ms. Megan Ambuhl told you about the two that she got to know and their families. Abdellah was one of the boys that she got to know very well.

And Amir, who heard Specialist—and or Ms. Ambuhl testify to you that she went out of her way and actually bought a refrigerator for the family, beds, clothes for the children.

This is who Specialist Sabrina Harman is.

Yes, Specialist Harman did very well in Al Hillah, she did well in representing the American soldier, but that was because she was in an environment where she could do so. Abu Ghraib was not an environment to do so for her. It was the wrong environment.

She takes full responsibility. She gives no excuses. She doesn't blame the chain of command. She does not blame the U.S. Army. She herself takes full responsibility. This young woman, so young, so inexperienced in the Army, takes full responsibility for her charges. She made a terrible mistake in judgment and she wishes she had the strength to have done things different.

But also, she did a lot of good as you see in these pictures. And we ask you to take these pictures back and look at it. We ask you to look at her sentencing book there's many more pictures in there. There's letters from family and friends who could not be here at Fort Hood today before you to testify to you, their feelings for her and of her.

At this point we beg for mercy. She has been punished. She had been in Iraq for over 19 months before she was let go and this case was moved to Fort Hood. Being in Iraq for 19 months is indescribable. That's the only word I could say.

Her lack of life experience was such—despite the fact that she's not 19 or 20, she's 27, but in essence she's not really 27-years-old. She is very childlike. She doesn't have much life experience. She was an assistant pizza—a Papa John's

Pizza Manager. She hasn't had a lot of college. She hasn't been really out into the world. The Army was her first chance to get away from home. She grew up in a farm, not that there's anything wrong with that, but she—her life experience is very small and the Army was the first time that she could have had a lot of life experience out there. A lot of contact with strangers; a lot of contact with authority. For her this is all new.

Dr. Mestrovic explained a lot of conditions to you, we ask you to look at that. We ask you to consider that seriously. We ask you also to understand her personality. This isn't, um, some 6 feet, 250 pound man who is afraid. This is 5 feet 3 inches, 100 and some pounds Sabrina Harman with no life experience who before she went Abu Ghraib had this as her Army experience. This is what she knew to be her mission in the U.S. Army when she got in to Iraq, not Abu Ghraib. She certainly didn't—she certainly wasn't warned about what she was going to face at Abu Ghraib. It was very, very different from Al Hillah.

You heard from Mr. Amjad Ismail Khalil al-Taie as I read the deposition for you. You heard from Mr. Thame Abed Salah Al-habasi as I read the deposition to you. They thought of her as a sister. Not just as a guard that was okay. Not just as a guard that treated them all right. Not even just as a friend, but as a sister. I submit to you that that speaks volumes.

Despite what the government would like you to believe that she treated people atrociously at Abu Ghraib, she treated people very well at Abu Ghraib, and these two detainees, who are still detainees, stepped forward to share that knowledge with you because that is the true Sabrina Harman.

The government talks about punishment and I submit to you the 19 months in Iraq was certainly punishment. The stigma of a court-martial conviction, which she already has at this point, is punishment. To be punitively discharged from the Army is a stigma that she will never get over. To have a federal conviction on her record at this age is something that she'll never get over. To lose a chance of a career in our U.S. Army is something that she'll never get over. To lose her benefits, her G.I. Bill, her Veteran status, and whatever else bonuses that she had earned at this point all gone, never a chance to get it back. Never a chance to be part of our U.S. Army, that is punishment. The punishment that she has basically given herself, in thinking about herself throughout this past year is punishment that none of us will ever understand.

We ask you to look at everything. Look at her inexperience in life as well as the military. Look at what you are really punishing her for, two nights basically, of some photos. We ask you to look at that and give her an appropriate punishment. We ask you, if you want to, feel that it's appropriate, give her a punitive discharge. Take some pay from her, give her a pay forfeiture, give her hard labor, if that's what you feel is appropriate. Give her a letter of reprimand. But we ask you not to give her any confinement. She had endured and has been punished enough. The 19 months that she had to live in Iraq and then the past year that she has to wait for this trial, and we ask you to not go back there only with pictures of Abu Ghraib, but we also ask you to balance that with the pictures of Sabrina in Al Hillah with the local Iraqis and the children. And we ask you for an appropriate punishment and we ask you that it not be confinement.

Thank you.

(May 17, 2005)

Sworn Statements

Lynndie Rana England
Sworn Statement
Baghdad Correctional Complex, Abu Ghraib, APO AE 09335
January 14, 2004
Time: 0347

I, Lynndie Rana England, want to make the following statement under oath:

Around the end of October 2003, I went to the Hardsite to visit with the soldiers working there. When I arrived at 1A/1B Wing CPL Graner and SPC Ambuhl were the only ones there. CPL Graner and SPC Ambuhl had said that there was a prisoner named "Gus," in solitude. He was arrested for attacks on Coalition Forces and was telling the soldiers working at the Hardsite that he "hated Americans and wanted to kills us." CPL Graner has suggested he take a picture of me with Gus pretending to drag him on a leash type thing. CPL Graner then got out a tiedown strap and went downstairs to solitude. He opened the door got Gus out. Gus was not handcuffed, but he was naked. CPL Graner had Gus lay down on the floor and he made a big loop in the tiedown strap. He then placed the tiedown strap loosely around Gus' head and neck. He gave me the end of the strap and took a picture. At any time, I did not drag or pull on the leash. I simply stood with the strap in my hand. Gus started to crawl on the floor and CPL Graner took another picture. We then took the strap off of him and placed back in his cell. SPC Ambuhl during that time was observing. On or about the 24th of October, I went back to the Hardsite to visit again. I got off work at 2200 and walked over to the prison. I arrived at about 2215. Shortly after I arrived SSG Frederick, SSG Elliott and SSG Davis had brought two prisoners from another block to 1A/1B. The two prisoners had supposedly raped a 15-year-old boy in the prison the night before. They were brought to 1A/1B to be questioned about the incident prior to this, MI had told us to "rough them up," to get answers from the prisoners. When they were brought in the prisoners were handcuffed wearing their civilian clothes and had sand bags on their hands. SSG Elliott and SSG Davis had shoved the two prisoners at myself, CPL Graner and SSG Frederick …

On 08 Nov 03 at 2200 I went back to the Hardsite to visit because it was my birthday and I wanted to see the soldiers who worked at the Hardsite. When I arrived at 2215 SPC Ambuhl was the only one on the block. I stayed there with her then at about 2400 CPL Graner and SSG Frederick returned and said that there was a riot at Ganci and they were bringing 7 prisoners over for initiating the riot. Then they arrived they were escorted by SSG Davis, SSG Frederick and SSG Elliott. The prisoners were brought in handcuffs, sand bags on their heads and wearing civilian clothes. They appeared to be exhausted from the riot. When they were brought in SPC Ambuhl and I stayed on the top tier. Everyone else was downstairs pushing the prisoners into each other and the wall. Until they all ended up in a dog pile. They just lay there because they were exhausted I guess. CPL Graner and SSG Frederick told me to grab the camera and get some pictures of them pretending to hit the prisoners. While I was taking the pictures at no time did they actually hit the prisoners. At that time, I went downstairs to get the paperwork. We started sorting through the dog pile of prisoners to match them with the paperwork. We'd get one at a time and stand them up, unhandcuff them and tell them to strip their clothes off. Once we had them all lined up against the wall naked with bags on their heads we decided not to PT them cause they were already exhausted ...

During this whole time various people had stopped cause they'd heard about the riot in Ganci. I can't remember who all stopped by, but they were only there for a few minutes at a time ...

CPL Graner and SSG Frederick wanted me to get beside him and pose pointing at him masturbating for a picture. I really didn't want to get that close him masturbating, but posed for the picture anyway. SPC Harman had returned at this time and she started taking pictures too.

Q: Who is CPL Graner?

A: CPL Graner was the NCO of nightshift for 1A wing with the 372nd MP Co.

Q: Who is SSG Frederick?

A: SSG Frederick is the NCO IC for nightshift at the hardsite with the 372nd MP Co.

Q: Who is SPC Ambuhl?

A: SPC Ambuhl is the NCO of nightshift for 1B with the 372nd MP Co.

Q: Who is SSG Davis?

A: SSG Davis is one of the NCO's for nightshift in one of the other blocks in the Hardsite with 372nd MP Co.

Q: Who is SSG Elliott?

A: SSG Elliott is the NCO who works in the office at the Hardsite who keeps accountability of all the prisoners with 372nd MP Co.

…

Q: Did you observe any acts against female detainees?

A: No.

…

Sabrina Dawn Harman
Sworn Statement
Baghdad Correctional Facility, Abu Ghraib, Iraq APO AE09335
February 2, 2004
Time: 1904

I, Sabrina Dawn Harman, want to make the following statement under oath:

Q: Why did you take the photographs?

A: To show what was going on?

Q: Whom were you going to show?

A: The media.

Q: Why did you want to give the photos to the media?

A: To show what was going on.

Q: What was your intent for the media to do?

A: Make it stop.

Q: Did you tell anyone in your Chain of Command?

A: My Chain of Command was there. CPL GRANER and SSG FREDERICK were there.

Q: Did you try to tell anyone higher in the Chain of Command?

A: No.

Q: Why didn't you report the incidents?

A: Some rumors were going around and I figure they already knew.

Q: Whom are you referring to when you said, "they already knew?"

A: People higher up.

Q: Did you let anyone other than the Chain of Command know about the incidents in this investigation?

A: My roommate back in the states.

Q: How did you tell your roommate?

A: I told her with letters. When something would happen I would write her.

Q: Where are the letters now?

A: At my house.

Q: At anytime did you attempt to stop the incidents in this investigation?

A: Yes, there was an inmate with a messed up hand, I would not let anyone get close to him because I felt sorry for him.

...

Q: Pertaining to photograph with an inmate who appeared to have wires connected to his extremities, who were present for that photo?

A: Myself, CPL GRANER, SSG FREDERICK and another inmate who had a deformity with his hand.

Q: Do you have anything to add to this statement?

A: Yes, I would like to add the following information that was not in my previous statements. An inmate was handcuffed to the front bar gate to the 1A side, behind his back so low that he was bending backwards. No pictures were taken. Further, the inmate known as the "Taxicab Driver," was handcuffed to his bed, naked in his cell with a pair of underwear donned on his head. Another incident with the "Taxicab Driver," was when he was handcuffed against the wall and an interpreter, named "Mike," was doing some karate moves on him and kicked him in the head, which why "Taxicab Driver" needed stitches. "Mike" was not allowed in the Tier again. Pictures were taken of "Taxicab Driver" getting stitches. In addition, a prisoner was handcuffed to his door for almost six hours straight. I uncuffed him with AMBUHL; HUBARD was removed from 1A for that incident. Pictures were not taken. I recall an occasion when two dogs were brought into 1A to scare an inmate. He was naked against the wall when they let the dogs corner him. They pulled them back enough and the prisoner ran to I think Addle and some else, straight across the floor like he was trying to jump in their arms. The prisoner was cornered and a dog bit his leg. A couple seconds later, he started to move again and the dog bit his other leg. The guy ran straight for the door where they tackled him. I ran up and got the first aid pouch, started cleaning him up; STROTHERS came down and we gave him a stitch. Pictures were taken, but not by us. The dog handlers have copies. I know that CID went to my house in the states and picked up the CD, which contains the pictures that were downloaded from my computer in November. But, I also have letters and notes, which I sent home to my friend, which documents all the incidents that I saw. I know she still has them because when I went home on leave I saw letters addressed to her from me, in the nightstand in the bedroom. She keeps everything I send her. Also, if you go into 1A, there are tack marks on the wooden wall, which symbolized how many stitches inmates have received in 1A: Further, MI, CID, OGA, etc. have all been involved. Many of the inmates are now at Ganci/Vigilant that was there during these incidents.

...

Q: What was documented in the letters you wrote to your friend?

A: Whatever went on that day.

Q: Are the letters dated?

A: Yes.

Q: You stated MI was involved. What were the names of the MI personnel involved?

A: I don't know names; I only know them by face. I'm pretty sure them went home by now.

Q: How was MI involved?

A: They were there during incidents and even participated in a few.

Q: How did they participate in the incidents?

A: One of the MI guys took two of the inmates naked down to Tier 3. I saw an Iraqi Policeman who told the MI guy that it was an insult for another man to see another man naked like that. I think there was an interpreter with him.

Q: Who was the interpreter?

A: Not sure.

Q: You stated Other Government Agency (OGA) personnel were involved. Can you name them?

A: No.

Q: How were they involved?

A: They present during some incidents. And as soon as International Red Cross came in, OGA wanted the prisoners to have their numbers, mattresses, blankets and clothes back.

Q: You stated CID was involved. What were their names?

A: Agent PIERON.

Q: How was he involved?

A: He was there during an incident.

Q: Do you recall which incident he attended?

A: I believed it was when the dogs bit the prisoner twice, but I'm not sure.

Q: What was his involvement?

A: He was just watching from the top Tier.

Q: How long was he watching?

A: I'm not sure.

Q: Did make any attempts to stop the incident?

A: No.

Sabrina Dawn Harman

Sworn Statement
Abu Ghraib Prison Complex, Abu Ghraib, Iraq
January 14, 2004
Time: 1420

I, Sabrina D. Harman, want to make the following statement under oath:

Late October/Early November around 12:30 am I was the runner for the night. I went to 1B to get SPC Ambuhl to go use the phones. When I got there five prisoners were escorted into 1A: They were handcuffed and bagged from Ganci accused of starting a riot. For some time they were laying on the floor, I ended up taking a picture of CPL Graner posing for a picture. They went to the wall where they were stripped. I came back in when they were getting into the pyramid. Myself and Graner posed for a thumbs up picture. I went back to 1B, Ambuhl and I got ready to leave, came down the steps and saw one on his knees and the other standing. We left and she returned about 1 and ½ hours later. Nothing follows that night. A man was in the shower of 1B when nightshift arrived. They said he was dead and on ice. He started to defrost and melt outside the shower into the hallway. We got the key and took photos of him. Nothing follows that day. Two females were brought into 1B. I got a picture with both. Nothing follows that day.

Q: During the night of the "pyramid" you discussed above, who ordered the five men to strip their clothes off?

A: I don't remember.

Q: Is it standard procedure to have them remove their clothes when they enter cell block 1A?

A: Yes.

Q: Who ordered them into the human "pyramid"?

A: I left the bottom floor of block 1A when the prisoners were taking off their clothes. I walked upstairs to talk to SPC Ambuhl, and return CPL Graner's digital camera to the office, SPC Ambuhl and I talked for a while and I looked down stairs and noticed the five prisoners were naked and getting into a human pyramid. I then walked back down stairs with the digital camera but SPC Ambuhl stayed up stairs. I then took about two pictures of the naked prisoners in the human pyramid with CPL Graner and SPC England in the photos. I do not know who ordered the prisoners into the human pyramid as they were already getting into the position when I walked back down stairs with CPL Graner's digital camera.

...

Q: After you took the pictures of the pyramid what happened?

A: I went back upstairs to get SPC Ambuhl and when we walked back down stairs the second time, I saw one male prisoner, naked, on his knees with another prisoner, naked, standing in front of him. I was standing by the doorway and the two prisoners were in the middle of the cell block. They appeared to be about 6 inches from each other. I do not think that was right for the prisoners to have to do.

Q: Who was present at this incident?

A: SSG Frederick, CPL Graner and SPC England?

Q: Did you see any contact between the two prisoners?

A: No.

Q: Which dead prisoners did you pose for photographs?

A: One dead man that the "OGA" brought into the prison and one dead man at the morgue.

Q: When did this happen?

A: The morgue incident was in August or September of 2003 and the dead OGA I can not remember.

Q: Did you ever give any order for any prisoner to do any sex acts?

A: No.

Q: Have you ever physically abused any prisoner?

A: No.

Q: Other than what you have told me, have you ever witnessed or heard about any prisoner being physically or sexually abused?

A: SGT Jones entered the room talking about one prisoner on his knees and the other standing above masturbating in front.

Q: Who were the prisoners?

A: I assume they were the same five as before.

Q: How do you know this?

A: SGT Jones just walked into the room I was in and told everyone. SGT Diaz, SPC Brown and myself were in the room.

…

Q: What is the procedure to strip search prisoners?

A: If a female is being searched only female guards can be present. If a male is being strip-searched both male and female guards can be present and can conduct the search.

Q: How do you know, it is standard operating procedure to strip-search all prisoners in cell block 1A?

A: I just heard it from different people.

Q: Have you ever seen this in writing?

A: No.

Q: Has an officer or NCO ever told you this?

A: No officer has and I don't think any NCO has either.

Q: Who told you this then?

A: Either MI, SSG Frederick or CPL Graner.

…

Sabrina Dawn Harman
Sworn Statement
Abu Ghraib Prison CIO Office
January 15, 2004
Time: 1609

I, Sabrina Harman, want to make the following statement under oath:

Q: At what point did you enter the prison area on the day that the seven detainees were made into the pyramid?

A: I got there about the same time as the detainees.

…

Q: Do you know who wrote the word rapist on the one detainee?

A: I did.

Q: Where did you write this?

A: On his right side, and I wrote it with a marker.

Q: Why did you write this on his leg?

A: Because that is what his sheet said he was.

…

Q: Were there any other incidents you were present for when detainees were not treated correctly?

A: There was one event where someone had handcuffed a detainee and the cuffs were not double locked. The detainee was left handcuffed for about 6 hours. I went with AMBUHL to uncuff him. His hands were cold and there were marks on his wrist from the cuffs. SPC HUBBARD was the person who did this. He is in my unit. I think he was written up for this, but I know he was taken off the tier.

Q: Have you any seen other photographs of detainees?

A: I know of some with a female detainee and one of a detainee that is standing with wires on his hands.

Q: What is the incident with the female's photographs?

A: There is one with her and me and I have my thumbs up. She was a thin and blue clothes. I believe she was in for prostitution.

Q: Describe the incident with the detainee with the wires on his hands?

A: He is nicknamed Gilligan, he is currently on tier 3. He was just standing in the MRE box with the sandbag over his head for about an hour. I put the wires on his hands. I do not recall how. I was joking with him and told him if he fell he would get electrocuted.

Q: Who took the pictures of this?

A: I took one and FREDERICK took one.

Q: Why did you do this to detainee "Gilligan"?

A: Just playing with him.

Q: Do you feel it was allowable to do this to the detainee?

A: We were not hurting him. It was not anything that bad.

Q: Was this your idea?

A: Just the wires part.

Q: Why did you have the detainee in standing on the box?

A: Just to keep him awake.

Q: Did MI ask you to do this?

A: Not me personally. They were talking to GRANER. MI wanted to get the OGA to get these people to talk. I do not recall anyone from MI or OGA saying this. I do not recall GRANER or FREDERICK ever saying that MI or OGA had told them to do this earlier.

Q: Do you have anything to add to this statement?

A: No. ///End of Statement///

Bibliography

Works Cited

Abbott, P. and Wallace, C. 1996. *Introduction to Sociology: Feminist Perspectives.* New York: Routledge.

ACLU. 2005. ACLU and Human Rights First Sue Defense Secretary Rumsfeld Over U.S. Torture Policies. *American Civil Liberties Union* [Online, March 1]. Available at: http://www.aclu.org/national-security/aclu-and-human-rights-first-sue-defense-secretary-rumsfeld-over-us-torture-policie [accessed: March 1, 2005].

Adorno, T. and Horkheimer, M. 1979. *Dialectic of Enlightenment.* London: Verso.

Ahmed, A.S. 1992. *Postmodernism and Islam.* New York: Routledge.

Bartky, S. 1988. Foucault, femininity and the modernization of patriarchal power, in *Feminism and Foucault: Reflections on Resistance*, edited by I. Diamond and L. Quinby. Boston, MA: Northeastern University Press, 36-42.

Baudrillard, J. 1981. *For a Critique of the Political Economy of the Sign.* St. Louis, MO: Telos Press.

Baudrillard, J. 1983a. Simulacra and simulations, in *Jean Baudrillard: Selected Writings*, edited by M. Poster. Stanford, CA: Stanford University Press, 169-187.

Baudrillard, J. 1983b. On seduction, in *Jean Baudrillard: Selected Writings*, edited by M. Poster. Stanford, MA: Stanford University Press, 152-168.

Baudrillard, J. [1977]1987. *Forget Foucault.* New York: Semiotext(e), Boston, MA: MIT Press.

Baudrillard, J. [1979]1990. *Seduction.* New York: St. Martin's Press.

Baudrillard, J. [1981]1994. *Simulacra and Simulation*, translated by Sheila Faria Glaser. Ann Arbor, MI: The University of Michigan Press.

Baudrillard, J. [1991]1995. *The Gulf War Did Not Take Place.* Bloomington, IN: University of Indiana Press.

Baudrillard, J. [1995]1996. *The Perfect Crime.* New York: Verso.

Baudrillard, J. [1995]2002. *America.* New York: Verso.

Baudrillard, J. [2002]2003. *The Spirit of Terrorism.* New York: Verso.

Baudrillard, J. 2003. *Passwords.* New York: Verso.

Bauman, Z. 1992. *Intimations of Postmodernity.* New York: Routledge.

Beauvoir, S. de [1949]1952. *The Second Sex.* New York: Vintage Books.

Bejerot, N. 1974. The Six Day War in Stockholm. *New Scientist*, 61:886, 486-487.

Berger, P.L. and Luckmann, T. 1966. *The Social Construction of Reality: A Treatise in the Sociology of Knowledge.* Garden City, NY: Anchor Books.

Best, S. and Kellner, D. 1991. *Postmodern Theory: Critical Interrogations.* New York: The Guilford Press.

Bianco, M.W. and Nicholson, W. 1976. *The Velveteen Rabbit: Or, How Toys Become Real.* Garden City, NY: Doubleday.

Bordo, S. 1988. Anorexia Nervosa: Psychopathology as the crystallization of culture, in *Feminism and Foucault: Reflections on Resistance*, edited by I. Diamond and L. Quinby. Boston, MA: Northeastern University Press, 56-71.

Bourdieu, P. 1979. *Distinctions: A Social Critique of the Judgment of Taste*, translated by Richard Nice. Boston, MA: Harvard University Press.

Bourdieu, P. 1980. *In Other Words: Essays Towards a Reflexive Sociology.* Cambridge, MA: Cambridge University Press.

Butler, J. 1991. *Inside/Out: Lesbian Theories, Gay Theories.* New York: Routledge.

Butler, J. 1993a. Imitation and gender subordination, in *The Lesbian and Gay Studies Reader*, edited by H. Aabelove, M. Barale, and D. Halperin. New York: Routledge, 307-320.

Butler, J. 1993b. *Bodies That Matter: On the Discursive Limits of "Sex".* New York: Routledge.

Butler, J. [1990]1999. *Gender Trouble: Feminism and the Subversion of Identity.* 2nd Edition. New York: Routledge.

Butler, J. 2004. *Undoing Gender.* New York: Routledge.

Caldwell, R.A. 2009. Gender queer productions and the bridge of cultural legitimacy: "Realness" and "Identity" in *Paris is Burning*, in *Co-opting Culture: Questions of Culture and Power in Sociology and Cultural Studies*, edited by B.G. Harden and R. Carley. Lanham, MD: Rowman & Littlefield/ Lexington Publishing, 77-90.

Caldwell, R.A. and Mestrovic, S.G. 2008a. Torture, what is it good for? Absolutely nothing! An analysis of the response to abuse at Abu Ghraib. *Theory in Action*, 1:4, 123-139.

Caldwell, R.A. and Mestrovic, S.G. 2008b. The role of gender in 'expressive' abuse at Abu Ghraib. *Cultural Sociology*, 2:3, 275-299.

Caldwell, R.A. and Mestrovic, S.G. 2010. The War on Terror in the Early 21st Century: Applying lessons from sociological classics and sites of abuse, in *The Routledge Handbook of War and Society*, edited by M.G. Ender and S. Carlton-Ford. London: Routledge, 88-99.

Connell, R.W. 1995. *Masculinities.* Berkeley, CA and Los Angeles: University of California Press.

Danner, M. 2004. *Torture and Truth: America, Abu Ghraib, and the War on Terror.* New York: New York Review of Books.

Davenport, M.M. 1980. The Post-Existential Blues. *Cross Currents*, Spring.

Derrida, J. 1978. *Writing and Difference.* Chicago, IL: The University of Chicago.

Durkheim, E. [1897]1951. *Suicide: A Study in Sociology*, translated by John A. Spaulding and George Simpson. New York: Free Press.

Durkheim, E. [1893]1965. *The Division of Labor in Society*, translated by G. Simpson. New York: Free Press.

Ebony, D. 2006. *Botero: Abu Ghraib*. New York: Prestel Publishers.

Ehrenreich, B. 2007. Forward: Feminism's assumptions upended, in *One of the Guys: Women as Aggressors and Torturers*, edited by T. McKelvey. Emeryville, CA: Feal Press, 1-5.

Enloe, C. 1988. *Does Khaki Become You? The Militarization of Women's Lives*. London: Pandora Press.

Enloe, C. 2000. *Maneuvers: The International Politics of Militarizing Women's Lives*. Berkeley, CA: University of California Press.

Ensler, E. 2007. I still don't get how you could put a leash on a human being, in *One of the Guys: Women as Aggressors and Torturers*, edited by T. McKelvey. Emeryville, CA: Feal Press, 17-21.

Falk, R., Genzier, I., and Lifton, R.J. 2006. *Crimes of War: Iraq*. New York: Nation Books.

Fausto-Sterling, A. 1992. *Myths of Gender.* New York: Basic Books.

Fausto-Sterling, A. 2000. *Sexing the Body*. New York: Basic Books.

Fay, MG G.R. 2004. AR 15-6 Investigation of the Abu Ghraib Detention Facility and 205th Military Intelligence Brigade, in *Investigation of Intelligence Activities at Abu Ghraib*. Available at: http://fl1.findlaw.com/news.findlaw.com/hdocs/docs/dod/fay82504rpt.pdf

Foucault, M. 1972. *The Archeology of Knowledge*. New York: Pantheon Books.

Foucault, M. [1975]1977. *Discipline and Punish: The Birth of a Prison*. New York: Vintage Books.

Foucault, M. 1978. *The History of Sexuality*. New York: Pantheon.

Foucault, M. 1988. *Michel Foucault: Politics, Philosophy, Culture*. New York: Routledge.

Fox-Keller, E. [1985]1995. *Reflections on Gender and Science*. New Haven, CT: Yale University Press.

Fox-Keller, E. and Longino, H.E. 1996. *Feminism and Science*. Oxford: Oxford University Press.

Fox News. 2011. Rumsfeld Memoir Draws Criticism From ACLU Over Abu Ghraib Depiction. *Fox News* [Online, February 3]. Available at: http://www.foxnews.com/politics/2011/02/03/rumsfeld-memoir-draws-criticism-aclu-abu-ghraib-depiction/ [accessed: February 3, 2011].

Fraser, N. and Nicholson, L.J. 1990. Social criticism without philosophy: An encounter between Feminism and Postmodernism, in *Feminism and Postmodernism*, edited by L.J. Nicholson. New York: Routledge, 1-18.

Frontline: The Torture Question (dir. Michael Kirk, 2005).

Gribaudo, P. 2003. *Botero Women*. New York: Rizzoli International Publications, Inc.

Haraway, D. 1991. A Cyborg Manifesto: Science, Technology, and the Socialist-Feminism in the Late 20th Century, in *Simians, Cyborgs, and Women: The Reinvention of Nature.* New York: Routledge, 149-181.

Haraway, D. 1997a. Universal Donors in a Vampire Culture: It's all in the Family. Biological Kinship Categories in the Twentieth-Century United States, in *Modest_Witness@Second_Millennium*. New York: Routledge.

Haraway, D. 1997b. Modest_Witness@Second_Millennium. FemaleMan©_ Meets_OncoMouse™, in *Modest_Witness@Second_Millennium*. New York: Routledge.

Harding, S. 1987. *Feminism and Methodology: Social Science Issues*. Bloomington, IN: Indiana University Press.

Harding, S. 1991. *Whose Science? Whose Knowledge? Thinking from Women's Lives*. Ithaca, NY: Cornell University Press.

Harding, S. 1993. *The 'Racial' Economy of Science: Toward a Democratic Future*. Bloomington, IN: Indiana University Press.

Harding, S. 1998. *Is Science Multicultural? Postcolonialisms, Feminisms, and Epistemologies*. Bloomington, IN: Indiana University Press.

Human Rights Watch. 2005. *Getting Away with Torture? Command Responsibility for the U.S. Abuse of Detainees*.

Human Rights Watch. 2005. *Leadership Failure Firsthand Accounts of Torture of Iraqi Detainees by the U.S. Army's 82nd Airborne Division*, 17:3(G).

Human Rights Watch. 2006. *By the Numbers: Findings of the Detainee Abuse and Accountability Project*, 18, 1-28.

Jameson, F. 1991. *Postmodernism, or, the Cultural Logic of Late Capitalism*. Durham, NC: Duke University Press.

Jones, LTG A.R. 2004. AR 15-6 Investigation of the Abu Ghraib Prison and 205th Military Intelligence Brigade, in *Investigation of Intelligence Activities at Abu Ghraib*. Available at: http://fl1.findlaw.com/news.findlaw.com/hdocs/docs/dod/fay82504rpt.pdf

Karpinski, J. 2005. *One Woman's Army*. New York: Miramax.

Kaufman-Osborn, T. 2005. Gender trouble at Abu Ghraib? *Politics & Gender*, 1:4, 597-619.

Kratochvil, A. 2007. *Homage to Abu Ghraib*. Available at: http://www.viiphoto.com/detail-story3.php?news_id=529

Levin-McCain Report, Senate Armed Services Committee, Executive Summary and Conclusions of Report on Treatment of Detainees in U.S. Custody. 2008. Available at: http://levin.senate.gov/newsroom/release.cfm?id=305735

Longino, H.E. 1986. *Can There be a Feminist Science?* Princeton, NJ: Princeton University Press.

Longino, H.E. 1990. *Science as Social Knowledge: Values and Objectivity in Scientific Inquiry*. Princeton, NJ: Princeton University Press.

Lorde, A. 1984. The Master's tools will never dismantle the Master's house, in *Sister Outsider*. Berkeley: The Crossing Press.

Lutz, C. 1995. The gender of theory, in *Women Writing Culture*, edited by B. Ruth and D.A. Gordon. Berkeley, CA: University of California Press, 249-266.

Lyotard, J.F. [1979]1984. *The Postmodern Condition: A Report on Knowledge*. Minneapolis, MN: University of Minnesota Press.

Mann, J. 2004. Civilian contractor involvement in Iraqi prisoner abuse. *CNN*. 8 September. Transcript: http://transcripts.cnn.com/TRANSCRIPTS/0409/08/i_ins.01.html

Mayer, J. 2005. Can the CIA legally kill a prisoner? *The New Yorker*. November 14.

McCain, J. 2005. Statement of Senator John McCain on Detainee Amendments on (1) The Army Field Manual and (2) Cruel, Inhumane, Degrading Treatment, *Amendment to the Defense Authorization Bill*, November 4.

McKelvey, T. 2007. *One of the Guys: Women as Aggressors and Torturers.* Emeryville, CA: Avalon Publishing Group.

McGowan, J. 1991. *Postmodernism and its Critics*. Ithaca, NY: Cornell University Press.

Mestrovic, S.G. 1988. *Emile Durkheim and the Reformation of Sociology*. Totowa, NJ: Rowman & Littlefield.

Mestrovic, S.G. 1991. *The Coming Fin de Siècle: An Application of Durkheim's Sociology to Modernity and Postmodernism.* London: Routledge.

Mestrovic, S.G. 1992. *Durkheim and Postmodern Culture.* New York: Aldine de Gruyter.

Mestrovic, S.G. 1993. *The Barbarian Temperament.* London: Routledge.

Mestrovic, S.G. 1994. *The Balkanization of the West: The Confluence of Postmodernism and Postcommunism.* London: Routledge.

Mestrovic, S.G. 1997. *Postemotional Society.* London: Sage.

Mestrovic, S.G. 2003. *Thorstein Veblen on Culture and Society.* London: Sage.

Mestrovic, S.G. 2005. *From the Hague to Abu Ghraib and Guantanamo: A Cultural Analysis of International Law Pertaining to Crimes of War.* Presented at the American Sociological Association Annual Meeting, Summer 2005, Philladelphia, PA.

Mestrovic, S.G. and Caldwell, R.A. 2006. *Analyzing the Role of Gender in an Abu Ghraib Courts-Martial.* Presented at the American Sociological Association Annual Meeting, Summer 2006. Montreal, Canada,

Mestrovic, S.G. 2007. *The Trials of Abu Ghraib: An Expert Witness Account of Shame and Honor.* London: Paradigm Publishers.

Mestrovic, S.G. and Caldwell, R.A. 2010. Durkheim's concept of *dérèglement* retranslated, Parson's reading of Durkheim re-parsed: An examination of post-emotional displacement, scapegoating and responsibility at Abu Ghraib, in *Durkheim and Violence*, edited by S.R. Mukherjee. Chichester: Wiley-Blackwell and UNESCO, 139-158.

Milgram, S. 1963. Behavioral Study of Obedience. *Journal of Abnormal and Social Psychology*, 67: 371-378.

Nestle, J. 1984. The fem question, in *Pleasure and Danger: Exploring Female Sexuality*, edited by C.S. Vance. London, UK: Pandora Press, 232-241.

Nicholson, L. 1990. *Feminism and Postmodernism.* New York: Routledge

Oliver, K. 2007. *Women as Weapons of War: Iraq, Sex and the Media.* New York: Columbia University Press.

Oudshoorn, N. 1991. *The Making of the Hormonal Body*. Netherlands: Vanderdav Studio.

Paris is Burning (dir. Jennie Livingston, 1991).

Parsons, T. [1937]1949. *The Structure of Social Action*. Glencoe, IL: Dorsey Press.

Parsons, T. 1951. *The Social System*. Glencoe, IL: Free Press.

Parsons, T. 1954. The kinship system of the contemporary United States, in *Essays in Sociological Theory*, edited by T. Parsons. New York: Free Press, 189-194.

Parsons, T. and Bales, R. 1955. *Family, Socialization, and Interaction*. Glencoe, IL: Free Press.

Quiet Rage: The Stanford Prison Study (dir. Ken Musen and Philip G. Zimbardo, 1991).

Rich, A. 1980. Compulsory heterosexuality and lesbian existence. *Signs: Journal of Women in Culture and Society*, 5:4, 631-660.

Riesman, D. [1953]1995. *Thorstein Veblen* (introduction by Stjepan G. Mestrovic) New Brunswick, NJ: Transaction Publishers.

Riesman, D. [1961]2000. *The Lonely Crowd*. New Haven, CT: Yale University Press.

Ritzer, G. 1993. *The McDonaldization of Society*. London: Pine Forge Press.

Ritzer, G. 2003. Rethinking globalization: Glocalization/grobalization and something/nothing. *Sociological Theory*, 21:3.

Ritzer, G. 2004. *The McDonaldization of Society: Revised New Century Edition*. Thousand Oaks, CA: Pine Forge Press.

Rojek, C. 1995. *Decentering Leisure: Rethinking Leisure Theory*. London: Sage.

Rorty, R. 1989. *Contingency, Irony, and Solidarity*. Cambridge, MA: Cambridge University Press.

Rosenau, P.M. 1992. *Postmodernism and the Social Sciences: Insights, Inroads, and Intrusions*. Princeton, NJ: Princeton University Press.

Rubin, G. 1984. Thinking sex: Notes for a radical theory of the politics of sexuality, in *Pleasure and Danger: Exploring Female Sexuality*, edited by. C.S. Vance. London: Routledge, 267-319.

Rubin, G. [1975]2002. The traffic in women: Notes on the "Political Economy of Sex." *Philosophy of Feminism Reading Packet*, Dr. A. Sowaal, Lubbock, TX: Texas Tech University. Fall 2002.

Rumsfeld, D. 2011. *Known and Unknown: A Memoir*. New York: Sentinel.

Said, E.W. 1978. *Orientalism*. New York: Pantheon.

Sartre, J-P. [1938]1964. *Nausea*. New York: New Directions Publishing Corporation.

Sarup, M. 1993. *Post-Structuralism and Postmodernism:* Second edition. Athens, GA: The University of Georgia Press.

Sawicki, J. 1994. Foucault, Feminism, and questions of Identity, in *The Cambridge Companion to Foucault*, edited by G. Gutting. Cambridge: Cambridge University Press, 193-214.

Schlisinger, Hon. J.R. 2004. *Final Report of the Independent Panel to Teview DoD Detention Operations, Schlesinger Report.* Available at: http://www.npr.org/documents/2004/abuse/schlesinger_report.pdf.

Sedgwick, E.K. 1990. *Epistemology of the Closet.* Berkeley, CA: University of California Press.

Shumway, C. 2004. Systematic pattern of rape by U.S. forces. *Znet* [Online, 6 June]. Available at: http://www.zcommunications.org/systematic-pattern-of-rape-by-us-forces-by-chris-shumway [accessed: June 6, 2004].

Sjoberg, L. 2007. Agency, Militarized Femininity and Enemy Others. Observations from the War in Iraq. *International Feminist Journal of Politics*, 9:1, 82-101.

Sontag, S. 2004. Regarding the torture of others. *The New York Times Magazine*, May 23.

Strasser, S. and Whitney, C.R. (eds). 2004. *The Abu Ghraib Investigations: The Official Independent Panel and Pentagon Reports on the Shocking Prisoner Abuse in Iraq.* New York: Public Affairs, Persus Book Group.

Terry, J. 1999. *An American Obsession: Science, Medicine, and Homosexuality in Modern Society.* Chicago, IL: The University of Chicago Press.

Taguba, MG Antonio. 2004. *Article 15-6 Investigation of the 800th Military Police Brigade of Abu Ghraib Prison, Taguba Report.* Available at: http://www.agonist.org/annex/taguba.htm

Taibbi, Matt. 2005. Ms. America. *Rolling Stone*, October 20, 47-48.

The Human Behavior Experiments (dir. Alex Gibney, 2006).

U.S. Department of the Army. 1987. *Army Operations Field Manual on Intelligence and Interrogation,* FM-34-52.

Vance, C.S. 1984. Pleasure and danger: Towards a politics of sexuality, in *Pleasure and Danger: Exploring Female Sexuality*, edited by C.S. Vance. London: Routledge, 1-27.

Veblen, T. [1899]1994. *Theory of the Leisure Class.* New York: Penguin Books.

Zagorin, A. 2005. Haunted by the 'Iceman'. *Time*, November 21.

Zimbardo, P.G. 1971. The power and pathology of imprisonment. Hearings Before Subcommittee No. 3, of the Committee on the Judiciary, House of Representatives, Ninety-Second Congress, *First Session on Corrections, Part II, Prisons, Prison Reform and Prospner's Rights: California. Congressional Record*, serial no. 15, Washington, D.C.: U.S. Government Printing Office, 10-25, October 25.

Zimbardo, P.G. 1972. The pathology of imprisonment. *Society*, 9, 32-37.

Zimbardo, P.G. 2007a. *The Lucifer Effect: Understanding How Good People Turn Evil.* New York: Random House.

Zimbardo, P.G. 2007b. Understanding how good people turn evil. Interview Transcript. *Democracy Now!* [Online, March 30]. Available at: http://www.democracynow.org/article.pl?sid=07/03/30/1335257 [accessed: March 31, 2007].

Zimbardo, P.G. *Stanford Prison Experiment: A Simulation Study of the Psychology of Imprisonment Conducted at Stanford University* [Online]. Available at: http://www.prisonexp.org/ [accessed: December 1, 2005].

Zimmerman, B. 1997. Feminism, in *Lesbian and Gay Studies: A Critical Introduction*, edited by A. Medhurst and S.R. Munt. London: Cassell Publishing, 82-89.

Works Considered

Ahmed, A.S. 2003. *Islam Under Siege.* Cambridge: Polity Press.

Amnesty International Report. February 22, 2005. *Iraq: Now Decades of Suffering, Women Deserve Better* [Online]. Available at: http://www.amnesty.org/en/library/info/MDE14/001/2005 [accessed: January 18, 2012].

Balsamo, A. 1996. *Technologies of the Gendered Body.* Durham, NC: Duke University Press.

Bourke, J. 2006. A taste for torture? *The Guardian*, September 13.

Camus, A. 1951. *The Rebel.* New York: Random House

Connor, S. 1997. *Postmodernist Culture: An Introduction to Theories of the Contemporary.* Malden, MA: Blackwell Publishers.

Danto, A.C. 2006. The body in pain. *The Nation*, November 27.

Eisenstein, Z. 2004. *Sexual Humiliation, Gender Confusion and the Horrors at Abu Ghraib* [Online: Znet: A Community of People Committed to Social Change]. Available at: http://www.zcommunications.org/sexual-humiliation-gender-confusion-and-the-horrors-at-abu-ghraib-by-zillah-eisenstein [accessed: June 22, 2004].

Freud, S. [1962]2000. *Three Essays on the Theory of Sexuality, 1856-1939.* New York: W.W. Norton and Company.

Freedberg, L. 2007. CALIFORNIA CULTURES/The art of Abu Ghraib. *The San Francisco Gate* [Online, January 22]. Available at: http://articles.sfgate.com/2007-01-22/opinion/17228074_1_abu-ghraib-fernando-botero-modern-art [accessed: January 22, 2007].

Giddens, A. 1990. *The Consequences of Modernity.* Stanford, CA: Stanford University Press.

Giddens, A. 1992. *The Transformation of Intimacy.* Stanford, CA: Stanford University Press.

Giddens, A. 1993. *New Rules of Sociological Method.* New York: Basic Books.

Goffman, E. 1967. *Asylums.* New York: Anchor Books.

Goffman, E. 1986. *Frame Analysis: An Essay on the Organization of Experience.* Boston, MA: Northeastern Press.

Haraway, D. 2004. *The Donna Haraway Reader.* New York: Routledge.

Harding, S. 1986. *The Science Question in Feminism.* Ithaca, NY: Cornell University Press.

Hoppen, J. 2007. Who's got your back? *Off Our Backs: The Feminist Newsjournal*, xxxvi(2), 14-16.

Huggins, M.K., Haritos-Fatouros, M., and Zimbardo, P.G. 2002. *Violence Workers: Police Torturers and Murderers Reconstruct Brazilian Atrocities*. Berkeley, CA: University of California Press.

International Committee of the Red Cross, 2004. *Report of Abuse at Abu Ghraib Prison, Iraq*. Available at: www.globalsecurity.org/military/library/ report/2004/icrc_report_iraq_feb2004.htm

Irigaray, L. 1985. This sex which is not one, in *This Sex Which is Not One*. Ithaca, NY: Cornell University Press.

Irigaray, L. 1985a. The power of discourse and the subordination of the feminine, in *This Sex Which is Not One*. Ithaca, NY: Cornell University Press.

Irigaray, L. 1985b. Women on the market, in *This Sex Which is Not One*. Ithaca, NY: Cornell University Press.

Irigaray, L. 1985c. Commodities among themselves, in *This Sex Which is Not One*. Ithaca, NY: Cornell University Press.

Kant, I. [1790]1988. *Critique of Judgment*, translated by James Creed Meredith. Oxford: Clarendon Press.

Kennicott, P. 2006. A conflict of images: Fernando Botero's chubby figures confront the torture of Abu Ghraib. *Washington Post*, October 14.

Klein, J. 2006. Art propaganda, Fernando Botero: Abu Ghraib invades the New York art scene. *Canadian Free Press*, October 23.

Lackey, P.N. 1987. *An Invitation to Talcott Parsons' Theory*. New York: Cap & Gown Press.

Meisel, S. 2006. State of emergency. *Vogue Italia*. September. Available at: http:// www.style.it/cont/home-style/home-style.asp

Merton, Robert K. 1957. *Social Theory and Social Structure*. New York: Free Press.

Mills, C.W. 1959. *The Sociological Imagination*. New York: Oxford University Press.

Molinski, D. 2005. Colombian artist depicts Abu Ghraib abuse. *The Associated Press*, Bogota, Colombia, April 30.

Moody, S. 2007. *Art and Violence*, Center for Latin American Studies, University of California Berkeley, January 31.

Priest, D. and Wright, R. 2005. Cheney fights for detainee policy as pressure mounts to limit handling of terror suspects, he holds hard line. *The Washington Post*, November 7, page A01.

Rosen, R. 2006. The hidden war on women in Iraq. *Mother Jones*, July 13.

Schmitt, E. 2004. Military women reporting rapes by U.S. soldiers. *New York Times*, February 26.

Sedgwick, E.K. 1985. *Between Men: English Literature and Male Homosocial Desire*. New York: Columbia University Press.

Snitow, A.1983. *The Powers of Desire: The Politics of Sexuality*, edited by A. Snitow. New York: Monthly Review Press, New Feminist Library.

Stapleton, K. 2000. In search of the Self: Feminism, Postmodernism, and Identity. *Feminism and Psychology*, 10:4, 463-469.

Tarrant, S. 2004. Who's accountable for the abuse at Abu Ghraib? *Off Our Backs: The Feminist Newsjournal*, September.

Index